Atlas of
American Religion

The Denominational Era
1776–1990

William M. Newman

Peter L. Halvorson

ALTAMIRA
PRESS

A Division of
ROWMAN & LITTLEFIELD PUBLISHERS, INC.
Walnut Creek • *Lanham* • *New York* • *Oxford*

ALTAMIRA PRESS
A Division of ROWMAN & LITTLEFIELD PUBLISHERS, INC.

Published in the United States of America
by AltaMira Press
A Division of Rowman & Littlefield Publishers, Inc.
1630 North Main Street, Suite 367
Walnut Creek, CA 94596
http://www.altamirapress.com

Rowman & Littlefield Publishers, Inc.
4720 Boston Way, Lanham, Maryland 20706

12 Hid's Copse Road
Cumnor Hill, Oxford OX2 9JJ, England

British Library Cataloguing in Publication Information Available

Library of Congress Cataloging-in-Publication Data

Newman, William M.
    Atlas of American religion : the denominational era, 1776-1990
    / by William M. Newman & Peter L. Halvorson.
    p.   cm.
    Includes bibliographical references and index.
    ISBN 0-7425-0345-3
    1. United States—Religion—History. 2. United States—Church history. 3. Christian sects—United
        States—History. I. Halvorson, Peter L. II. Title.
BR515 .N49   1999
277.3'08'0223—dc21   99-6320
                                                                       CIP

Printed in the United States of America

♾™ The paper used in this publication meets the minimum requirements of American National Standard for Information Sciences—Permanence of Paper for Printed Library Materials, ANSI/NISO Z39.48–1992.

Cover design: Joanna Ebenstein, Astropop Productions
Production services: ImageInk, San Francisco

Dedication

for

Judith Halvorson and Sylvia Marks-Newman

Table of Contents

Chapter 5

List of Tables and Figures

Tables

FIGURES

List of Maps

About the Authors

William M. Newman is Emeritus Professor of Sociology at the University of Connecticut in Storrs, Connecticut. He is an Associate Editor of the *Review of Religious Research*, and past editor of the *Society for the Scientific Study of Religion Monograph Series*. He is the author of *American Pluralism: A Study of Minority Groups and Social Theory* (1973), editor of *The Social Meanings of Religion* (1974), and co-author (with F. Boudreau) of *Understanding Social Life: An Introduction to Sociology* (1993).

Peter L. Halvorson is Professor of Geography at the University of Connecticut in Storrs, Connecticut, where he has chaired the department of geography. His writings have appeared in *The Professional Geographer*, *Geographic Perspective*, and *Academe*, of which he is a past member of the Editorial Board.

Together they have authored a series of books on American religion including *Atlas of Religious Change in America 1952-1971* (1978), *Patterns in Pluralism: A Portrait of American Religion, 1952-1971* (1980), *Atlas of Religious Change in America, 1971-1980* (1987), *Atlas of Religious Change in America, 1952-1990* (1994).

Acknowledgments

The authors gratefully acknowledge the Lilly Endowment and Fred Hofheinz, Director of its Religion Program for supporting our work through two generous grants. John L. Allen has provided considerable advice and support with regard to cartographic presentation. Both skill and dedication have characterized the manner in which Stephen Martin accomplished the data management tasks for the project, and Jeffrey Crocker produced the cartographic products for the book. They began this work as graduate students, but surely have become respected professional colleagues. Jeannie Pogmore, with her usual grace and good humor, has transformed everything from scritch, scratch, cut, and paste into a polished manuscript. Erin M. Milnes acted as copyeditor, Andrea Fox as proofreader, and Lisa Bravo at ImageInk provided graphic editing and page composition. Erik Hanson and the entire staff at the AltaMira Press have been supportive and helpful in giving the book its shape and form. Finally, Judy and Sylvia have been patient and forebearing through frequent interruptions to our domestic lives. To all of them we say thank you.

Preface

The present study is intended to be both an atlas and a thematic monograph. It is an atlas because, like any such work, it provides a compilation of cartographic exhibits. In the present instance, these maps focus on the historical development and growth patterns of American religious organizations from 1776 to 1990. It is a monograph because these maps entail a story, a story that requires both explanation and interpretation. What are the circumstances that have produced this blend of efforts? We previously have authored a series of atlas publications focused on American religious organizations during the latter half of the twentieth century (Halvorson & Newman, 1978, 1987, 1994). When we discovered that eighteenth and nineteenth century data are available, from materials in private collections as well as from the United States Census Bureau, which could then be matched with the twentieth century data with which we had worked previously, opportunity seemed to be knocking. The possibility that we might link these diverse data sources with a view toward displaying over 200 years of religious trends seemed just too inviting to ignore. Accordingly, we turned, once again, to the Religion Program of the Lilly Endowment for financial sponsorship.

Of course, the presentation of time-series data alone does not constitute the making of a scholarly monograph. Rather, throughout our work with these kinds of data, certain questions of an historical nature have been of interest. Clearly, by expanding the timeframe of our focus, a long-range vantage point could be established from which to address certain analytical questions. Most importantly, what are the typical processes of organizational change and development that have characterized religious communities in the United States? Is it possible to discern certain kinds of typical cases? To what extent does a typology illuminate the organizational processes of these many religious bodies? To be sure, our earlier efforts with data for the period 1952–1990 provided some clues. Yet, in the life span of social organizations, half a century is a short time.

It long has been argued by scholars of American history that religious expressions on these shores are diverse and pluralistic. Unlike the nations of Europe, in which state-sponsored national churches were the norm, the new American nation has experienced a diversity of religious organizations, none of which would enjoy state sponsorship per se. In everyday and scholarly parlance alike, the term *denomination* has been used for referring to these religious organizations. However, the terms *denomination* and *sect* have taken on somewhat unique and specific proportions. Indeed, though most of religious history may be viewed as the history of schism and division, in the twentieth century, American religion uniquely has been characterized by organizational mergers and consolidation. Our theme, simply put, is that the resulting pattern of organized religions in the United States at the dawn of the twenty-first century is a unique happening. The task of the present work, in part, is to reveal the social and organizational processes through which these denominational and sectarian organizations have been created.

From these concerns and questions, the structure of the present work unfolds in five chapters. The plan of the book begins with a revisiting of American religious history. Although this story has been told innumerable times and, to be sure, by historical scholars more qualified than we, our treatment is not simply history for the sake of history. Rather, the focus is on the historical emergence of organizational entities that encapsulate the various faith communities that either migrated to American shores, or that have been invented on American soil. As will be seen in some detail in Chapter 1, we wish to look anew at the religious patterning of American history. Our question is not simply which faith communities have populated the religious landscape, but in what kinds of organizational structures have they been expressed? As we will show, certain distinct families of denominations and sects have populated the religious landscape. A reconsideration of their patterns of emergence and organizational formations sets the stage for the analysis that follows.

As we noted at the outset, the occasion for the present effort was the opportunity to link eighteenth, nineteenth, and twentieth century data sources on American religion. Chapter 2 provides a detailed examination of the available data sources. These include privately collected data for the late eighteenth and mid-nineteenth centuries, the 1850 and 1890 United States Censuses, Census Bureau studies between 1906 and 1936, and the privately conducted Church Membership Studies of 1952, 1971, 1980, and 1990. Ultimately, the present work focuses on data sources for the years 1776, 1850, 1890, 1952, and 1990. To be sure, any social scientific study would have required a clear treatment of our data and methods, and that is exactly what is revealed in Chapter 2. However, the story of the Census Bureau's involvement in the collection of religious data is itself a fascinating chapter in the relationship between social science and religion.

If this book truly may be said to be monographic, then the linchpin of the monograph is provided in Chapter 3. Having examined the unfolding of religious organizations in American history (Chapter 1), and having reviewed in detail the data at hand for studying religious organizational patterns (Chapter 2), we present the issues of organizational types and the typical processes they exhibit in Chapter 3. We propose to employ some standard sociological criteria for distinguishing between Denominations and Sects. However, we have added to those criteria certain spatial criteria suggested by the field of cultural geography. The result is a fivefold classification system that distinguishes between types of Denominations and Sects. That typology, in turn, provides the framework for the display and analysis of the "atlas" materials in Chapters 4 and 5.

Two types of denominational organizations, here called National Denominations and Multiregional Denominations, are the focus of Chapter 4. While the United States has no single carrier of religious ideas that parallels European national churches, the National Denominations treated in Chapter 4 nonetheless qualify as "national" religions in an American context. Similarly, Multiregional Denominations constitute something short of national religions, but surely something more than Sects. Together these two forms of denominational organization represent the key expressions of mainstream religion in the United States.

Chapter 5 provides an examination of three forms of sect. Classic sects, multiregional sects, and national sects represent different forms of non-normative religious expression in American society. In addition to the stability of these types, we shall focus on the processes of transition through which some, though surely not all, religious organizations have migrated from one typological status to the next.

If it reasonably can be said that the twentieth century has been, in religious terms, a denominational era, then the task of this book is to depict its formation and its evolution into the array of organizational expressions that populate the American landscape. Toward that end, we begin, as it were, at the beginning—with the emergence of religious organizations at the point of the birth of the new nation. From there, we follow these religious organizations as well as the other immigrant and native religious movements that join them, to the close of the twentieth century.

Chapter 1

Organizing Religions in American History

The Founding Faiths and Organizational Beginnings

Perhaps it goes without saying that the relationship between general societal trends and developments within religious organizations is indeed complex. It is no more correct to maintain that societal trends entirely determine patterns among religious organizations than it is to contend that religious organizations have a life of their own, separate from social and cultural forces. This chapter explores the historical relationships between these two things in the American experience. To be sure, the focus here is upon religious organizations. Later chapters of this work provide cartographic portrayal and analysis of 39 such organizations. However, we begin here by examining how they make their entrance onto the stage of American society and how their organizational forms develop to the point where the available quantitative data allow a more detailed examination of them.

Although much has been made of the pluralistic elements, both ethnic and religious, present in eighteenth-century America, this "diversity" consisted largely of what might be described as trace elements within a predominantly white Anglo-Saxon Protestant (WASP) nation. The *Atlas of the Historical Geography of the United States* by Paullin (1932) long has been a touchstone for American historical geographers and contains a remarkable compilation of information on American churches in 1776. It identifies more than 3,200 individual congregations, of which only 18.9 percent fall outside of the WASP designation, with barely 2 percent being either Catholic or Jewish congregations. Whereas Paullin's compilation is of churches only, not membership or adherents, Finke and Stark (1986) have made an approximation of membership based on these and other data from the period. They estimate the average size of the typical congregation in a series of denominations at 75 persons. This procedure, in turn, generates a total estimated denominational membership of 242,100, which represents about 10 percent of the estimated total population (2.5 million) of the 13 colonies in 1776. Throughout this study we have employed "adherents" rather than "membership" counts, which

yield larger estimates. (Table 1-1, on the next page, presents the number of churches and estimated adherents in 1776 based on Paullin's data and Finke and Stark's estimation procedure.) That such a relatively low proportion of the population belonged to a church of some sort contradicts certain mythic notions about religiosity, churches, and church membership in the Colonial period. By way of example, one envisions the stern religious culture depicted in Hawthorne's *The Scarlet Letter* (1850). However, if the scant data on church membership during the Colonial period are correct, it must be concluded that tales like those told by Hawthorne are written from a very particular Puritan standpoint and may not so much represent the general culture of the time. This is not to suggest that religious values did not play an important role in the shaping of the soon to be new nation. But it is equally important to consider that just like the political leadership of the new nation, religious membership very likely was drawn from the more elite strata of the social structure. Although it is clear that in time, religious movements would hold great popular appeal in the United States, this does not yet seem to have been so on the eve of the nation's founding.

What geographic patterns existed with regard to individual religious communities during the period of the founding of the nation? Most of the 1775–1776 maps included in the *Atlas of the Historical Geography of the United States* (Paullin 1932) are reproduced here. The original source contains ten maps for individual organizations, which are listed here as 1-1 through 1-10. Two additional "composite" maps not reproduced here each display the locations of four religious communities numbering fewer than 50 churches in the colonies in 1775–1776 (see discussion, pgs. 22–23). The data collection process that lay behind the creation of these maps is recounted in considerable detail in Paullin's text, and no attempt has been made here to duplicate that effort. However, it must be said that these data and maps provide an unparalleled snapshot of the state of organized religion in the new nation at its founding.

Table 1-1 Churches and Estimated Adherents by Religious Organization in 1776

Name	Churches*	Adherents**
Congregational	668	71,643
Presbyterian	588	63,063
Episcopal	495	53,089
Baptist	494	52,982
Friends	310	33,247
German Reformed	159	17,053
Lutheran	150	16,088
Dutch Reformed	120	12,870
Methodist	65	6,971
Catholic	56	6,006
Moravian	31	3,324
Congregational/Separatist	27	2,896
Dunker	24	2,574
Mennonite	16	1,716
French Protestant	7	750
Sandemanian	6	644
Jewish	5	536
Rogerene	3	322
Total Adherents		**345,774**

* Paullin (1932)

** Estimated figures for adherents are calculated following the procedure of Finke and Stark (1986) plus the standard age-based adjustment for population under 14 (based on 1790 Census).

The distribution of Congregationalist churches is depicted on Map 1-1, for which reproduction is difficult given the intensity of the pattern in New England. The Congregationalists were the leading group with almost 700 churches in the colonies, yet their locational pattern is even more heavily concentrated in New England than might have been expected. In New England, it is virtually impossible to distinguish individual locations from southern New Hampshire to Connecticut, except in the Baptist enclave of Rhode Island. On the other hand, Congregational churches elsewhere stand in sharp relief and isolation. The four along the eastern border of New York may be thought of as an extension of the New England core, and the other four (two in South Carolina and one each in Georgia and New Jersey) are very solitary. As a result, the Congregationalists may have been the most numerous group at this time, but their spatial concentration in New England was extreme and provided them with a somewhat limited base for future growth and expansion.

The second largest group in 1775–1776 was the Presbyterians. As seen on Map 1-2, their geographic distribution contrasts sharply with that of the Congregationalists. Presbyterians were present in fairly substantial numbers everywhere except in New England, although it is worth noting that there were significantly more Presbyterian churches in New England than there were Congregationalist churches outside that region. The Presbyterians are sometimes thought of as a mid-Atlantic group, and it is apparent that there were substantial numbers of their churches in New Jersey and central Pennsylvania. However, it is also plainly evident that by this date, Presbyterian churches were well established in Virginia and the Carolinas, especially in the more interior areas of those states. Although the Presbyterians may have had somewhat fewer churches than the Congregationalists, they were much more broadly dispersed.

What would later become Protestant Episcopal churches in 1775–1776, of course, still were Anglican or Church of England congregations. As the representative of the officially sanctioned church of the "mother country," neither their fairly substantial numbers nor their fairly widespread distribution are surprising. They were located throughout the colonies, but were most numerous in Virginia and Maryland, as shown in Map 1-3 (p. 20). In New England, the various dissident churches were predominant. Thus, with the exception of Connecticut, Episcopal churches were not as common in New England as elsewhere. One additional comment seems appropriate. The Revolutionary War involved considerable dislocation for this body, as virtually all Anglican clergy were loyalists. When the Protestant Episcopal

Map 1-1

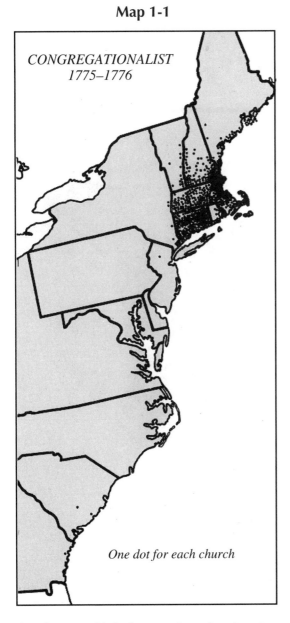

One dot for each church

Map 1-2

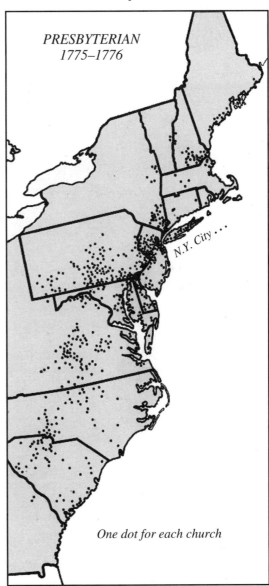

One dot for each church

Church was established as an independent American body only a decade later, it was a very small remnant of the organization portrayed here. In that sense, this particular "snapshot" is a bit misleading.

The Baptist movement, like the other manifestations of the English Reformation, was also well established in the colonies by 1775–1776. It is the stuff of grade school history that Roger Williams brought the movement to Rhode Island, and that pocket of Baptist churches is clearly evident on Map 1-4 (p. 20). However, it is equally as clear that there were numerous and widespread Baptist congregations in the area from Virginia through the Carolinas, as well as a substantial number in the Delaware Valley and New Jersey. Considering that the Baptists had not always been warmly received in the colonies, they

displayed considerable resilience, and by 1776 had become part of the Anglo-Protestant establishment.

The Friends, or more colloquially, the Quakers, whose distribution is shown on Map 1-5 (p. 21), Were, in 1775–1776, at a peak in terms of their relative position compared to other religious communities. From the perspective of their role in the colonies, they should be viewed as "one of the big five" Anglo-Protestant establishment churches. From the perspective of the twentieth century, they would be classified as something more apart from that establishment. These issues aside, the Friends were established in some number, with more than 300 congregations, or, in this case, "meetings." They were present in many areas beyond the Pennsylvania–Delaware Valley locations so generally associated

Map 1-3

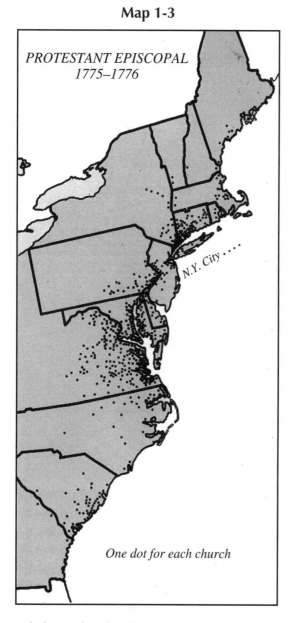

PROTESTANT EPISCOPAL
1775–1776

N.Y. City · · · ·

One dot for each church

Map 1-4

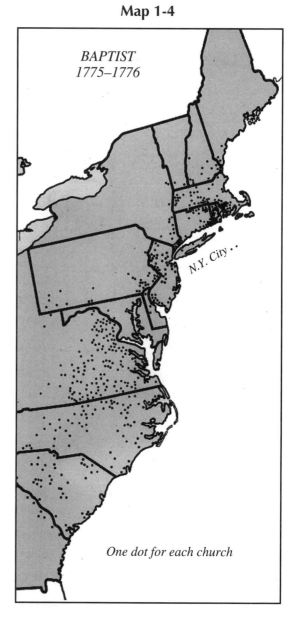

BAPTIST
1775–1776

N.Y. City · ·

One dot for each church

with their Colonial era history. Map 1-5 shows clusters of counties with Friends in Rhode Island, the Hudson Valley, and the Carolina Piedmont, as well as at least three meetings in each of the colonies. In short, they were quite widespread. One suspects that this distribution probably was quite thinly spread. Our estimates of total adherents are based on a congregation size of 75, which, in this particular case, very likely has resulted in an overestimation.

The German Reformed churches, whose location is shown on Map 1-6, represent the first of the non–Anglo-Protestant churches in the 1775–1776 enumeration. These were followers of Calvinism who had emigrated from Germany. Their geographic pattern at this date was quite simple. They were primarily located in Pennsylvania with smaller numbers of con-

gregations in the Hudson Valley and Carolina Piedmont. For readers unfamiliar with this church's history, in the twentieth century, this body was to disappear in two mergers; first with the Midwestern-based German Evangelical Church, creating the Evangelical and Reformed Church, and second, in the union of that body with the more Anglo-Protestant Congregational Christian Churches to form the present-day United Church of Christ. That later history aside, on the eve of the American Revolution, the German Reformed churches were present in considerable number, especially in Pennsylvania, where they helped to create a distinctive regional culture.

German migrants to the colonies were to carry with them a wide variety of religious traditions including, of course, Lutheranism. By 1775–1776, a

Map 1-5

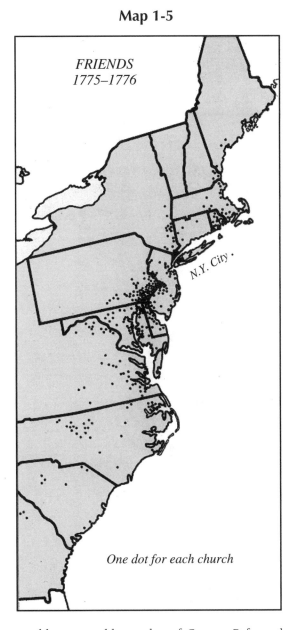

*FRIENDS
1775–1776*

N.Y. City

One dot for each church

Map 1-6

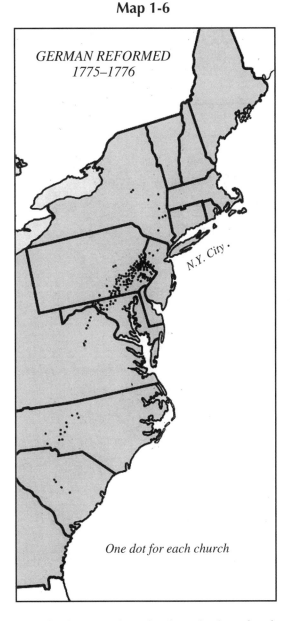

*GERMAN REFORMED
1775–1776*

N.Y. City

One dot for each church

roughly comparable number of German Reformed and Lutheran churches had been established, and in much the same general areas (see Map 1-7, p. 22). The Lutherans, too, had a core area in the mid-Atlantic states, centered in southeastern Pennsylvania with smaller numbers in the Hudson Valley and Carolinas. On both this map and those of the German and Dutch Reformed churches, the absence of any congregations in New England is striking. Nonetheless, with 150 churches in 1775–1776, Lutheranism was firmly planted in the United States.

On the European continent, Calvinism moved down the Rhine Valley through German territory to arrive in the Netherlands. Again, the story of the Dutch colony in New Amsterdam and its lasting imprint on the Hudson Valley is well known. Not sur-

prisingly, these Dutch settlers brought their church with them, and, despite the British dominance in the colonies, the Dutch Reformed Church prospered. As revealed by Map 1-8 (p. 22), the 120 Dutch Reformed churches were strongly concentrated in the vicinity of New York City, in the adjacent section of New Jersey, and from there northward up the Hudson Valley. Only a small handful of Dutch Reformed churches had been established outside this old Dutch settlement hearth, and those are in the Germanic settlement area in southern Pennsylvania, Maryland, and Delaware.

The number and distribution of Methodist churches in 1775–1776 is one of the more interesting of these maps. Methodism had originated in England around 1740, and, although Methodist preachers had

Map 1-7

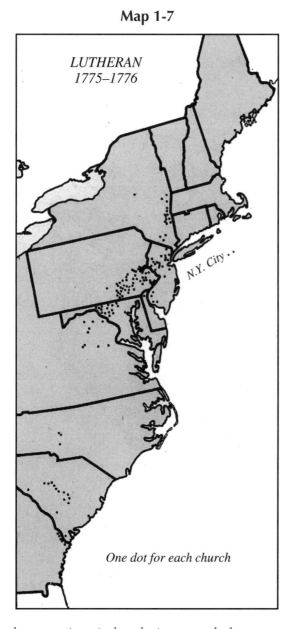

*LUTHERAN
1775–1776*

N.Y. City

One dot for each church

Map 1-8

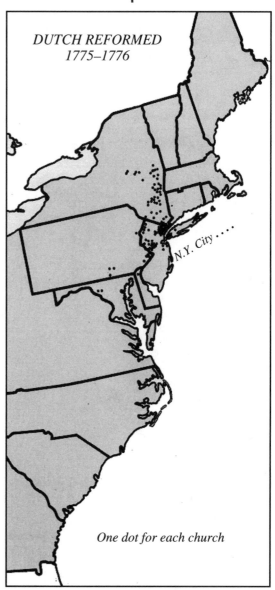

*DUTCH REFORMED
1775–1776*

N.Y. City

One dot for each church

been prominent in the colonies at an early date, separate Methodist churches did not appear until the 1760s. As a result, relatively few were present by 1775–1776. The enumeration here tallied only 65 Methodist churches, most of them between New Jersey and Maryland (see Map 1-9). Outside that central area, there were a few churches in New York and Virginia, two widely separated in North Carolina, one each in Pennsylvania and Massachusetts, and none in the other colonies. This represents a small base both numerically and geographically for a church that was to explode across the new country in the years following independence.

The same general statements pertain to the Catholic Church in 1775–1776. Catholic settlers had not been particularly welcome in the colonies,

suffering under restrictions in all the colonies including even Maryland, which typically is described as having been founded by and for Catholics. Those restrictions aside, it is clear from Map 1-10 that Maryland and Delaware were home to most of the 56 Catholic churches in the colonies, with small numbers also in Pennsylvania and New Jersey. In contrast, Catholic churches were generally absent not only in the Carolinas and Georgia, but also in New England. In this case, one suspects that the adherents estimate is probably an undercount, perhaps by a factor of two or even three, but the aggregate totals were surely quite small. This very modest base represented a sort of beachhead for Catholicism. Nineteenth-century immigrations would alter that picture drastically.

Map 1-9

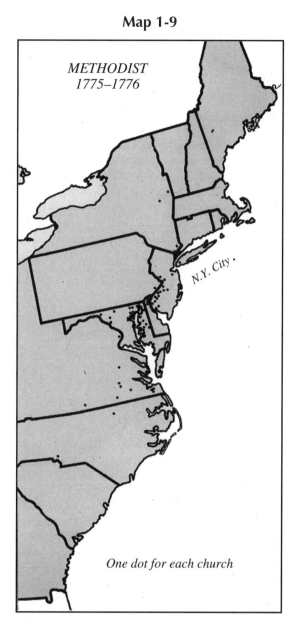

Map 1-10

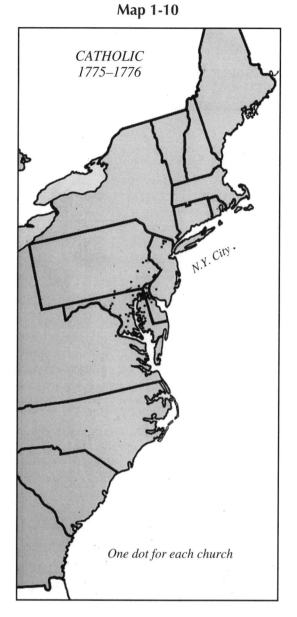

As stated earlier, the final two maps in Paullin (1932) are composite maps portraying the geographic distribution for each of four separate religious communities. Those communities all claim fewer than 50 local churches. Their adherents estimates are included in Table 1-1 (p. 18). Although they are not displayed here, the patterns on those two additional maps are quite predictable. Moravians exhibit two clusters of counties, one in the Carolinas and the other in Pennsylvania. The Dunkers and Mennonites are largely in Pennsylvania, whereas the five Jewish congregations are widely dispersed.

What then was the aggregate situation for religious organizations on the eve of the Revolution? Clearly, Anglo-Protestant churches were in the lead in terms of numbers of churches. Their dominance was greatest in New England, where neither the several Continental Protestant communities nor the Catholic Church had established any foothold. Alternatively, although Anglo-Protestants were numerous throughout the colonies, their dominance was challenged in the mid-Atlantic region by a wide variety of largely, but not exclusively, German Protestant organizations, and Catholics as well. That area, with its mix of peoples and traditions, was the closest approximation on the Colonial landscape to the pluralism of religious organizations that was to develop over the next two centuries.

What are the organizational developments within these religious communities that accompanied this early period in the life of the new nation? It is important to realize that although the colonists immigrated with their faiths intact, most did not bring religious organizations with them. Rather, the planting of churches on the North American continent occurred congregation by congregation, initially with no thought of the eventual establishment of organizational ties beyond those with their "home" offices in Europe. The American Revolution changed all of this.

It is an interesting historical puzzle that the great secular event of the birth of the new nation and the remarkable religious event of the Second Great Awakening (1780–1830) occurred nearly together. The French social observer Alexis de Tocqueville, upon his visit to the United States in the early 1800s would write in his classic *Democracy in America* (1835–39) that the new American nation was uniquely a nation of joiners of social associations of every conceivable type. Yet, modern religious historians (Miller 1965, Mathews 1964) have argued that the creation of formal organizations among religious adherents was one of the most significant and specific outcomes of the Second Great Awakening. Regardless of its cause, it is nonetheless clear that within the first decade of the new nation at least four theological communities would move in the direction of creating independent American national denominations. They were the Anglicans, Methodists, Presbyterians, and Baptists. Let's consider each of these briefly.

Anglican clergy in North America were predominantly missionaries operating under the auspices of the Society for the Propagation of the Gospel in Foreign Parts. The social and political position of Anglicans at the end of the war was, no doubt, precarious. The United States had fought a war of independence from England, and the Anglican Church was the established church in England. Its missionaries in North America had been predominantly loyalist Tories, many of whom emigrated by the end of the Revolution. The new name "Protestant Episcopal Church" was first used by Anglican clergy from Maryland, convening in 1783. A year later a new national denomination was born. In 1784, three regional committees representing eight of the thirteen states declared that the new Protestant Episcopal Church in the United States, while following doctrine and worship of the Church of England (Anglicanism), was to be independent of all foreign authority. The American Protestant Episcopal Church adopted an episcopal form of church government (polity) based on the election of a system of bishops, and by the late 1780s, following canonical law, had the sufficient number of bishops (two of English origin and one Scottish) to begin ordaining their own American clergy.

A similar process of gradual association between local churches at the state and later regional levels transpired among the Presbyterians, although much earlier than among the Anglicans. The form of church polity (presbyterial) among Presbyterians was essentially that of a representative democracy. In Europe, the practice of local Presbyterian churches electing representatives to higher church councils (presbyteries and synods) was well established. Thus, as early as 1706, self-governing religious organizations began to emerge among Presbyterians in North America. However, the sounding of the bell of secular independence in 1776 would be the signal for the creation of a national organization among the various branches of American Presbyterianism. In 1785, the Synods of Philadelphia and New York joined to create an American Presbyterian Church consisting of 11 presbyteries and representing two-thirds of all American Presbyterians. Though some branches of Presbyterianism would remain outside this growing national denomination (most importantly the Dutch and Associate Reformed Presbyterians), by 1789 the American Presbyterian Church had adopted a constitution and had formed the organizational structure to respond to the reality of the new nation.

The first Anglo-American denomination to achieve independent organization was the Methodist community, emerging in Baltimore in 1784 as the Methodist Episcopal Church. It has been argued (Sweet 1952) that the Methodist reliance upon lay preachers in the colonies greatly predisposed American Methodism to develop both a religious style and religious leadership that viewed itself as distinct from English Methodism. Whatever the reason, the Methodist Episcopal Church that emerged in 1784 stressed its independence from English control even as it adopted John Wesley's version of the Church of England's liturgy and hymns. The American Methodist Episcopal Church adopted an episcopal form of polity in which bishops would populate the structure of the new religious organization.

The case for an emerging national organization among the Baptist churches during this period is a bit more complex owing to the fact that Baptists, like Congregationalists, adhere to a congregational polity system. Under this form of church government, all authority is deemed to lie within the local congregation, and it is claimed that there is no theological justification for levels of organizational structure and authority beyond the individual church. Thus, among Baptists, national associations arose not between local churches, but among Baptists who had organized into bible tract societies, home missions boards, publishing societies, and the like. Although regional and state associations among Baptist churches were not uncommon, national organizations focusing upon such functions as evangelism, bible study, and Sunday school curriculum emerged during the period 1814 to 1832.

The movement to Americanize the churches was not restricted to these four larger Anglo-Protestant denominations. Among Roman Catholics, the appointment of John Carroll as Prefect Apostolic between 1784 and 1789 marked the first step in the creation of a distinctively American Catholic Church. The Dutch Reformed Church, though small in numbers, had been virtually self-governing in North America since the early 1770s. The General Synod of the Reformed (Dutch) Church in America became formally organized in 1794. German Reformed churches were under the supervision of the Church of Holland until the formation of an American Coetus in 1747. Official separation from Holland occurred in 1793. Finally, the Evangelical Lutheran Ministerium of North America was formed in 1781. The constitution and form of synodical organization adopted by this German Lutheran body would set the pattern for many ethnic Lutheran churches that would migrate to North America in the nineteenth century.

It is useful to pause briefly here to consider the main features of European Christendom, and especially developments within Protestantism, that would influence the North American religious landscape in the late eighteenth and early nineteenth centuries. As we have already seen, the presence of Catholics and Jews was a relatively small factor when compared to the diversity of immigrant Protestant churches. However, as we also have seen, during the early Federal period, not all forms of Protestantism enjoyed equal status.

Within European Protestantism, the Reformation had produced two major theological streams following the works of the two great reformers, John Calvin and Martin Luther. In the British Isles, Anglicanism already had provided an alternative to Catholicism. In turn, Calvinism would shape the major departures from Anglicanism. Thus, Anglicanism, Presbyterianism, Baptism, Methodism, Congregationalism, and Quakerism were the major forms of Anglo-Protestantism that migrated to North America. Later, both Unitarianism and Universalism would add to this Anglo-Protestant diversity. As we've already seen, four of these faith communities had apparent numerical dominance at the time of the birth of the new nation, Congregationalism, Presbyterianism, Baptism, and Anglicanism.

Both Lutheranism and Calvinism found expression on the main European Continent in a great diversity of forms. Calvinist churches on the European Continent would carry the name "Reformed." Thus, both the Dutch and German Reformed Churches that were present in small numbers in the colonies represented additional expressions of Calvinism. Although the various forms of Calvinism in the new republic give the appearance of diversity, the common root of both Anglo and Continental Calvinists in the same system of theology was the greater reality. In other words, though these faith communities worshipped under a variety of labels (Congregational, Presbyterian, and others), they were but one single family theologically. The Continental Lutheran churches most frequently carried the names "Evangelical" or Lutheran. Although present in the United States by 1790, they were a minor element.

For the uninitiated, the nomenclature of the many Protestant groups that play roles in the story to be told here may be confusing. Although the distinction between Reformed (Calvinist) and Evangelical (Lutheran) churches on the European Continent is clear enough, it also must be remembered that in time, many Anglo-Calvinist forms would migrate from the British Isles to the Continent, and subsequently to North America. Thus, in the United States, there are both English Baptists and German Baptists, and to confuse matters even more, the term *evangelical,* which in Europe means Lutheran, later would be used by American Protestant churches to indicate a spiritually based faith. So, for example, a small American group formed in 1981 named the Evangelical Presbyterian Church is, of course, Calvinist not Lutheran. For the moment, however, our main point is that in spite of the diversity of names involved, the religious landscape of the new American nation was decidedly Anglo-Saxon Protestant. We turn next to both the wider social factors and religious institutional changes that would transform these early patterns.

Social Change and Religious Diversification

At the point of the first census in 1790, the population of the then new republic was about four million people. Whereas, in the first half of the eighteenth century that population had been narrowly confined to the eastern coastal fringe, in the second half of the century, emboldened first by the peace of 1763 and then even more by the peace of 1783, settlers began to press further into the interior, into and beyond the eastern mountains. By the time of the initial census in 1790, a first wave of settlement had extended into the interior of New England, New York, and Pennsylvania, and even further west into

Kentucky, Tennessee, and what was then the western portion of Virginia. These changes reflect the added security for settlers and their settlements in former Indian territories, a security that resulted from the expansion of British and later American political and military control. Thus, although in 1790 the new nation still consisted only of the 13 colonies, population already had spread substantially; so much so that the first census in 1790 would provide the demographic evidence supporting the addition to the Union in the next decade of three new states, Vermont, Kentucky, and Tennessee.

From the perspective of changes to the landscape of American society, the century from 1790 to 1890 was dominated by three phenomena: (1) Manifest Destiny and the frontier; (2) slavery, states rights, and the Civil War; and (3) cultural diversification largely brought about by the "great immigration." Each served to alter American society dramatically, and each of these great social forces was felt in different ways, in different places, and times. In the period from 1790 to 1850, the first two of these were more in evidence, while the impact of the third was just beginning to be felt. Similarly, from the time of that first census to the middle of the nineteenth century, the geography of the country was altered drastically. The national territory was doubled by means of territorial purchase (Louisiana Purchase), treaty or territorial cession (Oregon and Florida, among others), and conquest (the Mexican-American War). These changes shifted the western boundary of the country from a line essentially along the Mississippi River to the Pacific, encompassing an area that, lacking only the Gadsden Purchase of 1854, basically conforms to the shape and area of today's lower 48 states.

The pattern of human settlement lagged behind this territorial expansion. Although settlement had reached westward to include most of the area bounded by the Atlantic, the Great Lakes, and the Mississippi, it still had not leapfrogged to the Pacific, nor filled the great expanses of the Great Plains and the Rockies. Nonetheless, expansion into the areas of Kentucky, Tennessee, and the Old Northwest had developed a new frontier mentality and society. These areas also were the birthplace of a constellation of new spiritual movements destined to occupy an increasingly important role in American religion. Among these were the Anti-Mission churches of the Baptists, most notably the followers of Barton Stone, Thomas and Alexander Campbell, and Walter Scott. By 1839 these churches, later to be called the Restoration Movement, had coalesced into an association known as the Christian Churches, Disciples of Christ. These Disciples would become the seedbed of three present-day denominations: The Christian Churches (Disciples of Christ), the

Christian Churches and Churches of Christ, and the Churches of Christ. Together, they account for nearly four million adherents in 1990, with local churches throughout the nation.

A second movement of the period, Adventism, emerged in the 1830s. Following the ideas of William Miller, whose theology focused on the second coming of Christ, the movement drew followers from a wide spectrum of Anglo-Protestant denominations (Methodists, Baptists, Presbyterians, Congregationalists, and others). Both the Seventh-Day Adventists (formally organized in 1855) and the Advent Christian Church (1860) are leading contemporary expressions of Adventism.

Mormonism, of course, would become one of the most controversial religious movements to emerge from the first half of the nineteenth century. Officially named the Church of Jesus Christ of Latter Day Saints, the movement was organized in Fayetteville, New York, in 1830. This small and persecuted group that followed the teachings of Joseph Smith would resettle in Utah, and from that base they would grow throughout the nation to a 1990 adherence level of almost three and a half million followers.

These several major religious movements do not, of course, exhaust the list of religious groups that originated during this period. They do, however, constitute the major religious organizations from this period that will continue to appear on the American religious landscape. As will be seen, the later half of the nineteenth century spawned even more indigenous religious movements and organizations. But, this is a bit ahead of our story. During the first half of the nineteenth century, the frontier also proved to be inhospitable to some of the more formally organized and established groups of the Colonial seaboard, with the result that some groups, most importantly Congregationalists, Episcopalians, and Friends, began declining in relative importance. Thus, territorial expansion played a much greater role in transforming the religious landscape than simply by enlarging the area occupied by various groups between 1790 and 1850. It provided a playing field on which some though surely not all of the older denominations expanded, while some important new religious movements were born. Clearly, the relative positions of faith communities, old and new, began shifting dramatically.

For the "old" religious groups, one of the dominating issues of the early years of the republic was to establish a new American identity independent of European control. As we have already seen, a series of "new" American national denominations emerged as a result. However, within a generation, the divisive force of the slavery issue began a process of fragmenting these organizations in ways that would have enduring consequences. The most obvious of these was the formation of the Southern Baptist Convention in 1845, a separation that continues to affect the American Baptist movement at the dawn of the twenty-first century. Other groups to feel this same impact were the Presbyterians, who split in 1858 not to be reunited until 1983, and the Methodists, who were split from 1845 to 1939. An interesting characteristic of the 1850 United States Census (Bureau of the Census 1854) is that in each of these cases, the enumeration essentially collapses these three identifications to the earlier undivided families (i.e., "Baptists," "Methodists," and "Presbyterians"). Although those divisions may have been viewed as temporary in 1850, subsequent enumerations were to be more realistic as to their enduring meaning. These issues are examined in detail in Chapter 2. Though these early schisms resulting from regional divisions over the slavery issue are of lasting significance, shifts in the relative numerical strengths of the various denominations is an equally important feature of the period between 1790 and 1850.

A comparison of the religious data for 1776 with those from the 1850 Census reveals the scope of these changes in the religious landscape (Bureau of the Census 1854). By 1850, the Methodists and Baptists had become the two predominant American forms of Protestantism. Methodism, which consisted of only 65 congregations in 1776, by 1850 reported some 13,300 congregations, representing more than a third of the nation's churches. The Baptists, with 9,360 churches in 1850, were the second most populous denomination. In contrast, the two most "established" denominations of the Colonial period, the Protestant Episcopal Church and Congregationalism, both experienced substantial relative decline. It is little surprise that the American form of Anglicanism did not grow during the early decades of the new republic. Anti-English feeling was still very high, and the Protestant Episcopal Church, even though independent from Anglicanism, still was viewed by many as being the "Church of England."

The reasons for the failure of New England Congregationalism to extend its numerical and geographic reach during this period are complex. In 1801, The General Assembly of the Presbyterian Church and the Congregational General Association of Connecticut entered into a Plan of Union. Under this agreement, which later was adopted by other New England state Congregational associations, these two faiths agreed to form union congregations in the Western reserve territories of Ohio, Illinois, Michigan, and beyond. The plan was intended to avoid competition and, thus, generally promote missionary efforts in the expanding territories (these were known as comity agreements). In practice, a disproportionate number of the new churches opted for affiliation with the widely dispersed national Presbyterian Church. It is argued that the connectional ties of presbyterial polity inherent in the national structure of Presbyterianism proved more advantageous to the new churches on the expanding frontier. In contrast, Congregationalism, lacking a national organizational structure, was not well equipped to respond to the needs of the new frontier churches. As a result, many New England Congregationalists who ventured into the frontier territories developed affiliation in Presbyterian churches.

However, the shifting of the relative strength between the several leading denominations of the Colonial period is but one part of the story. The other development that greatly impacted the religious composition of the nation was immigration. Between 1790 and 1850, the population of the United States increased from 4 million to 23 million, and it is estimated that by 1850, religious adherence had increased to something greater than 25 percent of the population (*Baptist Almanac and Annual Register* 1850). Both the growth in religious memberships and the general population growth reflect, in part, the great migration that had begun in the 1830s. The immigration is reflected in the religious diversity reported in the 1850 census materials (Bureau of the Census 1854), as illustrated by the presence of the German Reformed Church, Mennonites, Moravians, Lutherans, and Jews. However, the most notable change in religious diversity between 1790 and 1850 concerns the growth in the number of Catholics.

The addition to the growing nation of territories formerly held by the French and Spanish incorporated some Catholic populations into the country. However, events in Europe, specifically the Irish potato famine and political instability in several areas of the southern German states, led to substantial immigration from staunchly Catholic areas. As a result, whereas the Catholic presence had been only a trace element in 1776, by 1850, the Catholic Church had established 1,227 congregations. Although estimates of the number of adherents vary widely, the most conservative of these suggests a total of just over 1 million adherents (Finke & Stark 1992). As seen in Table 2-1 (p. 39), our own calculations based on the *Baptist Almanac and Annual Register* for 1850 suggest approximately 1.22 million. Whether we accept more conservative estimates or our own, these numbers still leave Catholics in a distinct minority status that would change sharply in the second half of the nineteenth century. Nonetheless, with more than one million adherents by 1850, Catholics already had become a substantial religious community in the United States.

Indeed, with some 1,227 churches, they ranked fifth out of the 22 religious identities supplied in the 1850 United States Census data on religion.

A third feature of the religious institutional environment evident by 1850 is the growing diversity of indigenous religious organizations being founded on the expanding American frontier. Although the Census of 1850 does not provide much detailed information about these new movements, the *Baptist Almanac and Annual Register* for 1850 does supply such documentation (see Table 2-1, p. 39). Among the Baptists are the Anti-Mission, Campbellite, and Church of God Movements. Both the Universalist and the Unitarian divisions within Congregationalism appear in these data, as do the Mormons. By 1890 these indigenous religious movements and others will have found expression as formal organizations.

Finally, no consideration of developments in American religion during this period would be complete without an examination of two sources of organizational schisms. The first of these was purely theological and surfaced among the Presbyterians as the distinction between "New School" and "Old School." This dispute was a contributing factor in the schism that produced the Cumberland Presbyterian Church in 1810 and subsequently led to a larger rupture in the short-lived national Presbyterian Church through a formal schism in 1837, with the more conservative synods situated predominantly in the Southern states. The second of these issues, slavery, has both its theological and secular aspects (Goen 1985). Interestingly, among Presbyterians, in 1836, the year just prior to the Old School–New School split, representatives from slave states and abolitionists had held separate caucuses at the denomination's General Assembly. However, it would not be until 1858 that the Southern wing of Presbyterianism would become formally organized as the United Synod of the Presbyterian Church in the United States of America.

Among Baptists the schism occurred even earlier. Here, it will be recalled, owing to the precepts of congregational polity, there was no single national denominational structure connecting Baptist congregations. Rather, there were state and regional associations and, of course, such national organizations as the Baptist Home Missions Society and other special purpose religious societies. It was in the latter that the slavery debate took on national proportions among Baptists. These disputes culminated in 1845 with the formation of the Southern Baptist Convention. It is perhaps not correct to describe this as a schism per se, as there would be no Northern Baptist Convention until 1907. Nonetheless, the 1845 organizing of the Southern Baptist Convention around the states rights issue created a division in the Baptist family that would survive into the twenty-first century.

The same slavery and states rights issues that had caused the formation of a separate Southern Baptist denomination, and that had precipitated formal division in the short-lived national Presbyterian denomination, also split the Methodist Episcopal Church. In this case, the division occurred on the basis of a formal plan of division that was adopted by the General Conference of 1844. In 1845, the new Methodist Episcopal Church, South, was formed, with the northern half of the original denomination retaining the name Methodist Episcopal Church. This division would last until a reunion in 1939.

Finally, even the Protestant Episcopal Church would be divided by the slavery issue. Although the schism did not occur until 1861, with reunion occurring immediately after the close of the Civil War, there was, for a brief time, a Protestant Episcopal Church in the Confederate States. Though its bishops continued to hold their offices in the Protestant Episcopal Church, the Southern organization was formed to carry out religious functions that the Northern-based denomination no longer could accomplish in the states of the Confederacy. On balance, it may be argued that two, if not three religious communities, Methodist, Presbyterian, and Baptist, were poised in the early 1800s to emerge as truly national denominations, widely dispersed and strong in numbers of adherents. Clearly, the issues of slavery and states rights fragmented these three potential national denominations. Two of them accomplished reunion in the twentieth century, whereas the third remained divided.

In general, religious diversity prior to 1850 was more a product of processes internal to the country than a result of the introduction of newcomers. The great migration from eastern and southern Europe was yet to begin, and the immigration from northern and western Europe was about to be forestalled by the outbreak of the Civil War. Both theological and secular disputes were causing organizational divisions among the predominant religious families, and new religious cousins of the established faiths were emerging on the expanding frontier. As we've already seen, the single most dramatic change in the American religious landscape by 1850 was the explosive expansion of Methodism. With only 65 congregations reported in 1776, by mid-century, the Methodists had expanded to more than 13,300 congregations representing more than one-third of the nation's churches. Even though Methodism was an "imported" religion, it had proved to be more successful in the United States than in its land of origin (England). Conversely, as we already have noted, prototypical Colonial groups, Congregationalists, Friends, and Episcopalians, were experiencing significant relative decline. The end product of these changes was a much expanded and far richer, albeit still largely Protestant, mix of religious groups than had been visible at the nation's founding.

These changes in the religious landscape of the United States were accompanied by significant increases in population. The first national census, in 1790, reported a total population of about 4 million people. By 1850, that total had grown to over 23 million. Our own estimates of religious adherents are based on the membership statistics originally reported in the *Baptist Almanac and Annual Register* (1850, 32) and subsequently reprinted in the 1850 Census (Bureau of the Census 1854, 138). As can be seen in Table 2-1 (p. 39), using those reports as a basis and making a standardized adjustment, in 1850 there are an estimated 6.1 million religious adherents, representing more than 26 percent of the total population. Using a different approximation technique based on "pew counts," Finke and Stark (1986, 186) estimate religious adherence in 1850 at 7.8 million people or 34 percent of the total population. Recognizing that both are but approximations, the fundamental point is that both estimates lead to the same conclusion; that by the mid-nineteenth century, with about three in every ten Americans identified as adherents, the nation had become far more "churched" than at its founding. In an environment of dizzying territorial and demographic expansion, as well as increasing social diversity, and in a time span of but two or three generations, organized religion was claiming as adherents an increasing share of the population of the United States.

What factors would account for the transforming of American society and its religious landscape during the second half of the nineteenth century? The "map" of the country would be much more complete in 1890 than it was in 1850. By 1850, although the total area of the lower 48 states largely had been claimed or acquired, much of the territory of the nation remained relatively unsettled, often containing only small numbers of isolated outposts. In contrast, a flurry of new states entered the Union in 1889 and 1890, among them Idaho, Montana, North Dakota, South Dakota, Washington, and Wyoming. Thus, in the area that would become the lower 48 states, this left only the territories of Arizona, New Mexico, Oklahoma, and Utah not yet advanced to statehood. Since much of our analysis in this study will involve data for county units, we are drawn to them for comparison here. In 1850, it is possible to match some 1,287 counties to corresponding 1990 county units. However, by 1890, that number has grown to 2,754, representing 89.6 percent of the total number of counties in the United States in 1990.

The "filling up" of the national territory between 1850 and 1890 is the end product of a series of important migrations. In the decade preceding the Civil War, the most notable migration involved movement across the continent to California and Oregon. Although these migrations continued throughout the entire period, in the 1870s and 1880s, spurred in particular by development of networks of railroads, settlements began filling the areas of the Great Plains. This process of occupying the land was a reflection of both a widely shared sense that it was America's destiny to do so, and of a very rapid expansion in total population. Despite the massive traumatic dislocation and loss of life in the Civil War, the nation's population grew by almost 10 million people per decade, reaching 63 million in 1890. Though it would be another twenty years before historians would date the "closing of the frontier," by 1890, the nation largely was formed geographically, with only a limited number of areas (Oklahoma and Arizona) yet to be populated.

As we already have noted, the process of sectional or regional divisions culminating in the Civil War was anticipated by schisms in religious organizations prior to 1850. The devastation of the war and the harshness of the period of Reconstruction extended its impacts well beyond the end of hostilities in 1865. In the years following the Civil War, economic expansion was typical of much of the country outside of the area of the Confederacy. This disparity was reflected in several social developments that, in turn, were reflected in the religious organizations of the United States.

First, it created a regional identity for the South as a distinctive entity in cultural terms. Southerners and Southern institutions developed a clearly defined sense of themselves as separate and distinct. Consider that in 1890 the Methodist Episcopal Church, South, remained separate from the Methodist Episcopal Church, as did the Presbyterian Church in the United States (Southern) from the Presbyterian Church (U.S.A). The Cumberland Presbyterians had two denominations, one white and one "colored," and even the Lutherans had a Southern synod, the United Synod in the South. Among the Baptists, the Southern Baptist Convention was far better organized than any Baptist organization outside of the South. Second, the economic gap between the South and much of the rest of the country meant that the massive immigrant populations of the last half of the nineteenth century largely settled elsewhere in the country, in areas where either jobs (as in the industrializing cities of the North) or land (as in the Great

Plains) were more readily available. The result was that the South retained its Anglo-Protestant cultural base much more than those areas entered by large numbers of diverse groups between the 1850s and the 1920s. Although in the twentieth century, the rise of the Sun Belt would both narrow the economic gap and bring a broader cross section of Americans to the South, these linked processes did not occur to any substantial degree in the nineteenth century. Thus, regional distinctiveness within the country would prevail until the mid-twentieth century.

Of course, the second half of the nineteenth century witnessed a dramatic increase in America's cultural pluralism through immigration. Historians of the great migration often divide it into two phases (Jones 1960) differentiating between the "old immigrants" who arrived before 1880 and the "new immigrants" who arrived after that date. Though the decade of the 1840s experienced a substantial influx of 1.4 million immigrants, the total over the next forty years was 12.7 million, more than 5 million of whom arrived in the 1880s. Most of the immigrants arriving prior to 1850 came from northern and western Europe, especially the British Isles and Germany. Even after mid-century, migration from Germany constituted the largest single stream of immigrants. However, during the 1860s, the migration was augmented by substantial numbers of Scandinavians and, therefore, Lutherans of various linguistic or national origins. Further, by the decade of the 1880s, these groups were joined for the first time by sizable numbers of people from Russia, Austria, and Italy. The latter will dominate the final great surge in immigration between 1890 and the enactment of the National Origins Quota Act of 1924. Thus, by 1890, new ethnic groups among Roman Catholics, and substantial numbers of Jewish migrants had begun to arrive, further augmenting the cultural and religious mosaic of the country. By 1890, one in four Americans had foreign-born parents and almost one in five (the highest level ever recorded by the Census Bureau) was foreign born.

The diversity of denominational organizations participating in the 1890 Census provides a convenient measure of the extent to which immigration was changing the landscape of American religion (Bureau of the Census 1894). Among Lutherans, the enumeration included two Norwegian organizations, two Danish Churches, and one each composed of Swedish, Finnish, and Icelandic immigrants. Another half dozen Lutheran organizations composed largely of people of German background who had settled in different regions of the country added to the overall picture of increased complexity and division among religious communities. The two participating Norwegian organizations were the Hauge Lutheran Synod Church and the Norwegian Lutheran Church in America. Regional Lutheran denominations of primarily German background include the Lutheran General Synod, the United Synod in the South, the General Council, and the Joint Lutheran Synod of Ohio and other states. Moreover, outside the Lutheran fold, German immigration had led to the formation of several new denominational organizations and the transplanting from Europe of others. Among these were the Evangelical Association, the German Evangelical Synod of North America, the Dunkard (Conservative) Church, the Moravian Church, the Mennonite Church, the Amish Mennonite Church, and the United Brethren in Christ. By 1890, the Reformed tradition (originally Dutch) was represented by both the Reformed Church in America (Dutch) and the Reformed Church in the United States (Swiss and German). Finally, the American Jewish population had become sufficiently large and diverse to be represented by two denominational bodies, Orthodox (largely eastern European) and Reformed (primarily German).

However, it should not be presumed that immigration was the only source of the growing diversity in the American religious landscape during the second half of the nineteenth century. Two movements, the Holiness Movement and Pentecostalism, would be nineteenth-century seedbeds of new American churches. The National Holiness Movement emerged in the late 1860s as a reaction against the secularism and religious indifference that followed the Civil War. Followers of this movement, which occurred almost exclusively among Methodist congregations, adhere strictly to Biblical precepts in seeking purification and sanctification. After the turn of the century, a number of new denominations for which data are available in the present study had been organized. The largest of these, the Church of the Nazarene (1907) emerged through mergers of several smaller bodies that were organized in the 1890s. By 1990, the Nazarenes would number just under 700,000 adherents. A number of Holiness groups would adopt the name "Church of God." One of the largest of these, the Church of God (Anderson, Indiana), began as a movement among existing churches in the 1880s. As will be seen, its twentieth-century growth has been substantial, numbering just under a quarter of a million adherents by 1990.

Closely related to the Holiness movement, but more focused on the ability of believers to evidence the receiving of gifts, especially speaking in tongues, are the Pentecostal churches. With their roots in this late nineteenth century movement, most Pentecostal organizations were formally organized early in the twentieth century. The largest of these, the Assemblies of God, was organized in 1914 and would grow to become a national organization of more than two million adherents by 1990. The Church of God (Cleveland, Tennessee) is yet another such group. It emerged through schism with its parent organization in 1909. Two other Pentecostal organizations are included in the present study. They are Pentecostal Holiness Church, International, which was first organized in 1898 as the Fire-Baptized Holiness Church. Subsequent mergers in 1911 and 1915 resulted in its final twentieth-century organization. Finally, the International Church of the Foursquare Gospel was founded under the leadership of Aimee Semple McPherson in 1921. Like many such groups, the Foursquare Gospel is at once fundamentalist, adventist, and perfectionist.

What then was the sum of all these influences? Historian Robert H. Wiebe (1975, 37) describes America as "a segmented society" within which "institutions grew locally to serve localities." This was particularly true in the nineteenth century, and perhaps more the case in terms of religious organizations than in almost any other aspect of American life. The influences of spatial or geographic distance and separation, distinct regional economies and histories, compounded by ethnic and cultural distinctiveness, resulted in a patchwork of regional and local religious communities with relatively little organizational cohesion. This degree of fragmentation was to provide a primary element of the agenda for consolidation among religious organizations in the century ahead. Nonetheless, it is remarkable that in the face of all of this diversity and segmentation, the United States by 1890 had become still more "churched," with fully 45 percent of the total population tallied as adherents of the groups identified in the 1890 Census.

Religious Consolidation in Modern America

If the primary forces driving the nineteenth-century American social experience resulted in regional separation and organizational fragmentation, those of the twentieth century would lead in the opposite direction. Pierce Lewis (1987, 411) has identified several underlying forces driving the creation of a "new geography" in twentieth-century American society. First are technological innovations in communication and transportation. These contribute to an astounding process of what geographers call space-time convergence, which erodes the isolation caused by distances. Second are inter-regional or internal migrations. Tremendous flows of internal migrants in the twentieth century have emphasized mobility as a central characteristic of American society and have blurred distinctive images of regional identity. To these, we would add a third factor entailing the emergence and dominance of larger scale, even national, organizations. Such organizations are as apparent in the organized religious life of the United States as in its corporate life. Let's take a closer look at these three trends.

Turning first to technological innovations, it has been observed that whereas in 1850 it took 24 days to travel from New York to California, with the completion of the transcontinental railroad, it took only 4 days. By 1930, the trip could be completed in less than a day by air, and, with the advent of jet travel by 1960, the same trip could be completed in about five hours (Haggett 1983, 339). Of course, the car and the accompanying development of a system of roads was

essential to these processes of space-time convergence. These same travel times prevailed with regard to the speed of "snail mail" in the nineteenth century. By 1929, 40 percent of American families had a telephone and, by the end of the Second World War, both the telephone and the radio were universally available to the American population, meaning that voice communication had become instantaneous. Similarly, the impact of the new mass media was to bring about an acceleration of cultural convergence, as people in all parts of the country heard the same messages over the airwaves. With the development of television in the years since mid-century, the process of cultural convergence has continued unabated so that insularity has become nearly impossible. The cumulative impact of these changes in transportation and communications technology has been the decline in geographic regionalism and the simultaneous dispersion of a more homogeneous national culture.

Second, the 100 years between 1890 and 1990 have witnessed tremendous changes in the human geography of the nation as a result of migration. The nineteenth-century version of mobility emphasized the settlement of an ever-moving frontier. However, the migration patterns of the twentieth century have been more complex, involving at least three different sorts of movements; from rural to urban, from cities to suburbs, and from cold climates to warm ones (Lewis 1987, 428).

America's process of "filling up" the land continued until well into the twentieth century, peaking with a farm population of more than 30 million people. Although this number remained relatively constant until the Second World War, outmigration from rural areas to urban centers already had begun by the 1920s. Most Americans recognize the significance of the great trans-Atlantic migration that brought almost 33 million people to the country between 1820 and 1920. However, it is equally important to recognize the magnitude of the internal migration that saw 50 million Americans leave the farm for the city between 1920 and 1970. This internal shift has progressed to the point where true "rural" residents (farmers) represent only a tiny fraction of the population, causing the United States Census Bureau to adopt new terms such as "rural non-farm" and "ex-urbanites" to identify non-traditional rural residents. In the 1990s, almost four of every five Americans were classified as urban. In contrast, in 1890, only a bit more than one in three were so classified. Standard theories about the impact of urbanization emphasize the difficulty of maintaining traditional value systems in the diverse cultural environment of the city. The implications of rampant urbanization for religious organizations are considerable.

The influx of people into urban areas augmented by developments in transport technology also produced massive suburbanization. Though this process had antecedents in the mid-nineteenth century United States, it became a broadscale phenomenon in the era of economic and demographic expansion following the Second World War. The American population became more suburban than either rural or urban, with migration from suburb to suburb representing the largest single stream of migration in the nation. This suburbanization process has involved local churches following their parishioners to the suburbs. It also has necessitated churches adapting to a new social and spatial environment. It is not surprising that sociologists of religion have debated the effects of suburbanization upon religious organizations (Winter 1961, Newman 1976).

However, in the context of traditional patterns of regional culture, the most significant twentieth-century migration pattern has been the relative shift from North and East to South and West. This realignment of population into the Sun Belt has been under way since the beginning of the twentieth century. The net effect of this geographic shift has been a transformation of the Western states from a region containing a relatively minor portion (8.9 percent) of the national population in 1890, to one of relatively equal population size as compared to the other regions.

As is seen in Table 1-2, whereas the South has maintained its relative position, the West has grown as the result of relative declines in the Northeast and Midwest regions. Although this shift of population has involved sizable numbers of seniors moving toward the sun, a greater number of younger people have moved in search of the opportunities associated with rapidly expanding regional economies in both the South and West. In this environment, religious organizations have confronted decisions about whether to break out of their old regional bases to "follow their flocks," while individuals have faced decisions about switching their personal affiliation when entering new communities with social and cultural features different from those they left (Hoge et al. 1995, Roof & McKinney 1987, 172–85).

Finally, the nature of corporate behavior in a wide array of organizations has shifted dramatically from the local and regional level toward the national level during the twentieth century, as distinctly local organizations have found it increasingly difficult to compete with more broadly dispersed organizations. Two different processes appear to be at work here, one that is geographic and driven by demographic shifts, and one rooted in the economic benefits of an increased scale of operations.

The process of "going national" can be understood in the context of products from fast food (McDonalds) to breweries (Coors vs. Lone Star). A telling example from the realm of professional sports is supplied by DeVita (1996, 7). In 1960, all eight

Table 1-2　United States Population by Region in 1890, 1950, 1990

	1890		1950		1990	
	Regional Population (in 000,000)	**% of National Total**	**Regional Population (in 000,000)**	**% of National Total**	**Regional Population (in 000,000)**	**% of National Total**
Northeast	18.6	29.6	42.1	28.0	56.7	22.8
Midwest	22.4	35.6	44.5	29.5	60.9	24.5
South	16.3	25.9	34.6	23.0	60.4	24.5
West	5.6	8.9	30.1	20.0	70.3	28.3

Source: Compiled from state-level totals provided in respective editions of the United States Census.

National Basketball Association franchises were located in the Northeast or Midwest. By the 1990s, though there were 10 teams located in those two regions, following the lure of new markets, 19 "new" teams had been created outside of those regions, with 17 located in the South and West. This transformation, though facilitated by jet travel and television, is founded on the demographic and economic expansion of new markets. The expansion of the "big leagues" to encompass the whole country whether in sports, media, or retailing is a central phenomenon of the late twentieth century United States. As we will show, religious organizations exhibit this trend as well, most especially through processes of organizational mergers.

Among economic organizations, a first phase of organizational mergers took place in the period from 1890 to 1904 (Niemi 1980, 332). This period saw the emergence of integrated firms seeking more monopolistic control of markets in a wide range of areas. Some of the mergers in this period took the form of trusts against which there was a strong reaction leading to the "trust busting" of the early twentieth century. This flurry of organizational mergers has parallels in the lives of the nation's religious organizations, with the emergence through merger processes of groups such as the Assemblies of God (1914), Pentecostal Holiness Church (1911), Church of the Nazarene (1907), and the United Lutheran Church (1918), all of which previously had held to strictly local organizational forms.

A second spurt of merger activity among economic organizations was tied to the economic growth of the 1920s. This set of mergers was halted by the Depression, and the period from 1929 to the end of the Second World War did not see sizable amounts of business merger activity. However, in the general prosperity beginning in the 1950s and continuing through to the 1990s, economic mergers, many taking the form of conglomerates, have occurred at a rapid pace. Among religious organizations similar processes have eradicated much of the differentiation and fragmentation that prevailed among nineteenth-century bodies. Perhaps the greatest instance of organizational consolidation has been among the Lutherans, where three twentieth-century organizations—the Evangelical Lutheran Church in America; the Lutheran Church - Missouri Synod; and the Wisconsin Evangelical Lutheran Synod—now account for 90 percent of the adherents that at one time were represented by as many as 150 different organizations (Mead 1975, 169, Nelson 1975). Although the Lutheran mergers are more numerous than those in other American theological communities, they do illustrate certain features common to most religious organizational mergers. Most are between theological cousins and entail the bridging of ethnic or regional differences.

As seen in Table 1-3 (p. 34), in the twentieth century there have been at least 33 (that is, we could identify 33) organizational mergers among American Protestant organizations. Of these, only eight reach across theological or family boundaries, and four of the eight culminated in a single denomination, the United Church of Christ (UCC) (1961). The UCC merger was preceded by mergers between the Congregational Church and the Evangelical Protestant Church of North America (1925), the Congregational Churches and the Christian Churches (1931), and that between the Evangelical Church in the United States and Reformed Church in America (1934). The remaining 25 organizational mergers in Table 1-3 represent mergers within theological families, in which either ethnic or regional differences or both are bridged. The greatest ethnic blending has been among Lutherans, though not exclusively so, whereas the Anglo-Protestant bodies have focused upon repairing sectional differences. Overall, the result has been the emergence of a uniquely twentieth-century assortment of religious organizations, organizations that have shed their regional localism and their ethnic parochialism.

A unique subset of these twentieth-century religious mergers has involved the reunification of groups split apart in the middle of the nineteenth century in anticipation of the Civil War. The Methodists were reunited North and South in 1939 and subsequently absorbed the Evangelical United Brethren in 1968. A similar process of mergers among the Presbyterians culminated in 1983. Of the major groups fractured by the Civil War, only the Baptists remain divided at the close of the twentieth century. Despite that division, or perhaps even in part because of it, the Southern Baptist Convention now has emerged as the nation's numerically largest Protestant denomination.

In the face of such an array of geographic mobility, technological innovation, and organizational change, it is not surprising that diverse religious organizations have experienced different patterns of growth, stability, or decline during the twentieth century. Untangling those patterns has occupied many scholars of American religion during the past 30 years, including ourselves. However, for the moment, we wish to focus on a different point. From 1890 to 1990, the proportion of the American population identified as affiliated with these religious organizations has remained virtually constant, varying only from 45.2 percent to 46.2 percent (see Table 2-4, p. 49). Thus, despite a staggering amount of

Table 1-3 Twentieth-Century Religious Organizational Mergers in the United States

Year New Name Approx. Size	Constituent Organizations	Ethnic, Regional, and Theological Factors
1906 Presbyterian Church (U.S.A.) [1.6 million]	Presbyterian Church (U.S.A.) Cumberland Presbyterian Church	Old School welcomes in New Light frontier churches of Midwest.
1907 Pentecostal Church of the Nazarene [30,000]	Association of Pentecostal Churches Church of the Nazarene	East and West Coast Holiness groups merge.
1908 Pentecostal Church of the Nazarene [32,000]	Pentecostal Church of the Nazarene Holiness Church of Christ	East and West Coast Holiness groups adopt Texas branch.
1911 American Baptist Convention [1 million]	Northern Baptist Convention Free Baptist Churches	Large Anglo group absorbs smaller New England branch.
1911 Pentecostal Holiness Church [12,000]	Pentecostal Holiness Church Fire-Baptized Holiness Church	Holiness churches consolidate.
1915 Pentecostal Holiness Church [12,000]	Pentecostal Holiness Church Tabernacle Holiness Church	Holiness church absorbs smaller cousin.
1915 Pentecostal Church of the Nazarene [32,250]	Pentecostal Church of the Nazarene Pentecostal Mission	Holiness group absorbs Tennessee-based cousins.
1917 Evangelical Lutheran Church [1 million]	Hauge Norwegian Evangelical Synod Synod of Norwegian Evangelical Churches of America	Norwegian Lutherans unite.
1918 United Lutheran Church [1 million]	General Synod of Lutheran Churches General Council of Lutheran Churches United Synod of the South	Regional branches of Norwegian Lutherans unite.
1920 Presbyterian Church (U.S.A.) [2 million]	Presbyterian Church (U.S.A.) Welsh Methodist Calvin Church	Scotch-Irish Calvinists absorb Welsh version.
1922 Evangelical Church in America [200,000]	United Evangelical Church Evangelical Association	Regional branches of German Pietists merge.
1924 Reformed Church [400,000]	Reformed Church in the United States Hungarian Reformed Church	Swiss and German Calvinists absorb Hungarian cousins.
1925 Congregational Churches [800,000]	Congregational Churches German Congregational Churches Evangelical Protestant Churches North America	"Free church" Anglos absorb German and Scandinavian branches.
1930 American Lutheran Church [260,000]	Lutheran Synod of Buffalo Evangelical Lutheran Synod of Iowa Joint Evangelical Synod of Ohio	German Lutherans merge regional groups.
1931 Congregational Christian Churches [1 million]	Congregational Churches Christian Church	Small "free church" group absorbed by Congregationalism.
1934 Evangelical and Reformed Church [700,000]	Reformed Church in America Evangelical Church in the United States	Two German churches cross theological divide.
1939 Methodist Church [8 million]	Methodist Episcopal Church, South Methodist Episcopal Church	North and South wings of Methodism make national denomination.

Year New Name Approx. Size	Constituent Organizations	Ethnic, Regional, and Theological Factors
1946 Evangelical United Brethren Church [700,000]	Evangelical Church Church of United Brethren in Christ	German Methodist–type groups in in Pa., Md., and Va. unite.
1958 United Presbyterian Church (U.S.A.) [2.6 million]	Presbyterian Church (U.S.A.) United Presbyterian Church in North America	North and Midwest Presbyterians make near national denomination.
1958 American Baptist Convention [1.5 million]	American Baptist Convention Danish Baptist Convention	Anglos absorb smaller Danish Communion.
1961 American Lutheran Church [2 million]	Evangelical Lutheran Church American Lutheran Church United Evangelical Lutheran Church	Norwegian, German, and Danish Lutherans unite.
1961 United Church of Christ [2 million]	Congregational Christian Churches Evangelical and Reformed Church	New England Anglos and Midwest Germans form national denomination.
1961 Unitarian-Universalist Association [170,000]	Unitarian Association Universalist Church of America	Merger of New England upper- class and Midwest middle-class Anglos.
1962 American Lutheran Church [2.5 million]	American Lutheran Church Lutheran Free Church	German Lutheran church absorbs Norwegians.

1962
Lutheran Church in America
[3 million]
	American Evangelical Lutheran
	  Church
	United Lutheran Church in America
	Augustana Evangelical Lutheran
	  Church
	Finnish Evangelical Lutheran Church
		Danish, Norwegian, Swedish, and
		Finnish churches unite to make
		pan-Scandinavian denomination.

1964 Lutheran Church - Missouri Synod [2.6 million]	Lutheran Church - Missouri Synod National Evangelical Lutheran Church	German Lutherans absorb smaller group.

1965
Reformed Presbyterian Church
  Evangelical Synod
[15,000]
	Reformed Presbyterian Church of
	  North America
	Evangelical Presbyterian Church
		Two small orthodox groups merge.

1966
Wesleyan Methodist Church of
  America
[35,000]
	Reformed Baptist Church of Canada
	Wesleyan Methodist Church of
	  America
		Small American Methodist group
		unites with small Canadian Baptist
		group.

1968 United Methodist Church [10 million]	Methodist Church Evangelical United Brethren	German Methodists enter Anglo Methodist fold.
1968 Missionary Church [24,000]	Missionary Church Association United Missionary Church	Two Mennonite bodies sharing Holiness tradition and evangelism focus unite.
1968 Wesleyan Church [87,000]	Wesleyan Methodist Church of America Pilgrim Holiness Church	Two missionary-oriented Methodist groups unite.
1983 Presbyterian Church (U.S.A.) [3.2 million]	United Presbyterian Church Presbyterian Church (U.S.A.)	North and South branches become a national denomination.
1985 Evangelical Lutheran Church in America [5.3 million]	American Lutheran Church Lutheran Church in America Evangelical Lutheran Churches	German and Scandinavian Lutherans unite to become a national denomination.

Sources: The original list for the period 1906 to 1957 was taken from Robert Lee (1960) and was updated by the present writers. For the period 1957 to 1990, there is no single published source.

social and economic change, and despite almost continual lamentations regarding secularization or moral decay, the nation's people appear to be at least as "churched" in 1990 as they were in 1890. This is a remarkable fact that reinforces the view that religious affiliation is an enduring element of American society.

In summary then, whereas the nineteenth century was characterized by the proliferation of small religious organizations, the twentieth century has seen that process reversed. In the first century of the American experience, religious organizations tended to be more narrowly defined, whether by theology, the ethnic heritage of their members, or the geographic location of their origin. In contrast, during the twentieth century, forces tending toward blurring regional distinctiveness or conversely toward national cultural convergence have promoted the development of larger religious organizations whether through organizational mergers or evangelism. A central task of this book is a portrayal of the paths followed by individual religious organizations over the period 1850 to 1990 within the context of the general social and geographic patterns just described.

Chapter 2

Counting the Faithful
Religion and the United States Census

Data Sources on Religion in America

The present study represents a classic case of what social science refers to as secondary analysis. The lion's share of the data were collected by persons other than the present writers, and for purposes other than those at hand. In any scientific study, and surely in one based on secondary analysis, it is important to understand the limits of the available data and the constraints they impose on both analysis and interpretation. Moreover, when, as in this case, the data have been assembled from a variety of sources and were compiled over a lengthy period of time, the question of comparability is of paramount significance. This chapter addresses that concern as well as other methodological questions. First, it describes the data sets as they were originally collected and then as they have been reformatted for use here. Second, it focuses on the issue of comparability and the adaptations made in the original data to arrive at materials suitable for longitudinal or time-series analysis. Finally, special limitations or potential problems are examined, particularly those that have influenced choices as to which of the various data sets available would become the focus of this study.

Data collection activities regarding statistics on religious adherence in the United States fall most conveniently into three general stages. First, from the beginnings of the Colonial period up to the middle of the nineteenth century, "data" on religion in America are found largely in individual accounts of people or parishes and seldom extend to broader identities of even denominational scope. Substantial portrayals of American religion in this period may be found in sources as disparate in style as Edwin Gaustad's *Historical Atlas of Religion in America* (1962) and the much more current *The Churching of America: 1776–1990* by Finke and Stark (1992). We, of course, have leaned heavily on the treatment of early American religion contained in an earlier and widely regarded source, Charles O. Paullin's *Atlas of the Historical Geography of the United States* (1932). Paullin's maps, nearly all of

which already have been viewed here in Chapter 1, contain privately collected counts from various sources for the numbers of churches by denomination in the years 1775 and 1776. Following procedures developed by Finke and Stark (1992), we have calculated from the churches data an estimate of congregational size statistics. Finally, we have transformed the membership data into adherents figures, using a county population adjustment formula that was first employed in the 1971 study *Churches and Church Membership in the United States* (Johnson, Picard, & Quinn 1974). We have applied the latter formula to all denominational statistics in this publication, thereby arriving at comparable adherents statistics across all time periods. Tables 1-1 and 2-4 (pgs. 18 and 49) contain the results of these adjustments.

There is yet one additional source of information regarding religious organizations in the mid-nineteenth century. As the nation's fledgling religious communities were becoming more organized, it appears that many of them occasionally published reports about the size and location of their parishes. These statistics were but a small part of the information appearing in religiously sponsored publications of the era ranging from periodic newsletters to annual almanacs. Fortunately, some of these data are aggregated and reprinted in the 1850 United States Census materials. The latter draws specifically upon the *Baptist Almanac and Annual Register* of 1850. Archives containing this Baptist publication, as well as similar ones published by the Methodists, Congregationalists, Episcopalians, and Catholics, are available in some library collections. In the present instance, a reasonably complete picture of religious organizational patterns for 1850 has been obtained by supplementing United States Census counts with the more detailed listings provided in the *Baptist Almanac and Annual Register* for that year.

Second, in 1850, and at varying points thereafter up to 1936, the United States Bureau of the Census collected information and published a series of reports containing systematic data on American religious organizations. To our thinking, these census data constitute an often neglected source on the roots of American religious organizations, and much of our attention here is focused on them. For reasons that have been described in detail elsewhere, and largely involving "separation of church and state" and "freedom of religion" issues (Petersen 1962), after the Second World War, the Census Bureau ceased collecting data on American religion. The controversial 1957 sample survey is the one notable exception to this policy (Bureau of the Census 1958, Mueller & Lane 1972).

Third, in an attempt to fill the void created by the departure of the Census Bureau from the field, in the early 1950s, the National Council of Churches of Christ (NCCC) undertook a voluntary collection of membership statistics on a county-by-county basis. This report (Whitman & Trimble 1956) represents a mid-century landmark that was used widely but, unfortunately, not replicated until a less formal consortium of denominations under the leadership of the Glenmary Research Center initiated a voluntary, self-reported denominational enumeration in 1971 (Johnson, Picard, & Quinn 1974). This effort was repeated in 1980 (Quinn et al. 1982) and 1990 (Bradley et al. 1992) to coincide with the decennial census. These enumerations represent one of the most widely utilized broad-based data sources relative to American religious affiliation (Carroll, Johnson, & Marty 1979; Shortridge 1976, 1977; Halvorson & Newman 1978, 1987, 1994; Zelinsky 1961; Hale 1977; Newman & Halvorson 1980, 1984; Roof & McKinney 1987; and Stump 1984, 1986).

The balance of this chapter provides a detailed consideration of both the various Census Bureau enumerations (1850–1936) and the Church Membership Studies (1952–1990). Throughout, we wish to clarify exactly what has been counted, how was it counted, and the extent to which these different enumerations together allow for longitudinal analysis of religious trends over the period of two centuries. Additionally, this chapter addresses problems of comparability of the nation's county units during the period under study. The chapter concludes with a consideration of the cultural regions of the United States, for as we will demonstrate, regional settings are an important aspect of religious organizational development. On the one hand, this chapter may be viewed as the traditional "data and methods" drill that, for good reasons, is obligatory in any contemporary social scientific study. However, from the very beginning of our own work with these kinds of data, it has been clear to us that religion has had a somewhat unique place in the workings of the United States Census Bureau. Therein lies a tale, and this chapter seeks to tell it.

Early Private and Census Enumerations

The United States Census of 1850 was the first to include a substantial collection of data on religion in the United States. As such, it marks an important reference point and deserves substantial description. Census reports prior to 1850 included a limited set of what best are described as demographic variables differentiating people largely on the basis of gender, age, race (or "white" vs. "colored"), and free vs. slave status. The 1840 enumeration was expanded to include about two dozen additional variables involving employment types and educational activities. While the 1800 and 1810 enumerations included only 20 variables, by 1840, the list had expanded to 82. In contrast, the 1850 Census contains some 200 variables and involves two separate reports, one at the state level and one including both state- and county-level reporting of variables. Most importantly, for our present concerns, included in these county-level data are statistics on the number of churches, aggregate religious accommodations (often referred to as the "pew count"), and the total value of church property. These data are provided for a total of 23 religious identities that are shown in Table 2-1.

The 1850 United States Census data provide a great deal of social information about American society at a critical moment in its history. It is coincident with the opening of the era of the great trans-Atlantic migrations of the last half of the nineteenth century that so altered the cultural fabric of the nation. However, these data also pose serious problems in terms of direct comparison with later enumerations in at least three distinct areas. These are the areal units (counties) for which data are reported, the religious entities that are identified, and the measures that are employed. First, and most obvious, the national territory of the United States was not fully settled in 1850. Though conventional wisdom depicts the nation as expanding across the Mississippi and reaching Oregon and California by this time, actually

Table 2-1 Religious Organizations in the 1850 United States Census for Which County-Level Data Are Available (Based on the *Baptist Almanac and Annual Register* (1850) with additions based on the United States Census of 1850)

Name of Group	Number of Churches	Members as Reported in *Baptist Almanac*	Estimated Adherents[a]
Methodist[b]	13,338		
Methodist Episcopal		629,660	886,561
Methodist Episcopal South		465,553	655,499
Methodist Protestant		64,313	90,553
Methodist Wesleyan		20,000	28,160
Baptist Regular	8,406	686,807	967,024
Baptist Anti-Mission	2,035	67,845	95,526
Baptist Seventh-Day	52	6,243	8,790
Baptist Six Principle	21	3,586	5,049
Baptist Free Will	1,252	56,452	79,484
Baptist Church of God	97	10,102	14,224
Baptist Campbellites	1,848	118,618	167,014
Baptist Christian (Union)	607	33,040	46,520
Congregationalists (Orthodox)	1,971	197,196	277,652
Congregational Unitarian	244	30,000	42,240
Protestant Episcopal	1,192	67,550	95,110
Presbyterians Old School	2,512	200,830	282,768
Presbyterians New School	1,555	139,047	195,778
Presbyterians Cumberland	1,250	50,000	70,400
Presbyterians Associate	530	45,500	64,064
Dutch Reformed	276	32,840	46,239
German Reformed	261	69,750	98,208
Lutherans	1,604	163,000	229,504
United Brethren	800	15,000	21,120
Evangelical (German)	600	16,000	22,528
Moravians	22	6,000	8,448
Mennonites	400	58,000	81,664
Swedenborgians	42	3,000	4,224
Universalists	918	60,000	84,480
Mormons		20,000	28,160
Roman Catholic[c]	812	1,173,700	1,220,446[c]
Subtotal		4,509,632	5,917,437
Jewish Population[b]	37		19,588
Friends[b]	728		82,002
Free Church[b]	389		43,817
Tunker	52		22,400
Estimated total adherents			6,085,252
Proportion of total U.S. population			26.2%

a   The estimation procedure is derived from that employed in the *Churches and Church Membership in the United States* studies of 1971, 1980, and 1990.

b   Churches counting only adults as members are adjusted upward based on the proportion of the population 14 years old or younger in 1850. The *Baptist Almanac and Annual Register* (1850), while providing more detailed information than does the census, omits three groups enumerated by the census. In those instances the number of churches reported for the group by the Census Bureau has been used and has been multiplied by 80 (an estimated average congregation size based on the Congregationalists and Presbyterians in 1850) and further adjusted for the members vs. adherents differential.

c   The *Baptist Almanac and Annual Register* (1850) reports data for 812 Catholic churches whereas the United States Census of 1850 reports 1,227 Catholic churches. The *Baptist Almanac and Annual Register* (1850) membership has been adjusted upward to compensate for the difference by a procedure described in the preceding note.

the portion of the country settled and "organized" was relatively limited. Maps 2-1 through 2-4 allow comparing of the county units in the nation as of 1850 with those units present in 1890, 1952, and 1990. These include both directly comparable units, as well as some where relatively simple aggregation or partition will yield comparable units. In 1850, there are 1,287 comparable units constituting 42 percent of the 1990 total of 3,073 counties. This disparity represents a significant difference and severely limits comparability even, as will be seen, over a relatively short period of time.

Second, the process of identifying and "labelling" the religious communities in 1850 also is problematic. The list in Table 2-1 (p. 39) is a curious mixture of what today, at best, can be described as religious "families" (Baptist, Jewish, Lutheran, and Presbyterian), "denominations" (Episcopal and Roman Catholic), and "sects" (Swedenborgian and Tunker). Other religious communities (Protestant, and minor sects) defy categorization by contemporary terminology. By way of example, while the 1850 Census reports national-level membership data drawn from another source (*Baptist Almanac and Annual Register* 1850) for a wide variety of small religious organizations, the county-level data actually collected and reported by the Census Bureau lump these organizations into a single "minor sect" category. As a result, for many groups it is impossible to make county-level alignments with later data sources. Alternately, in 1850, another group, the Free Church, represents an association of abolitionist congregations drawn from a variety of denominational backgrounds. By 1870, the Free Church no longer exists as a distinct entity because individual congregations had merged back into the denominations or families from which they originally came. As a result, though the 1850 data may be used to provide a variety of portraits of American religion at the mid-point of the nineteenth century, these data entail identifiers that limit the ability to engage in detailed longitudinal analysis.

Moreover, the census takers in 1850 curiously ignore several schisms that already had occurred in several major denominations. National-level statistics taken from the *Baptist Almanac and Annual Register* of 1850 and reported by the Census Bureau distinguish between Methodist Episcopal and Methodist Episcopal, South, and between New School and Old School Presbyterians. However, in the census reports Regular Baptists comprise a single category, despite the fact that the Southern Baptist Convention already had been formed in 1845. Moreover, the state- and county-level data collected by the Census Bureau use the generic (i.e., family) categories,

Methodist, Presbyterian, Baptist, even though, as we have just noted, various divisions among all three appear in the national-level statistics of the *Baptist Almanac and Annual Register*.

Two measures of religion are provided in the 1850 Census. The number of churches is a clear and unambiguous measure that is replicated in subsequent Census Bureau and privately administered enumerations. However, the matter of a head count of participants is much more troublesome. The closest approximation in 1850 to the modern idea of members or adherents is "accommodations," sometimes referred to as the "pew count." The transformation of pew counts into an estimate of membership has been discussed by sociologists and historians alike (Bonomi & Eisenstadt 1982, Bonomi 1986, Finke & Stark 1986, 1992). Finke and Stark (1992) caution against estimating membership from pew counts at the county level and have undertaken a conversion to membership estimates only at the state level. However, in our view, the greater problem is that the 1850 United States Census data provide comparability with later data sets for only a very small number of modern denominations.

As we already have noted, in 1850, in addition to the data collected by the Census Bureau that has just been described here, the Bureau also published denominational-level statistics for the entire nation drawn from the independently published *Baptist Almanac and Annual Register* (1850). This publication, which apparently began annual editions in the year 1842 and published continuously under several different names through at least 1866, drew statistics from a diversity of other religious organizational publications. As the editors of that almanac themselves state in the 1846 edition, these statistics "may be considered as a fair approximation to correct religious statistics of those that in a general sense are denominated 'evangelical Christians,' in our country" (p. 27).

From citations found in various editions of the *Baptist Almanac and Annual Register,* it is apparent that it was common practice for religious organizations and societies to publish "almanacs" on an annual basis. In addition to containing self-collected statistics for the respective denominations, these publications also contained various kinds of information, including population statistics collected by the United States Census Bureau, as well as lunar tables, which were useful to the general population in agricultural pursuits at this time. The 1857 version of the almanac contains a humorously interesting note of interest to those who have, in the twentieth century, dealt with the difficulties of collecting statistics of this type. The editors write, "although we have

Map 2-1

COUNTIES IN THE UNITED STATES: 1850

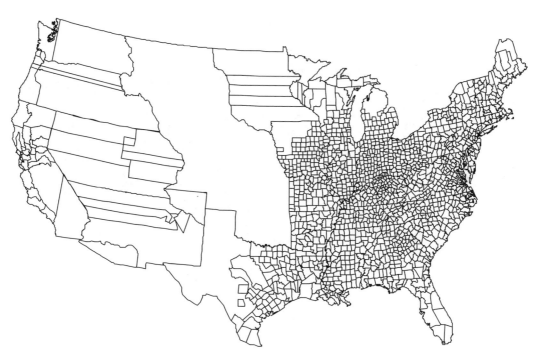

Map 2-2

COUNTIES IN THE UNITED STATES: 1890

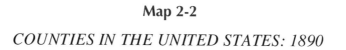

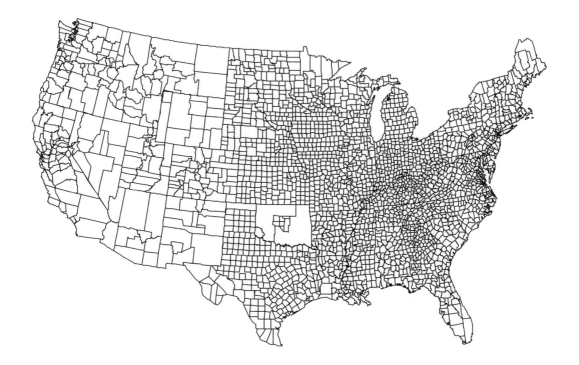

Map 2-3

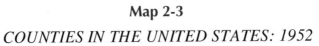

COUNTIES IN THE UNITED STATES: 1952

Map 2-4

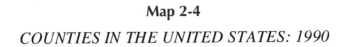

COUNTIES IN THE UNITED STATES: 1990

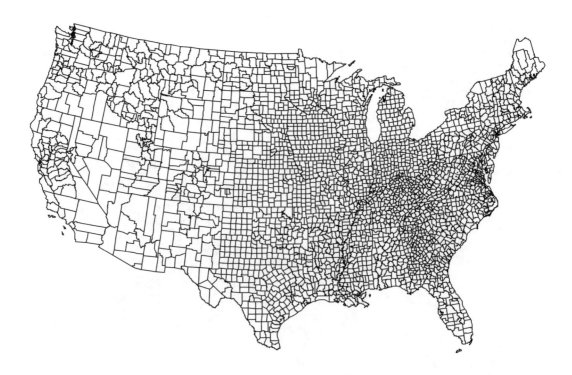

made every effort to procure minutes of the associations generally, we have been but partially successful, and have been obliged in many instances to give returns of previous years: hence the result is only an approximation to the actual number of Baptist churches, ministers, and members" (p. 46). A similar dilemma faced statisticians at the National Council of Churches of Christ during the early 1950s when they attempted to produce a self-reported census of church adherence for the entire nation. Clearly, the problem of "counting every member" is no different in the twentieth century than it was in the nineteenth century.

As we will show later in this chapter, 1890 appears to be the only year in which the United States Census Bureau actually undertook its own headcount of religious adherents. In all other instances, and clearly beginning with these publications in the 1850s and 1860s, the Census Bureau itself relied upon statistics provided by religious organizations themselves. In this regard, the data supplied by the *Baptist Almanac and Annual Register* are remarkably compatible not only with later census data collected early in the twentieth century, but also with the private enumerations undertaken in 1952, 1971, 1980, and 1990 (Whitman & Trimble 1956; Johnson, Picard, & Quinn 1974; Quinn et al. 1982; Bradley et al. 1992). Some scholars (Finke & Stark 1992) have focused on the Census Bureau's data for 1890 and have employed that data to estimate retrospectively adherence statistics for earlier periods. In our own estimation, the privately collected statistics generated by religious organizations themselves such as those printed in the *Baptist Almanac and Annual Register* and subsequently reprinted by the Census Bureau represent superior estimates of the extent of religious adherence by organization for these early time periods. Accordingly, we have relied heavily on these privately assembled organizational data for the mid-nineteenth century and emphasize again the extent of their compatibility with both twentieth century census and privately collected data described later in this chapter.

We have chosen to use the 1850 Census data simply to identify counties within which particular religious organizations had become established. Doing so allows us to identify points of origin from which their subsequent history of growth and dispersion can be traced. For estimates of the national membership strength of the various organizations in 1850, for the several reasons already noted, we have chosen to use the data reported by the Census Bureau from the *Baptist Almanac and Annual Register*. Although these data are incomplete because they omit a number of groups present by 1850 (the Chris-

tian Church, Jews, and Friends most notably), they do encompass most major religious organizations. As with all subsequent data sets, membership numbers have been adjusted upward to create adherents numbers that account for the portion of the society under age 13 and thus not yet advanced to full religious membership. This statistical adjustment creates comparability across religious groups and time periods (See Newman, Halvorson & Brown 1977).

The version of the 1850 Census county-level data employed here is a computer file entitled "Historical, Demographic, Economic, and Social Data: The United States, 1790–1970." This file was assembled by the Interuniversity Consortium for Political and Social Research (ICPSR) at the University of Michigan. In the instance of the 1850 Census, the file appears to be virtually a complete replication of the original printed source (albeit minus some explanatory text). This means that there have been no apparent editorial modifications limiting the interpretation of the data. Unfortunately, as was previously noted, the original manuscripts do not provide county-level data for many individual "minor sects" that register substantial numbers of adherents in later data sets. Nonetheless, using the computer file version of the data does not enlarge that problem.

In the census enumerations of 1860 and 1870, roughly comparable data on religious communities are assembled. The measures, "number of churches," "aggregate accommodations," and "value of property" are repeated in 1860, whereas the 1870 county-level data include only two measures labelled "organizations" and "sittings." The "value of property" measure is reported in 1870 only at the state level. The sorts of data collected in these enumerations are a reflection of the process utilized in their collection. The data were gathered by tax assessors at the county level and then aggregated. Both this indirect process of data collection and the information at hand for tax assessors as the enumerators of religious bodies represent fascinating aspects of these data collections. Nonetheless, the measures of organizational presence are roughly comparable across the 20-year interval from 1850 to 1870.

More difficulty in comparability is encountered in the area of the several identities for which data are reported. The 1860 enumeration contains 30 different religious identities, plus a residual minor sects category. Included are seven brands of Baptists (including one separately identified in 1850), four kinds of Presbyterians, and four new identities: Adventist, Mormon, Shaker, and Spiritualist. One religious group identity appearing in 1850 does not reappear, and it does not seem that the "Free" identity of 1850 is the same as the "Free Will Baptists" of

1860. These difficulties are accentuated by the 1870 enumeration, which returns Baptists and Presbyterians to single, apparently inclusive, categories but eliminates three identities used in the two previous enumerations as well as the minor sect category. Suffice it to say that these variations are troublesome, and since the manuscript versions do not provide thorough documentation as to procedures and aggregation techniques or criteria, attempts at reconciliation of these differences are fraught with uncertainty. We have not attempted to deal with this in any but the most general sense and, therefore, will not employ the 1860 and 1870 data for detailed analysis here.

The 1880 Census did not include information on religious organizations comparable to that found in the three previous enumerations. The "state" and "county" files are totally lacking such data, and the "state only" file includes a report of the "number of newspapers and periodicals" for 24 distinct religious communities but does not contain information on numbers of churches or a pew count. According to Christiano (1987), an extensive religious census was undertaken in 1880, but a shortage of funds prevented the Census Bureau from publishing the data that was collected. Thus, the omission of a published standard measure of religion in 1880 represents a major gap in the United States Census record.

To summarize, though it is possible to establish a baseline of data for 1850, it is virtually impossible to link that baseline with the data reported subsequently. Even where reasonably consistent measures of religion are available, there are not consistent categories of religious denominations, organizations, families, and the like. Thus, for social scientists attempting to reconstruct the story of how religious organizations came to populate the American landscape, these early Census materials provide some benchmark information, but not much data suitable for constructing time-series longitudinal analyses. However, this disappointing prospect brightens enormously with the 1890 Census.

Later Census Enumerations

The Census of 1890 is a unique resource for the study of American religion. First, as seen in Map 2-2 (page 41), in 1890, the stage is substantially more set than it was in 1850 in terms of the settlement of the country. By 1890, it is possible to identify 2,720 counties that can be aligned with the 3,073 present in 1990. This represents an 89 percent degree of compatibility. There are significant gaps in the map in only five states; Idaho, Montana, New Mexico, Oklahoma, and Wyoming. Everywhere else, the county-level map is remarkably complete. In only forty years, the basic geographic framework of counties for the entire country has been completed to a degree that permits broad comparability with patterns occurring 100 years later.

Second, the 1890 enumeration contains data regarding a large number of religious identities that are comparable to the organization-oriented files in subsequent Census Bureau enumerations (1906, 1916, 1926, and 1936), as well as in the voluntarily collected enumerations of the second half of the twentieth century (1952, 1971, 1980, and 1990) (Whitman & Trimble 1956; Johnson, Picard, & Quinn 1974; Quinn et al. 1982; Bradley et al. 1992). From this point forward, tracing denominational or organizational histories in terms of growth and spatial dispersion is far more possible because a consistent approach to labelling religious groups has been followed in the original data sources. Tracking changes in the names of denominations, as well as organizational mergers and schisms among them, become the major challenges. Unfortunately but understandably, the Interuniversity Consortium for Political and Social Research (ICPSR) computer-accessible rendition of the 1890 census is an abridged version of the original print document. The ICPSR file contains data for 60 distinct groups, whereas the printed volumes provides data for an additional 84 groups, as well as "independent congregations." Apparently, in the interest of streamlining the data conversion task, smaller groups were eliminated. Only ten of the "missing" religious organizations reported more than 100 churches nationwide. Although some of these might be of interest because they have persisted into the twentieth century, in general, those eliminated are relatively minor. Thus, the organizations available in the ICPSR file provide the basic framework for an analysis of the religious landscape at the end of the nineteenth century. The groups included in the ICPSR computerized version of the 1890 Census are listed in Table 2-2. Although many changes in name have occurred since 1890, the list includes most of the religious organizations still present in 1990 with two types of exceptions. First, there are a number of significant bodies that had not yet been founded. Included are the Assemblies of God (1914), the Churches of Christ (circa 1906), the Church of the Nazarene (1906), the International Church of the Foursquare Gospel (1927), and the Pentecostal Holiness Church (1898). More glaring omissions that are absent from

Table 2-2 Religious Organizations in the 1890 United States Census

Advent Christian Church	Joint Lutheran Synod of Ohio and Other States Church
Seventh-Day Adventist Church	Hauge's Lutheran Synod Church
Regular Baptist (North) Church	Norwegian Lutheran Church in America
Regular Baptist (Colored) Church	Mennonite Church
Freewill Baptist Church	Amish Mennonite Church
General Baptist Church	Methodist Protestant Church
Primitive Baptist Church	African Methodist Episcopal Church
Old Two-Seed-in-the Spirit Predestinarian Baptist	African Methodist Episcopal Zion Church
Roman Catholic Church	Wesleyan Methodist Connection of America Church
Christian (Christian Connection)	Methodist Episcopal Church (South)
Christian Scientist Church	Colored Methodist Episcopal Church
Independent Churches of Christ in Christian Union	Free Methodist Church of North America
Church of God Church	Moravian Church
Church of the New Jerusalem (Swedenborgian)	Presbyterian Church in the U.S.A. (Northern)
Congregationalist Church	Cumberland Presbyterian Church
Disciples of Christ Church	Cumberland Presbyterian (Colored) Church
Dunkard (Conservative) Church	Welsh Calvinistic Methodist Church
Evangelical Association Church	United Presbyterian Church
Friends (Orthodox) Church	Presbyterian Church in the U.S.A. (Southern)
Friends (Hicksite) Church	Protestant Episcopal Church
German Evangelical Synod of North America Church	Reformed Church in America
Jewish (Orthodox) Congregations	Reformed Church in the United States
Jewish (Reformed) Congregations	Salvation Army
Church of Jesus Christ of Latter Day Saints	Spiritualist Church
Reorganized Church of Jesus Christ of Latter Day Saints	United Brethren in Christ Church
Lutheran General Synod Church	Unitarian Church
United Synod in the South (Lutheran) Church	Universalist Church
General Council (Lutheran) Church	

both the ICPSR files and the original Census enumerations and that also are explained less easily include the Christian Reformed Church, the Church of God (Anderson), the Wisconsin Evangelical Lutheran Synod, the Baptist Missionary Association, and the Christian and Missionary Alliance, all of which by 1990 number in the hundreds of thousands of adherents. Even more perplexing, due to their numerical size, and also among the missing, are the Eastern Orthodox Churches for whom reliable numbers still are difficult to obtain, and the then recently organized American National Baptist Convention, which would become the founding group for the two largest, present-day black Baptist organizations. For these several organizations, one can only presume that either they refused to respond to Census Bureau inquiries or that they lacked the organizational infrastructure to do so. Despite these exceptions, and to continue a metaphor, it can be argued that by 1890, the stage basically is set, and most of the cast of players (denominations and sects) has been assembled for telling the story of religion in the twentieth-century United States.

The degree of comparability between county units and denominational labels alone would serve to distinguish the 1890 Census data from its predecessors as uniquely appropriate for longitudinal analysis. However, the picture gets even better in terms of the measures that are employed. The 1890 enumeration includes five separate measures of religious communities: organizations, edifices, seatings, the value of property, and communicant members. In two very important ways, this array of variables provides a check as well as a mechanism for calculating conversions of data reported in the 1850, 1860, and 1870 Censuses. First, as has been reported by Finke and Stark (1986, 1992), the parallel collection and reporting of both "communicant membership" and "seating" permits an estimation of the relationship between these two variables at different points in time. Utilizing this link, they have made retrospective estimates of the state-level "memberships" of the various religious organizations in 1850, when, it will be remembered, only "pew count" data are provided by the census. We have not pursued such an estimate at the county level in 1850 both because our prime concern is with the location of the organization rather than its exact size in each county, and because such estimates would be highly prone to error. However, these 1890 data provide the first unambiguous direct measures of the strength of the various religious organizations, a conspicuous asset. Again, it should be noted that we have converted the 1890 members count to an adherents count by utilizing the same procedure employed in the 1952 National Council of Churches of Christ (NCCC) enumeration and those at later dates. This conversion to adherents permits comparability between these 1890 Census Bureau data and those data sets collected privately in the latter half of the twentieth century.

Second, the potential confusion of meaning that occurred with the 1870 Census regarding the number of churches also has been addressed in the 1890 Census. It will be recalled that after reporting "number of churches" in both 1850 and 1860, in 1870 the Census Bureau used the somewhat more general term "organizations." The manuscript versions of these Census reports do not clarify whether the measures consistently involve all religious bodies or only those having their own places of worship (i.e., buildings). However, the 1890 enumeration, once again, provides both types of measures of the presence of a church. This creates at least some limited opportunity for clarifying the meaning of the statistics published in earlier reports. For all of these reasons, the 1890 Census enumeration is a particularly valuable source of data on American religion.

The magnitude of the 1890 data file on religious organizations apparently triggered a number of changes in later census studies. The most important of these is that subsequent United States Census Bureau enumerations of religious bodies became part of what are sometimes called "special counts." These are focused topical enumerations that take place in years other than that of the general decennial census. Subsequent census reports on religious bodies are dated 1906, 1916, 1926, and 1936. As a result, changes in religious organizations may not be measured readily against changes for the same interval in either general demographic or socio-economic conditions that might be reflected in the decennial census. In other words, general census variables are available for the beginning of each decade (1900, 1910, 1920, etc.), whereas census materials on religion appear closer to mid-decade (1906, 1916, 1926, and 1936). Comparisons may be undertaken only after creating estimated values for the non-religion variables. Although this is not impossible, it does create an uncertainty as to the validity of the statistics produced, particularly over the first two

decades of the twentieth century (1900 to 1910 and 1910 to 1920), when population change in the United States was highly dynamic due to massive immigration.

The census enumerations after 1890 also vividly illustrate some of the perils of the sort of secondary research we have undertaken here. In 1906, in place of the five measures reported in 1890, the Census Bureau collected data on a total of 19 variables including the amount of debt on local churches, the salary of ministers, and the language in which services were conducted. By 1916, the data base again was expanded and includes a schedule consisting of 24 separate variables for each local congregation, with a detailed report of annual expenditures. A separate questionnaire for ministers is composed of an additional 12 variables including data on individual salaries and educational background. In 1926, the list was further subdivided and expanded, and by the 1936 enumeration, it had reached a total of 51 variables—a testament to the seemingly manic behavior of data gatherers. It should be noted that starting in 1890, the enumeration procedure changed from using local tax assessors as enumerators to canvassing local church bodies directly. It is little wonder that by 1936, the Census Bureau began to encounter "refusniks" who failed to report as requested and that the rate of such non-reporting increased to even greater levels in 1946. In some senses, over-zealous data collection fueled the fires of both paranoia and resentment in ways that could only compromise the data collection effort. The results include a significant problem of incomplete reporting in 1936 and yet another reason for the abandonment of the 1946 enumeration when it had been only partially completed.

Vexing as these problems may seem, they have been further compounded in two ways. First, starting in 1906, the Census Bureau adopted a convention of reporting local membership numbers at the county level only for a selected set of the larger denominations in each individual locality. Thus, while state-level reporting is all inclusive, full county-level analysis for all denominations is not possible with the 1906 data. During the 1970s, a consortium of scholars, working under a National Science Foundation grant, computerized these early census data files. However, the resulting ICPSR tapes, which represent the most readily useable version of the 1906, 1916, 1926, and 1936 enumerations, contain *only* the number of members variable for religion. Although this represents an obvious choice in terms of an economy of data processing, it further compromises data analysis for users wishing to focus on other indicators such as the number of churches. The enumerations of 1906, 1916, 1926, and 1936 represent an intriguing and comprehensive data archive. However, in their present form, they are most amenable either to extremely detailed local-level study or aggregated state-level analysis based on the original manuscript versions. For all of these reasons, it should be easy to understand our decision to focus on the 1890 enumeration as the most appropriate data point in proximity to the turn of the century.

Given the general climate of continued immigration and population growth, as well as of organizational development, it is hardly surprising that these special censuses include even more sects and denominations than did the earlier census studies. Between 1890 and 1906, the number of sects and denominations grew from 60 to 91, and reached a peak of 108 in 1916. As might be expected, the added numbers of denominations include most branches of the Eastern Orthodox Church and, by 1916, both the Assemblies of God and Church of the Nazarene. The inclusion of these organizations surely enhances the usefulness of these enumerations for analysis of membership trends at the state or aggregate national level. However, for nationwide county-level analysis, the 1890 data set remains the most useful.

Strangely, after 1916, the completeness of the census data files begins to diminish. The 1926 enumeration includes only 82 denominations, and that of 1936, only 73. Though some of this may be accounted for by the fact that religious organizational mergers were occurring during this period, it also appears that groups may have become less cooperative. Indeed, by 1936, some participating denominations provide incomplete statistics. This kind of reporting, with its resultant incomplete files, sets the stage for the Census Bureau's abandonment of its enumeration after the Second World War, a decision buttressed by any number of arguments against such an enumeration based on "separation of church and state" and similar positions. Viewed in this perspective, it may be argued that the 1890 data file represents the high-water mark of the Census Bureau's enumerations of religion. Therefore, we have yet another reason for focusing a good deal of attention on the 1890 data.

The Church Membership Studies

Not surprisingly, the decision by the Census Bureau to discontinue the practice of collecting and publishing data on American religious institutions eventually led to a private effort to replicate the census enumerations. This effort was coordinated by the National Council of Churches of Christ (NCCC) Department of Survey, Research, and Evaluation, which was headed by Lauris B. Whitman. In the early 1950s, the NCCC approached all denominations included in its *Yearbook of American Churches* with a request to provide county-level enumerations of their churches and memberships. Ultimately, they secured cooperation and reporting by 114 religious bodies, 32 of which reported more than 100,000 members (Whitman & Trimble 1956, Series A, No. 1, p. 3). The data were requested for calendar year 1952 but, in fact, range from 1951 to 1954. This enumeration also includes data on Jews and Mormons that were estimated from other sources (see Halvorson & Newman 1978, 1994, and Newman & Halvorson 1982, 1993). In total, the study covers an aggregate membership of more than 74 million persons, as compared to a total United States population of slightly more than 150 million in 1950. As reported by Whitman and Trimble (1956, Series A, No. 1, pp. 3–4), among the most noticeable non-participating bodies were the Churches of Christ, Negro Churches, Eastern Orthodox churches, and Christian Science organizations.

Despite these gaps, this very ambitious project was successful due in no small part to the study director's significant efforts to ensure greater comparability and accuracy by correcting and adjusting the reported data. The final product is published at multiple levels of aggregation in several series of reports including a general introduction and summary tables (Series A); denominational statistics by regions, divisions, and states (Series B); denominational statistics by state and county (Series C); denominational statistics by metropolitan area (Series D); and analysis of socio-economic characteristics (Series E). These data, published as a series of booklets, can also be found as a bound volume in some libraries (Whitman & Trimble 1956).

Though the specific measures reported in Series A through D vary as to the unit of observation, they all derive from the same basic variables reported in Series C: "number of churches" and "reported membership." In that and other reports, comparisons also are made to "total population," based on the 1950 Census counts as adjusted by the subtraction of the "Negro" population to reflect the absence from the enumeration of most of the denominations labelled "Negro Churches." These data became the touchstone for a spate of research efforts (Gaustad 1962; Halvorson & Newman 1978, 1987, 1994; Newman & Halvorson 1980; Sopher 1967; and Zelinsky

1961). They also provided the procedural model for subsequent private census-type studies undertaken in 1971 (Johnson, Picard, & Quinn 1974), 1980 (Quinn et al. 1982), and 1990 (Bradley et al. 1992).

A small sampling of data from this 1952 census-type report is preserved in the ICPSR 1790–1970 computerized data file, which, it will be remembered, is the primary source for the various earlier United States Census enumerations. However, that sampling of the 1952 NCCC enumeration only aggregates certain denominations into "families" (Baptist, Lutheran, Presbyterian, and others), and includes only nine such groupings. In the 1970s, we undertook a much more complete conversion of the 1952 manuscript reports into a computer-accessible data archive (Newman & Halvorson 1982, 1993; Newman, Halvorson, & Brown 1977). That archive is housed at the Roper Center at the University of Connecticut and is the version of the 1952 NCCC data set utilized here.

The precipitating event leading to the creation of that archive was the publication in 1974 of the successor to the NCCC enumeration. Entitled *Churches and Church Membership in the United States, 1971* (Johnson, Picard, & Quinn 1974), that report includes 53 religious denominations providing self-reported 1971 data to a consortium led by the Glenmary Research Center. Subsequent enumerations timed to coincide with the decennial census in both 1980 (Quinn et al. 1982) and 1990 (Bradley et al. 1992) are essentially extensions of the 1971 effort. All three of these studies vary from the NCCC format only by the inclusion of a measure called "adherents." That measure attempts to reconcile the differences between organizations counting all members from birth (adherents), as opposed to those that only count adult members. For organizations that do not report both types of statistic, the adherents measure is estimated by increasing the members count by a proportion equivalent to the proportion of the county population under 14 years of age. This modification, which results in a uniform adherents statistic for all religious communities, provides greater comparability than is attained by using the self-reported members statistic (see Newman, Halvorson, & Brown 1977). We have employed the same technique retrospectively to both census data

and privately collected nineteenth-century data prior to undertaking longitudinal analysis.

Finally, it should be noted that following the example of Whitman & Trimble (1956), we have used statistics for American Jews taken from the *American Jewish Yearbook* (American Jewish Committee, annual editions). These data, rather than providing estimates of denominational memberships (Reform, Orthodox, Conservative, etc.) are Jewish population estimates at the community level. We have allocated these data to county locations, and believe that, given incomplete Jewish denominational data in the several studies, these "population" estimates best approximate the adherents statistics used for Christian denominations.

Unfortunately, the 1971 data collection included the smallest representation of organizations of any of the voluntarily collected data sets. Since employing it here would have meant losing numerous religious bodies for which data can be matched for 1890, 1952, and 1990 but not 1971, we have decided not to use the 1971 data. Given severe constraints of time and money during our process of automating the 1952 NCCC data, we selected 58 denominations from the original set of 114 groups. After aggregations to account for organizational mergers, this was further reduced to 39 denominations. Fortunately, most of the omitted organizations are extremely small. Consequently, new "repairs" or additions to the 1952 data file that we created have not been undertaken and that data file remains our primary data source for the middle of the twentieth century.

What then do these various attempts at counting the religious communities of the United States yield? Table 2-3 provides a summary of what, after all the changes in enumeration practices, is a surprisingly stable series of data sets. The most recent count provides a base for comparison. The organizations included in the 1990 portion of the data archive total more than 115 million adherents and constitute more than 46 percent of the total national population. This aggregation, encompassing close to half of the total population, is remarkably inclusive and begins to approach the proportion of practicing Judeo-Christian religionists that might be expected based on survey research studies of religious practice.

Table 2-3 Religious Adherents as a Percentage of United States Population: 1850, 1890, 1952, 1990

	1850	1890	1952	1990
Number of adherents (millions)	6.1	28.1	69.3	115.4
United States population	23.1	62.1	150.7	250
Percentage of United States population	26.4	45.2	46	46.2

Table 2-4 Number of Adherents and Percent Change for Religious Organizations in 1890, 1952 & 1990

Name	Adherents			Percent Change		
	1890	1952	1990	1890–1952	1952–90	1890–1990
Advent Christian Church	39,061	30,765	23,794	n/a	n/a	−39.1
African Methodist Episcopal Zion Church	599,836	n/a	1,142,016	n/a	n/a	90.4
American Baptist Churches in the U.S.A.	1,310,799	1,577,977	1,870,923	20.4	18.6	42.7
Assemblies of God	n/a	459,256	2,139,826	n/a	353	n/a
Baptist General Conference	n/a	49,127	167,874	−61.9	241.7	30.2
Brethren in Christ Church	2,688	6,007	19,769	223.4	229.1	n/a
Catholic Church	9,037,129	29,689,148	53,108,015	228.5	79.8	490.7
Christian Church (Disciples of Christ)	1,020,541	1,836,104	1,037,757	356.5	n/a	1.7
Christian Churches and Churches of Christ	n/a	n/a	1,210,319	n/a	n/a	n/a
Christian Reformed Church	17,557	155,355	225,852	884.8	45.4	n/a
Church of God (Anderson, Indiana)	n/a	105,564	227,887	n/a	115.9	n/a
Church of God (Cleveland, Tennessee)	n/a	136,461	691,563	n/a	406.8	n/a
Church of Jesus Christ of Latter Day Saints (Mormons)	261,633	845,689	3,540,820	n/a	n/a	1,253.40
Church of the Brethren	33,234	189,277	186,588	469.5	−1.4	461.4
Church of the Nazarene	n/a	249,033	683,245	n/a	174.4	n/a
Churches of Christ	n/a	n/a	1,677,711	n/a	n/a	n/a
Cumberland Presbyterian Church	293,671	92,656	91,040	−68.4	−1.7	−69
Episcopal Church	784,852	2,555,063	2,427,350	225.5	−4.3	211.6
Evangelical Congregational Church	n/a	28,596	33,166	n/a	16	n/a
Evangelical Lutheran Church in America	745,335	4,225,063	5,226,798	283.2	23.7	374.1
Free Methodist Church of North America	34,260	49,052	70,394	43.2	43.5	105.5
Friends	155,664	95,029	130,484	−39	37.3	−16.2
International Church of the Foursquare Gospel	n/a	66,181	250,250	n/a	278.1	n/a
Jewish Population	193,708	5,146,634	5,982,529	2,556.90	16.2	2,988.40
Lutheran Church - Missouri Synod	357,153	1,856,638	2,603,725	5,198.40	40.2	126.5
Mennonite Church	41,496	66,652	154,259	60.6	131.4	271.7
Moravian Church in America, UF	18,137	48,618	52,519	168.1	8	189.6
North American Baptist Conference	n/a	35,431	54,010	n/a	52.4	n/a
Pentecostal Holiness Church, International	n/a	41,541	156,431	n/a	276.6	n/a
Presbyterian Church (U.S.A.)	1,601,681	3,415,837	3,553,335	113.3	4	121.9
Reformed Church in America	133,818	194,157	362,932	45.1	86.9	171.2
Salvation Army	13,018	n/a	115,320	n/a	n/a	785.9
Seventh-Day Adventists	43,956	252,917	903,062	475.4	257.1	1,954.50
Seventh Day Baptist General Conference	9,143	6,425	6,439	n/a	0.2	n/a
Southern Baptist Convention	2,177,908	8,122,346	18,891,633	272.9	133.2	769.8
Unitarian-Universalist Association	165,575	160,336	174,004	−3.2	−11.9	8.5
United Church of Christ	1,473,458	2,009,642	1,993,459	36.4	−0.8	35.3
United Methodist Church	6,243,337	9,509,418	11,077,728	52.3	16.6	77.7
Wisconsin Evangelical Lutheran Synod	n/a	316,692	418,820	n/a	32.2	n/a

Working backward, the enumerations of 1952 and 1890 yield surprisingly similar results despite having been compiled by two different organizations. The 1952 data reveals 46 percent of the total national population to be religious adherents, while the 1890 count shows just slightly less than that. This degree of stability, added to the factors already mentioned regarding enumeration practice and comparable county units, reinforces our decision to begin time-series mapping with the data for 1890 and to focus on developments in 1952 and 1990 for the century since that benchmark data collection. Tables 2-4 through 2-6 provide a complete list of the

39 religious organizations for which comparable data are available in the years 1890, 1952, and 1990. This exceedingly representative list of American religious organizations are the "players" for the historical drama to be examined here. Table 2-4 (p. 49) gives the number of adherents and percent change for these years. Table 2-5 presents the number of churches by religious organization, and Table 2-6 provides the number of counties in which these organizations were present and the percent change for these years.

Obviously, the 1850 materials are not very compatible with any of the later data collections.

Table 2-5 Number of Churches by Religious Organization: 1890, 1952, 1990

Name	1890	1952	1990
Advent Christian Church	294	396	329
African Methodist Episcopal Zion Church	1,587	n/a	1,962
American Baptist Churches in the U.S.A.	7,066	5,871	5,801
Assemblies of God	n/a	6,396	11,149
Baptist General Conference	n/a	343	786
Brethren in Christ Church	45	113	188
Catholic Church	8,776	15,726	21,863
Christian Church (Disciples of Christ)	5,324	7,559	4,035
Christian Churches and Churches of Christ	n/a	n/a	5,238
Christian Reformed Church	106	346	716
Church of God (Anderson, Indiana)	n/a	2,015	2,336
Church of God (Cleveland, Tennessee)	n/a	2,617	4,996
Church of Jesus Christ of Latter Day Saints (Mormons)	266	n/a	9,208
Church of the Brethren	338	1,019	1,121
Church of the Nazarene	n/a	3,818	5,167
Churches of Christ	n/a	n/a	13,097
Cumberland Presbyterian Church	2,024	910	737
Episcopal Church	5,019	6,467	7,333
Evangelical Congregational Church	n/a	167	159
Evangelical Lutheran Church in America	5,170	9,527	10,912
Free Methodist Church of North America	620	1,117	1,038
Friends	995	674	1,296
International Church of the Foursquare Gospel	n/a	511	1,445
Jewish Population	301	n/a	3,975
Lutheran Church - Missouri Synod	1,531	4,651	6,020
Mennonite Church	198	544	1,242
Moravian Church in America, UF	114	139	153
North American Baptist Conference	n/a	210	267
Pentecostal Holiness Church, International	n/a	932	1,490
Presbyterian Church (U.S.A.)	9,784	12,841	11,433
Reformed Church in America	670	773	917
Salvation Army	27	n/a	1,167
Seventh-Day Adventists	418	2,796	4,214
Seventh Day Baptist General Conference	78	61	83
Southern Baptist Convention	13,502	29,381	37,922
Unitarian-Universalist Association	1,256	819	965
United Church of Christ	7,968	8,005	6,260
United Methodist Church	22,844	41,048	37,238
Wisconsin Evangelical Lutheran Synod	n/a	831	1,228

Table 2-6 County Statistics for Religious Organizations: 1890, 1952, 1990

Name	Counties			Percent Change		
	1890	1952	1990	1890-1952	1952-90	1890-1990
Advent Christian Church	281	n/a	185	n/a	n/a	-34.2
African Methodist Episcopal Zion Church	289	n/a	448	n/a	n/a	55.1
American Baptist Churches in the U.S.A.	1,307	1,152	1,227	-13.2	8.1	-6.1
Assemblies of God	n/a	2,064	2,546	n/a	18.9	n/a
Baptist General Conference	n/a	181	352	-61.6	94.5	-25.3
Brethren in Christ Church	n/a	57	90	n/a	57.9	n/a
Catholic Church	1,960	2,564	2,965	30.8	15.6	51.3
Christian Church (Disciples of Christ)	1,500	n/a	1,379	n/a	n/a	-8.1
Christian Churches and Churches of Christ	n/a	n/a	1,300	n/a	n/a	n/a
Christian Reformed Church	n/a	121	235	n/a	94.2	n/a
Church of God (Anderson, Indiana)	n/a	990	1,020	n/a	3	n/a
Church of God (Cleveland, Tennessee)	n/a	1,073	1,497	n/a	39.5	n/a
Church of Jesus Christ of Latter Day Saints (Mormons)	316	n/a	1,671	n/a	n/a	428.8
Church of the Brethren	152	460	420	202.6	-8.7	176.3
Church of the Nazarene	n/a	1,680	1,852	n/a	10.2	n/a
Churches of Christ	n/a	n/a	2,397	n/a	n/a	n/a
Cumberland Presbyterian Church	649	307	275	-52.7	-10.4	-57.6
Episcopal Church	1,604	1,946	2,089	21.3	7.3	30.2
Evangelical Congregational Church	n/a	34	36	n/a	5.9	n/a
Evangelical Lutheran Church in America	996	1,420	1,709	50.1	20.4	80.7
Free Methodist Church of North America	463	577	515	24.6	-10.7	11.2
Friends	319	260	666	-18.5	156.2	108.8
International Church of the Foursquare Gospel	n/a	290	537	n/a	85.2	n/a
Jewish Population	202	481	748	138.1	55.5	270.3
Lutheran Church - Missouri Synod	645	1,423	1,779	50.3	25	87.9
Mennonite Church	137	230	445	67.9	93.5	224.8
Moravian Church in America, UF	42	50	64	19	28	52.4
North American Baptist Conference	n/a	146	163	n/a	11.6	n/a
Pentecostal Holiness Church, International	n/a	371	509	n/a	37.2	n/a
Presbyterian Church (U.S.A.)	2,028	2,435	2,381	20.1	-2.2	17.4
Reformed Church in America	106	150	232	41.5	54.7	118.9
Salvation Army	238	n/a	778	n/a	n/a	226.9
Seventh-Day Adventists	612	1,466	1,802	139.5	22.9	194.4
Seventh Day Baptist General Conference	n/a	46	69	n/a	50	n/a
Southern Baptist Convention	1,176	1,789	2,513	52.1	40.5	113.7
Unitarian-Universalist Association	490	365	546	-25.5	49.6	11.4
United Church of Christ	1,347	1,401	1,270	4	-9.4	-5.7
United Methodist Church	2,573	2,890	2,966	12.3	2.6	15.3
Wisconsin Evangelical Lutheran Synod	n/a	248	503	n/a	102.8	n/a

However, as will be seen in later chapters where time-series maps are presented on a group-by-group basis, we have incorporated county-level 1850 churches data into the maps and analyses for those organizations for which it is possible.

The litany of problems in the form of uncertainties or inconsistencies regarding all these data might well convince others that it would be folly to attempt any serious analysis based on such shaky ground. On the contrary, we have long since determined that we would press ahead since these data represent both the best available and the only available. At the same time, we also understand that much of what we see and conclude must be tempered by a certain degree of hesitation and humility. Perhaps like all researchers who engage in secondary analysis, we proceed with the credo that knowing what is knowable is superior to remaining uninformed. In the present case, we have reasonably extensive knowledge about both the groups in the data and the factors that could account for distortions in the data. Convinced that these problems are not excessive, we employ these United States Census data and privately conducted census-type data to better understand the life histories of a wide assortment of American sects and denominations.

Regional Considerations

One of the primary objectives of this book is to develop an approach to the classification of American religious organizations. In addition to focusing on factors such as organizational character, position in American society or culture, and size, all relatively conventional criteria, we also shall focus on their geographic distribution across the country. Doing so requires a consistent partitioning of the country into a set of regions that can be used as a framework for examining and comparing patterns of national dispersion or regional concentration among the various religious organizations for which time-series data are available.

This issue poses a modest problem. On the one hand, regional partitions of the United States are numerous and quite diverse. They include general schemes based on environmental characteristics, such as landforms or climate, as well as those that reflect cultural or economic differences. A number of researchers have attempted to identify religious regions including Zelinski (1961), Shortridge (1976, 1977), and the present writers (Newman & Halvorson, 1980). Such regionalizations all have merit for a variety of purposes. However, most are not particularly suited to our present purposes because they tend to divide the country into more rather than fewer regions. Given the large number of variables already at hand in this work (39 religious organizations viewed over four data points), employing a schema based on a large number of spatially discrete regions would complicate rather than elucidate the resulting spatial patterns. To facilitate comparison, this study requires a basic division of the territory of the lower 48 states to create a limited number of preferably state-based regions of essentially similar population size. The regional scheme selected is derived from, but is slightly different than, the traditional version most frequently used by the United States Bureau of the Census. The latter divides the country into four regions, Northeast, Midwest, West, and South. We have modified this basic scheme in two ways, as can be seen in Maps 2-5 and 2-6.

First, most regional schemes involving cultural or economic patterns in the Northeast would involve a coastal corridor including metropolitan areas such as Baltimore and Wilmington as part of a larger Northeastern complex. This has prompted us to merge the states of Maryland and Delaware with the Northeast region identified by the census. Thus constituted, in 1990, this Northeastern Region includes more than 56 million people and contains almost 23 percent of the total United States population.

Two of the other regions identified by the Census Bureau make intuitive sense, but do present a bit of a problem with regard to proportionality. As drawn by the Census Bureau, the South (minus Maryland and Delaware) contains more than 80 million people, whereas the West contains only 50 million. This creates a substantial variation in the proportional size of the four regions. This is a classic boundary problem caused, in part, by the sharp differences between the eastern and western segments of Texas and Oklahoma. Most geographers would identify a cultural boundary falling somewhere roughly midway between East and West in Texas and Oklahoma, reflecting divisions of climate, agriculture and historical settlement, and development that extends northward into the northern Great Plains. The Census Bureau places both Texas and Oklahoma within the South. In the interest of creating a set of regions more balanced in terms of population, and perhaps more consistent with current social, demographic, and economic patterns, we have opted instead to place Texas and Oklahoma in the region labelled West. This region is the largest of the four in territorial extent, and, not surprisingly, also is the most diverse in terms of its cultural history and geographic settings. So configured, it contains 70 million people and more than 28 percent of the total national population. The residual South region consisting of the traditional Southern states contains 60 million people or more than 24 percent of the total national population. Essentially, with compelling arguments based on cultural patterns for Texas and Oklahoma to be on either side of this boundary, we have opted for a scheme creating a more balanced division of the country in terms of population.

Finally, the region of the Midwest is one of the most consistently identified areas of the country. Though many regionalization schemes would divide areas of the western segments of the Great Plains states from the more humid and more settled eastern

Map 2-5

STANDARD UNITED STATES CENSUS REGIONS

Map 2-6

MODIFIED UNITED STATES REGIONS

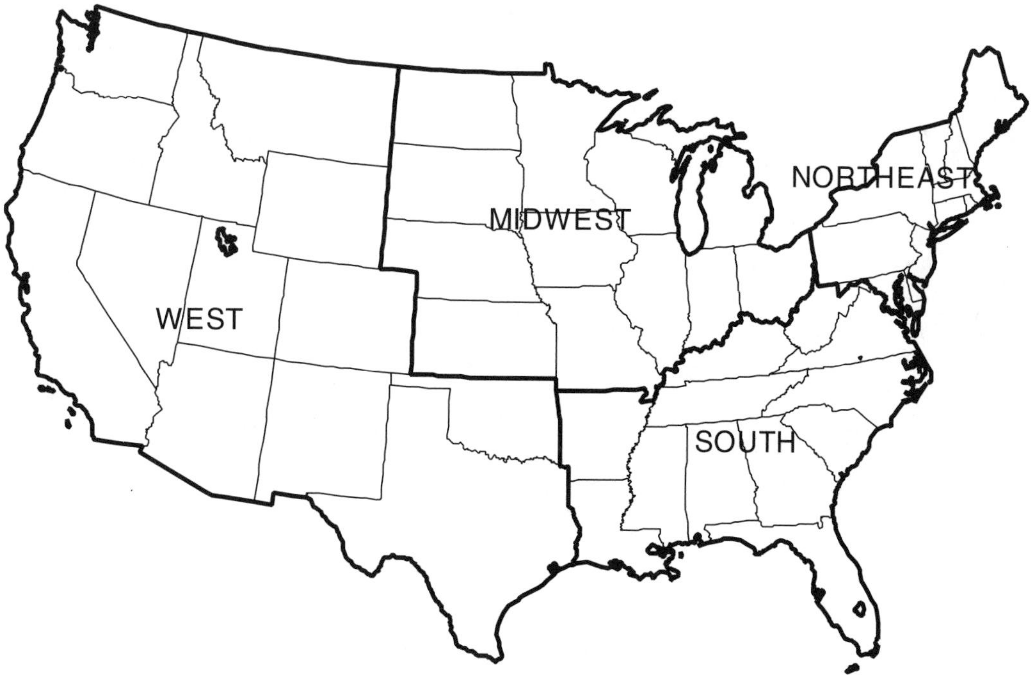

portions of those states, the Census Bureau allocation of the entire states of Kansas, Nebraska, and both South and North Dakota to the Midwest matches our desire for relative population balance between regions. This configuration yields an area with a 1990 population of just over 60 million people representing just under 25 percent of the total population.

This regionalization scheme will be employed in developing our classification of religious organizations (Chapter 3). As stated earlier, this regional framework has four regions, each of which contains roughly the same portion of the total population. Additionally, the four regions coincide in general form with popular notions about the partition of the country into cultural areas generally labelled Northeast, Midwest, South, and West. A final issue pertains to the elimination of the states Alaska and Hawaii from the analysis that follows here. Although the 1990 study *Churches and Church Membership in the United States* (Bradley et al. 1992) appropriately included both states, owing to the dates of their entrance into the union, neither state is included in any of the other data sources (1850, 1890, and 1952) used in the present study. Accordingly, all statistics employed in the present study reflect only the 48 continental American states.

In conclusion then, this chapter has attempted to tell the story of the United States Census Bureau's involvement in the collection of information about religion, as well as both the prior and subsequent enumerations by private agencies. From this rather substantial body of statistical materials, we have selected four data points that allow longitudinal analysis of a representative number of religious organizations.

Chapter 3

The Denominational Matrix

In Search of Types and Processes

One of the primary tasks in any scientific enterprise is sorting empirical cases—placing the experiences of real life into categories that promote meaningful analysis and understanding. In the present instance, we wish to know how America's religious organizations have come to populate the landscape over the nearly century and a half between 1850 and 1990, as well as what typical statuses these religious organizations occupy in American society near the close of the twentieth century. In scientific terms, these empirical questions translate into a concern for both types and processes. In this chapter, we have chosen initially to focus on the issue of organizational types. Can the 39 religious organizations for which data are available be categorized into a set of types that illuminate common elements among them? It is our presumption that such a typology also will facilitate an understanding of the typical social processes through which these religious organizations have arrived at their twentieth-century standings in American society. Thus, our concerns about the various types of religious organizations and the processes of organizational development through which they evolve are but two means of approaching the same set of questions. In that context, we've made an operational decision to begin with a typology of these religious organizations circa 1990 and, from that vantage point, to scrutinize their processes of development.

The student of American religious organizations is confronted by a dizzying array of empirical cases. As we already have seen, American society has served as fertile soil for the propagation of religious flora. Theological criteria alone suggest distinctions between Protestants, Catholics, and Jews; among Catholics, between Roman and various Eastern traditions; and among Protestants between such diverse movements as Calvinists and Lutherans, Holiness and Evangelical traditions, Adventists and Restorationists, not to mention those defining themselves as outside Protestantism, such as Latter Day Saints. The data we analyze in this atlas focus on historical trends for some 39 American religious organizations. With

the notable exception of the various Eastern religious traditions, representatives from nearly all of the theological categories just noted are available for analysis.

The task of classifying religious organizations long has been a focus of sociologists of religion. However, determining appropriate criteria has been a point of contention, and thus there is less than universal agreement about which categories or types best assist in the interpretation of developmental patterns among American religious organizations. We propose here to employ some old concepts in new ways.

Contemporary American sociologists have relied heavily upon categories derived from European sociology at the turn of the twentieth century, most notably the work of two German scholars, Ernst Troelstch (1865–1923) and Max Weber (1864–1920). Their focus on religious developments in Europe led to the conceptualization of the church-sect typology. As it was first conceptualized by Troelstch (1912) and Weber (1904–5, 1922), the church type is understood as a large, even bureaucratic, religious organization. Most importantly, the church is the carrier of society's cultural traditions and treasured values, and, in the ideal case, enjoys state sponsorship. It is the religion of the realm. Anglicanism in England, Roman Catholicism in Spain and Italy, and the various Scandinavian state Lutheran churches all provide examples. In contrast, the sect type of religious organization is defined as a small religious protest movement that emerges in opposition to the established church and the societal values it promulgates. As Benton Johnson (1957, 1963, 1971) and more recently William Sims Bainbridge (1997) have suggested, in the ideal-typical case, the religious sect stands in a position of high tension with its social and religious environment. Typically, emergent sect movements lack many of the organizational trappings of the church type. In Western European history, Christianity itself began as a small minority sect. By the third century, it grew to become the established faith of the Roman Empire. At the close of the Middle Ages, small sects within Christianity emerged as religious protest (thus, *Protestant*) or reform (hence, the term *Reformation*) movements against the Catholic Church. It is important to see that the church-sect typology, in its early formulation, envisions a typical process of organizational development through which sects grow into churches. Thus, religious protest movements such as Lutheranism in Sweden begin as sects that evolved to become established churches.

Of course, as is illustrated by the cases of Congregationalism and Unitarianism in England, Pietists and Mennonites in Germany, and others, not all sects grow to become established churches. In time, even the most established European churches would need to tolerate the enduring presence of a variety of sects. Although most European sects did not become "established" in the sense of state sponsorship, many have come to be viewed as respectable and legitimate religious options. There are, of course, many empirical issues that pertain to church and sect in the European setting that need not concern us here. The important question is, How well do these concepts serve for the understanding of religious organizational processes in the United States? Unfortunately, not so well!

To be sure, at the outset of European immigration to North America, different religious communities attempted to become "established" from one colony to the next. The patterns of religious dominance and also religious persecution varied according to the ethnic and religious characteristics of each colony's sponsor, and thus its early immigrant population. English Puritans (Congregationalists) quickly took hold in much of New England, and their religious community remained legally established well into the nineteenth century. Maryland became a refuge for Catholics, whereas Presbyterians were the mainstream in Virginia, as were Baptists in Rhode Island. As we have already seen (Chapter 1), for a time, a number of Anglo-Protestant churches seemed to provide an established religion of sorts. However, this apparent religious monolith was short-lived. Moreover, in the context of both new immigrant churches as well as new indigenous movements, the Fourteenth Amendment to the Constitution of the United States would promote two powerful guiding principles that distinguish the American from the European experience with regard to the religious landscape.

First, the "disestablishment clause" of the Fourteenth Amendment meant that no American religious organization would enjoy national establishment in the way that European national churches did. In the United States, there would be no religion of the realm, and alas, for American sociologists, there would be no clear empirical referent for what Weber and Troelstch had called the church type in their church-sect typology. Second, the separation of church and state had the consequence of allowing the emergence of religious pluralism. Indeed, if no single religious organization enjoyed the legitimacy of state sponsorship, then all religions enjoyed equal legitimacy in the religious marketplace (Littell 1962, Mead 1963).

Gradually, two important descriptive terms would shape the lens of the social scientific approach to studying religious organizations in the United States: *denomination* and *sect*. Following the pioneering work of H. Richard Niebuhr (1929), denominations would be viewed as large religious bodies that command the allegiance of substantial numbers of persons and that exhibit complex social structural characteristics (O'Dea 1966). They have full-time professional leaders, official criteria for membership, and regularly conduct rituals that appeal to broad and even diverse constituencies. Although these denominations don't enjoy the benefit of direct state sponsorship, they do reflect mainstream culture, so much so that writers like Herberg (1955) and Bellah (1967) would depict denominational religion as contributing to America's civic religion or cultural religion. In short, the term *denomination* would become a catch-all label for describing large religious organizations that embody mainstream cultural values in the United States. With the proviso that denominations are multiple in number, it may be argued that denominations are the North American counterpart to European churches. Niebuhr (1929), viewing the plurality of denominations in the United States, lamented the inability of Christian churches to unify into a single church. His quip that denominations are "churches that failed" betrays a decidedly European bias. Contemporary American sociologists depict denominationalism, in part, as an outcome of theological innovation and ethnic diversity in a free market environment (Finke & Stark 1992).

Unfortunately, social scientists have provided little if any specification about types of denominational organizations (Swatos 1998). There is, of course, the descriptive typology that classifies religious organizations according to their internal governance or polity systems (congregational, presbyterian, episcopal, and papal) (Harrison 1959). Additionally, as the wave of quantitative empirical research began to crest in the 1960s and 1970s, sociologists of religion stressed the distinction between theologically liberal and conservative denominations and demonstrated that religious conservatism generally goes hand in hand with political and social conservatism (Glock & Stark 1965, Stark & Glock 1968). However, if the term *denomination* has remained somewhat amorphous, quite the reverse is true for the term *sect*.

Again, based on empirical studies first emerging during the 1960s and 1970s, the concept of sect gained greater and greater conceptual specification. It has been demonstrated that in the North American setting, sects—generally viewed as smaller rather than larger religious communities, and as communities that define themselves as elect or religiously exclusive—are encountered in many different varieties. They have different thematic foci that, in turn, produce different patterns of interaction with the surrounding society (Johnson 1957, 1963, 1971; Stark 1967; Wilson 1961, 1970; Yinger 1970). Moreover, contrary to Weber and Troelstch's view of European sects, in the American case, contemporary researchers do not maintain that sects eventually become churches or, better stated, denominations. Rather, sectarianism, like denominationalism, can be a somewhat fixed organizational and doctrinal modality, not just an early stage of denominational or church development. Indeed, by the middle of the twentieth century, some American sects had become so large, even while proclaiming their distinctiveness from the religious mainstream, that Yinger (1946, 1970) and other sociologists (O'Dea 1957, 1966) coined the term *established sect* to describe them as a type.

In summary then, the task at hand is a reformulation of the terms *denomination* and *sect*. Clearly, most contemporary scholars seem to agree that the term *church*, understood in the Weberian sense as an organizational type, has little utility for the analysis of American religious developments. Rather, the larger religious communities in the United States are best described as denominations. However, there remains a need for a specification of the terms *denomination* and *sect* in a manner that illuminates their relationships in the context of American religious organizational processes. As will be seen, we propose here to focus on two widely used criteria for distinguishing sects from denominations, while also adding some new spatial criteria.

Defining Criteria for Denominations and Sects

As we already have noted, American sociologists have produced a rich literature describing the diversity of sectarian religious movements in the United States. In so doing they have employed, either implicitly or explicitly, a number of defining criteria for distinguishing sects from denominations. First, and most importantly, without exception, sects are described as religious organizations that depart in some significant manner from the religious and/or general cultural mainstream.

In this sense, sectarian organizations are the religious expression of social deviance. The sociological concept of "deviance" focuses on the fact that nearly all societies contain subgroups that define themselves as different or distinct, and, in turn, are so defined by the surrounding society. Among sociologists, so-called labelling theorists (Becker 1963, Lemert 1967) emphasize the reciprocity involved in the establishing of a social label between those in the subculture and those in the wider or dominant culture. Religious sects, typically focusing on elements of theological distinctiveness, exemplify this reciprocal labelling process. Sectarian religious organizations describe themselves as an elect, chosen, and separate people, and the general culture adopts this as a lens for labelling such groups as well. It is precisely for this reason that sociologists of religion view sects as being in a state of high tension with the host culture.

In contrast, mainstream religious organizations—denominations—link themselves with national civic values and practices. Denominations tend to advertise not their exclusiveness, but their inclusiveness (Wilson 1959). Simply stated, denominations, unlike sects, serve diverse constituencies. We reaffirm then, these first criteria of definition for the terms *sect* and *denomination*.

Secondarily, there is the prescription that sects are smaller and denominations are larger. We, too, affirm this general prescription. However, this criterion of definition is, in fact, at best, secondary. As we already have noted, Yinger (1946, 1970), O'Dea (1957, 1966), and others have puzzled over the fact that some deviant religious movements (sects) become extremely large in size while maintaining their theological exclusiveness. Though we do not adopt Yinger's terminology (*established sect*), we shall take account of such cases in the typology proposed. Thus, although there is the general tendency for sects to be smaller than denominations, there are sufficient exceptions to justify a typological accounting of large sects. However, for the moment, we affirm the perception that denominations are large, typically more than one million adherents, and sects are small, typically not more than half a million adherents. The issue of how some religious organizations migrate between these two organizational types will be addressed later.

Our own previous work with the spatial patterns of American religious communities (Halvorson & Newman 1978, 1987, 1994; Newman & Halvorson 1980) suggests that at least two features of spatial distribution should be considered in formulating a typology of religious organizations in the United States. Obviously, the degree of spatial extent, as measured by the number of counties in which a religious organization has adherents, is a primary variable. Of equal significance is the spatial dispersion of the counties in which a religious organization is encountered. As we already have suggested (pp. 52–54), geographic regions provide a ready-made yardstick for measuring spatial dispersion and have the added advantage that in the United States, geographic regions are understood to have cultural distinctiveness as well.

We propose, then, to operationalize four criteria of definition: cultural normativeness, organizational size, spatial extent, and spatial dispersion. Of these four criteria of definition, the first alone requires qualitative rather than quantitative measurement. Simply stated, those religious organizations that define themselves and, in turn, appear to be viewed as "mainstream" are classified as denominations. Those that define themselves as "different," and thus experience theological or cultural tension with their environment, are defined here as sects. The second criteria employed is size, as measured by the organization's 1990 national adherence statistic (Bradley et al. 1992). Denominations number greater than 1 million adherents. Sects typically number fewer than 500,000 adherents.

As spatial criteria are added to these first two criteria, it becomes apparent that important subtypes of both denominations and sects exist. Let's first consider types of denominations, within which we shall distinguish between national denominations and multiregional denominations. Once these two types of denominations are introduced, we next shall examine the several types of sects. The continental United States in 1990 contained 3,073 county units. National denominations are the culturally normative (mainstream), large (1 million or more adherents) religious organizations that occupy at least two-thirds of the nation's counties (i.e., more than 2,000 counties). National denominations also exhibit significant spatial dispersion across the nation's cultural regions. Specifically, national denominations are present in at least 50 percent of the counties in each of the four major regions.

Multiregional denominations, like their national counterparts, are culturally normative organizations numbering at least 1 million adherents. However, they differ from national denominations in both spatial extent and dispersion. First, as contrasted with national denominations in terms of spatial extent, multiregional denominations occupy fewer than two-thirds of the nation's counties. Second, in terms of spatial dispersion, multiregional denominations are present in 50 percent of the counties in at least two but not more than three of the four regions of the nation. Thus, multiregional denominations populate a smaller number of counties overall than do national denominations (fewer than two-thirds), and do not typically reach a norm of 50 percent of counties in all four regions. Tables 3-1 to 3-5 show the division into these categories of the 39 religious organizations discussed in this study.

According to these four criteria, the United States in 1990 had seven national denominations. As shown in Table 3-1, they are the Catholic Church, the Southern Baptist Convention, the United Methodist Church, the Presbyterian Church (U.S.A.), the Episcopal Church, the Assemblies of God, and the Churches of Christ. The first five of these national denominations represent Colonial-period immigrant organizations that were well established by 1850. In this sense, it appears that time plays a significant role in the American version of religious establishment.

Table 3-1 National Denominations

Name	Adherents 1990	Counties 1990	Percent Counties in Region, 1990			
			Northeast	Midwest	Southeast	West
Catholic Church	53,108,015	2,965	100	99	91	98
Southern Baptist Convention	18,891,633	2,513	71	60	99	91
United Methodist Church	11,077,728	2,966	100	97	100	88
Presbyterian Church (USA)	3,553,335	2,381	82	80	77	72
Episcopal Church	2,427,350	2,089	98	60	67	71
Assemblies of God	2,139,826	2,546	95	82	78	59
Churches of Christ	1,677,711	2,397	76	61	55	62

Table 3-2 Multiregional Denominations

Name	Adherents 1990	Counties 1990	Percent Counties in Region, 1990			
			Northeast	Midwest	Southeast	West
Evangelical Lutheran Church in America	5,226,798	1,709	84	76	31	50
Lutheran Church - Missouri Synod	2,603,725	1,779	60	81	30	64
American Baptist Churches in the U.S.A.	1,870,923	1,227	87	52	12	28
United Church of Christ	1,993,459	1,270	85	64	17	29
Christian Church (Disciples of Christ)	1,037,757	1,379	27	47	42	52
Christian Churches and Churches of Christ	1,210,319	1,300	38	61	45	44

Table 3-3 Multiregional Sects

Name	Adherents 1990	Counties 1990	Percent Counties in Region, 1990			
			Northeast	Midwest	Southeast	West
Wisconsin Evangelical Lutheran Synod	418,820	503	9	28	6	16
Reformed Church in America	362,932	232	22	12	2	5
International Church of the Foursquare Gospel	250,250	537	25	16	10	35
Christian Reformed Church	225,852	235	11	12	2	10
Church of the Brethren	186,588	420	25	19	11	7
Unitarian-Universalist Association	174,004	546	56	13	13	18
Baptist General Conference	167,874	352	16	21	1	10
Pentecostal Holiness Church, International	156,431	509	6	4	29	21
Friends	130,484	666	63	21	12	22
Salvation Army	115,320	778	61	23	19	22

Table 3-4 Classic Sects

Name	Adherents 1990	Counties 1990	Percent Counties in Region, 1990			
			Northeast	Midwest	Southeast	West
Mennonite Church	154,259	445	39	17	10	9
Cumberland Presbyterian Church	91,040	275	0	5	17	21
Free Methodist Church of North America	70,394	515	36	24	6	15
North American Baptist Conference	54,010	163	8	9	0	6
Moravian Church in America (Unitas Fratum)	52,519	64	9	2	2	1
Evangelical Congregational Church	33,166	36	8	1	0	0
Advent Christian Church	23,794	185	17	3	9	3
Brethren in Christ Church	19,769	90	14	2	2	2
Seventh-Day Baptists General Conference	6,439	69	7	2	2	2

Table 3-5 National Sects

Name	Adherents 1990	Counties 1990	Percent Counties in Region, 1990			
			Northeast	Midwest	Southeast	West
Jewish Population	5,982,529	748	78	21	28	21
Church of Jesus Christ of Latter Day Saints (Mormons)	3,540,820	1,671	80	41	49	69
African Methodist Episcopal Zion Church	1,142,016	448	42	4	26	4
Seventh-Day Adventist Church	903,062	1,802	84	55	52	61
Church of God (Cleveland, Tennessee)	691,563	1,497	55	31	78	33
Church of the Nazarene	683,245	1,852	76	61	55	62
Church of God (Anderson, Indiana)	227,887	1,020	32	33	34	26

The remaining two of these seven denominations, the Assemblies of God and the Churches of Christ, represent late nineteenth century American theological and organizational developments. These are indigenous brands of American Protestantism that have made impressive numerical and spatial advances during the twentieth century. Not surprisingly, the three largest American denominations, the Catholic Church, the Southern Baptist Convention, and the United Methodist Church, are included in this group of seven. All seven of these denominations fit uniformly the criteria of definition we have specified. In actuality, 2,500 counties appears to be a norm, with all national denominations attaining more than 50 percent county coverage in all four regions.

Another six religious organizations may be classified as multiregional denominations. As shown in Table 3-2, they are the Evangelical Lutheran Church in America, the Lutheran Church - Missouri Synod, the United Church of Christ, the American Baptist Churches in the U.S.A., the Christian Church (Disciples of Christ), and the Christian Churches and Churches of Christ. Only two of these denominations, the American Baptist Churches in the U.S.A. and the United Church of Christ (in its Congregational origins), can claim to have been a significant presence in the United States for periods that compare to those of the five national denominations mentioned previously. In fact, the first four denominations listed in Table 3-2 have accomplished their 1990 numerical and spatial status through organizational merger processes. The largest of these is the Evangelical Lutheran Church in America, which was formed in 1988 through a merger of the American Lutheran Church, a merged denomination formed in 1930, and the Lutheran Church in America, also a merged denomination, formed in 1961. The second largest of these is the Lutheran Church - Missouri Synod, which began with an 1847 merger of various Germanic Lutheran Synods in Missouri, Ohio, and other states. In 1971 it absorbed the Synod of Evangelical Lutheran Churches, which itself had been formed through a union between several Slovak Lutheran Synods in 1902. Thus, both of these contemporary American Lutheran denominations represent organizational bridgings of ethnic and regional differences.

The United Church of Christ was formed in 1961 through a merger of the Congregational Christian Churches, itself formed by a merger in 1931, and the Evangelical and Reformed Church, also a merged denomination (1934). The United Church of Christ merger brought together religious communities from diverse theological traditions, ethnic backgrounds, and regional settings. The last of these merged

denominations, the American Baptist Churches in the U.S.A., surely can claim Colonial period origins, but did not accomplish organizational solidarity until a series of mergers beginning in 1909 that united Northern and Western branches of the Baptist Home Missions, Publishing, and Missionary societies and later joined the Northern Baptist Convention and the Free Will Baptists into the American Baptist Convention (1911). The last two denominations in Table 3-2, the Christian Church (Disciples of Christ), and the Christian Churches and Churches of Christ, have emerged from a single nineteenth-century religious movement, often referred to as the Restoration Movement, which also spawned the smallest denomination listed in Table 3-1: the Churches of Christ.

Although the sizes of the denominations in Tables 3-1 and 3-2 overlap one another, we still can distinguish clearly between national denominations and multiregional denominations regarding the number of counties they occupy and the uniformity (or lack of it) of their representation across regions. In contrast to the norm of 2,500 counties among the national denominations, the multiregional denominations exhibit a norm of only 1,400 counties with none as great as 1,800. Whereas none of the national denominations register a presence in fewer than 55 percent of the counties in any region, the multiregional denominations typically exhibit at least one "weak" region (31, 30, 17, 12, 27, and 38 percent respectively). Moreover, whereas national denominations typically occupy more than 80 percent of the counties in several regions, multiregional denominations reach as high as 80 percent of a region's counties in only four instances. In fact, only two of these multiregional denominations, the Christian Church (Disciples of Christ) and the Christian Churches and Churches of Christ, fail to meet precisely the last of the four criteria of definition being employed.

In this regard, it is worth recalling Max Weber's observations (1904) concerning the use of typologies, or as he called them "ideal types," in the sociocultural sciences. Weber cautioned that it is unlikely for all empirical cases of a given type to fulfill maximally all the criteria of definition for their type. Each "type" in a classification scheme is but an idealized or hypothetical construct, which real cases will, at best, approximate. Any typology is successful if it highlights important features for comparison, and if it really does assist in grouping together those empirical cases that are the most alike to one another. This precisely was Weber's technique in his famous essay about religious movements entitled *The Protestant Ethic and the Spirit of Capitalism* (1904–5). Similarly, in the present study, we wish to bring into common groupings those religious organizations from among the 39 that share similar social standing in American society and have shared similar paths to that standing. In this context, the organizations identified here as national denominations and multiregional denominations exhibit a high level of conformity to their defining criteria and, as we will show, may be clearly distinguished from the several types of sects to be examined next. The national denominations and multiregional denominations are examined in detail in Chapter 4.

Among the sects, three subtypes are proposed. The first of these are called multiregional sects. As distinguished from denominations generally, sects depart from general cultural and/or religious norms in some manner. They are not mainstream brands of religion. As seen in Table 3-3 (p. 59), multiregional sects often represent theological departures from mainstream denominational religion (Foursquare Gospel, Salvation Army, Friends, and Brethren) and may be ethnically distinct (as in the Swedish Baptist General Conference of America, now called the Baptist General Conference). They also may represent schisms from the mainstream (Unitarians) or from one another (Reformed Church in America and Christian Reformed Church). Consistent with the traditional literature on sects, these organizations tend to be relatively small, characteristically with fewer than 500,000 adherents. However, multiregional sects consistently possess more than 100,000 adherents. Similarly, as might be anticipated from their numeric size, their spatial extent is limited, apparently clustering around a norm of 500 counties. They do, however, exhibit spatial dispersion, typically with county locations in all regions, but seldom exceeding 25 percent of the counties in more than one of the four regions. This latter tendency illustrates the propensity of sects to remain spatially centered in a single core region, typically the region of movement formation (International Church of the Foursquare Gospel and the Pentecostal Holiness Church, Int.) or of initial settlement for immigrant religions (Wisconsin Evangelical Lutherans, Reformed Church in America, and Christian Reformed Church). This tendency contrasts greatly with the regional strength and dispersion patterns of multiregional denominations.

Perhaps those sects most resembling the image of sects in American popular culture are here called classic sects. As seen in Table 3-4 (p. 59) the nine classic sects are small, culturally non-normative religious communities. Schismatic divisions from larger theological families appear here (Cumberland Presbyterians, Free Methodists, and Evangelical Congrega-

tionalists). Although unique theology (Adventists, Seventh Day Baptists, and Brethren), which sometimes combines with ethnic uniqueness (Mennonites and Moravians), also contributes groups to this type. These classic sects are small, typically with fewer than 100,000 adherents, and they rarely appear in more than 20 percent of the counties in more than one region. They represent religious-subcultural pockets of faith. They contrast in all statistical criteria with the multiregional sects shown in Table 3-3.

We arrive finally at a group of apparently vexing empirical cases because they truly are mixed types. For reasons that will become readily apparent, we have labelled these national sects. It often has been argued in both the social and physical sciences that empirical cases seeming to depart from general norms are highly instructive regarding those norms (deviant case analysis). To some extent we feel that way about the seven religious organizations that here are classified as national sects (shown in Table 3-5, p. 59). These organizations underscore some of the normative processes affecting the other types.

Why do we label them sects at all? Some religious organizations achieve large adherent numbers while still maintaining a non-normative theological or cultural position. Thus, though they exhibit size characteristics more typical of denominations, the core of their theological stance is culturally non-normative. Three of the national sects in Table 3-5 reflect long standing non-normative traditions, two of them theological (Jews and Mormons) and one of them ethnic (AME Zion). The remaining four examples in Table 3-5 represent instances of indigenous American sects that have grown in both adherent size and spatial dispersion to such a degree that they no longer are simply multiregional and may, in fact, be reaching the point of transition from national sect to national denomination. They are the Seventh-Day Adventists, the Church of God (Cleveland), the Church of the Nazarene, and the Church of God (Anderson).

It is hardly surprising that these national sects, though sometimes as large as denominations, contrast sharply with national denominations in their spatial features. They do not approach (yet?) the county coverage of denominations and might be expected not to exhibit the extent of regional dispersion of national denominations. However, aggressive spatial dispersion by a national sect may well signal its entering a transition into the status of a national denomination. Three organizations listed in Table 3-5, the Seventh-Day Adventists, the Church of the Nazarene, and the Church of Jesus Christ of Latter Day Saints (Mormons) seem to be moving in such a direction. If so, we would expect to find growing societal acceptance of those religious communities as "normal" not "different." However, to the extent that they presently may be viewed as sects, these national sects also differ, especially in adherent strength and county dispersion, from other types of sects. The three types of sects introduced here are the focus of Chapter 4.

Toward a Process Model

As we noted at the outset of this chapter, the analysis of types of religious organizations inevitably leads to a consideration of the typical processes through which organizations migrate from one type to the next. In other words, the typology introduced in this chapter is but a set of stopping points through which actual religious organizations may pass as their life histories unfold. Figure 3-1 depicts these categories as a set. Our final task here then is to consider some of the typical processes that may be encountered in Chapters 4 and 5 as we examine in detail the geographic and numeric changes that have shaped these 39 religious organizations during the nineteenth and twentieth centuries.

Traditional church-sect theory, of course, envisions a process in which religious communities begin as small sects and gradually evolve into large churches. Though it now is clear that not all sects evolve into churches or denominations, it is reasonable to view the classic sect as the starting place for most, if not all, religious communities. In this sense, we are tempted to paraphrase a well-known political proverb, "all religion is local."

By way of example, even the Anglican Church, which in the seventeenth century was the officially established church in Great Britain, was transported to the North American colonies in a variety of local communities. Only in time did a national denominational structure for the Protestant Episcopal Church emerge (Swatos 1979). Classic sects in the United States have been formed through at least three distinct processes, immigration, indigenous movements, and schisms.

The transition from a classic sect to a multi-regional sect is a requisite step for most religious organizations that eventually will achieve denominational status in the United States. However, it is equally clear that the movement between these two types of sects does not in any way guarantee an inevitable transition to the denominational type. Consider

Figure 3-1 Types of Denominations and Sects

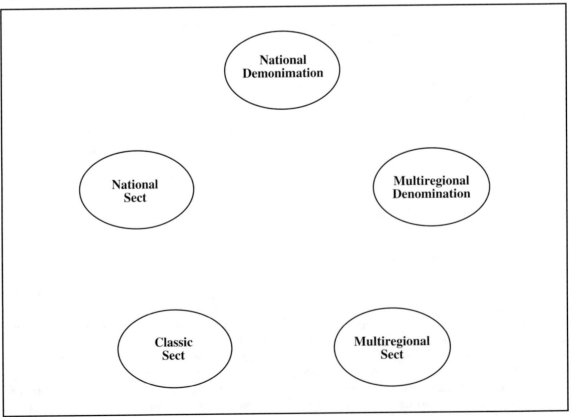

that there is virtually no overlapping of the adherent size ranges of the classic sects in Table 3-4 (p. 59) as compared to those of the multiregional sects in Table 3-3 (p. 59). None of the classic sects in Table 3-4 appear to be evolving toward more mainstream spatial patterns. Indeed, only one of them, the Evangelical Congregational Church, which was created by a 1922 schism, is of twentieth-century origin and yet only one of them (the Mennonite Church) possesses total adherents comparable to that of the multiregional sects.

Turning again to Table 3-3, though several of these sects have attained multiregional status through adherent growth (Foursquare Gospel and Baptist General Conference), mergers between smaller sects and schisms from within larger sects and denominations are the more common routes to multiregional status for these sects. Merger has been the route through which the Unitarian-Universalists and the Pentecostal Holiness organizations moved beyond being very localized organizations. However, schism has resulted in the twentieth-century organizations the Christian Reformed Church and the Reformed Church in America. The Wisconsin Evangelical Lutheran Synod, though not the product of a schism, has emphasized its opposition to fellowship with other religious bodies and has remained outside the merger processes through which a great many other American Lutheran Churches have united. In the absence of aggressive adherent growth, a multiregional sect may remain in this category for a substantial time. As we will demonstrate a bit later, at least one of these multiregional sects, the International Church of the Foursquare Gospel, has had an aggressive twentieth-century growth pattern and may have the potential of moving to a different status early in the twenty-first century.

However, movement away from the category of multiregional sect can occur in at least three different directions, producing national sects, multiregional denominations, and classic sects. First, multiregional sects that fail to replace or multiply their numbers may shrink back into the status of a classic sect (the Cumberland Presbyterian Church). Further schism may produce this transition as well. Second, multiregional sects that retain their cultural or theological distinctiveness while growing in adherent size and geographic extent can become national sects. There are four organizations in these data, the Seventh-Day Adventists, the Church of God (Cleveland), the Church of God (Anderson), and the Church of the Nazarene that appear recently to have made this transition. Additionally, if the present growth trajectory of the International Church of the Foursquare Gospel is sustained over another quarter

century, it too could become a national sect. However, it also must be remembered that the extent to which any of the organizations just noted may be called "sects" is a function of their differences from generally accepted cultural norms for religious communities. If one argues that the more "evangelical" forms of Protestantism are becoming more widely accepted, then what for a time are national sects, may become national denominations.

In this regard, it is worth re-examining the various criteria employed here to distinguish these five types of denominations and sects. The most critical of them, cultural normativeness, clearly cannot be quantified. Yet, it is the most important for understanding the organizational processes that transpire. Denominations are religious organizations with beliefs and practices culturally defined as mainstream. In simple terms, these organizations practice expressions of religion that most Americans see as normal, reasonable, and acceptable. Sects, in various ways, are viewed to deviate from that path of cultural acceptance. In some manner, each is different from and outside of the mainstream. Exactly what falls within the boundaries of "culturally normative" varies over time.

The usefulness of the typology proposed here presumes the ability of the analyst to "read" the culture and thus make reasonable judgments about which religious faiths and practices are normative. Beyond this, if there is a general process that might be called "denominationalization," then the quantitative features involved are somewhat obvious. Denominations are bigger and sects are smaller. Becoming a denomination means growing in numbers of adherents, numbers of counties, and within different regions. Most sects do not increase in all three of these quantitative dimensions. It is clear from Tables 3-1 through 3-5 (p. 58 and 59) that religious organizations that become denominations, and especially national denominations, are uniformly different across all statistical categories from their sectarian counterparts (e.g., compare multiregional sects and denominations, and national sects and denominations).

Of course, the anomalous case is the national sect, which at least in adherent size seems like a denomination. However, there are differences both quantitative and qualitative between national sects and national denominations. First, national sects, even when larger than some denominations, fail to attain the county coverage and regional dispersion typical of denominations. Second, and most importantly, they are not viewed as within the cultural norm for the time.

Thus, for religious organizations undergoing denominationalization, increases in adherent size, counties occupied, and significant dispersion into different regions all are clues to the process. However, not all religious organizations become denominations and not all large religious organizations are denominations. Social policies both internal to the religious community (e.g., the small sect as a chosen people) and those that evolve between the religious organization and the host society (e.g., viewing speaking in tongues as non-normative) are key determinants in these processes. We return then to the assertion that the unique compilation of time-series data employed here can be used to discern typical patterns in these types and to interpret individual organizational histories.

Third, it is equally likely that a multiregional sect, through either adherent growth or organizational merger, will become a multiregional denomination. To do so, it is presumed that some form of theological or cultural accommodation will be involved. Some guidance on this issue can be gained by examining multiregional denominations.

It is significant that four of the six multiregional denominations present in Table 3-2 (p. 59) have been involved in organizational mergers. The formation of the Evangelical Lutheran Church in America (ELCA) in 1985 is the most complex of these because it involved over time a great many mergers between ethnic cousins among the theological family of Lutheranism. Clearly, the prior formation of the American Lutheran Church (ALC) (1962) and the Lutheran Church in America (LCA) (1930) represented classic ethnic sects forming two multiregional bodies. However, to judge these two prior organizations as multiregional sects is to maintain that Lutheranism somehow was theologically or culturally distinct from the generally Calvinist cast of most of American Protestantism. They were multiregional because the ALC membership was primarily in the Midwest and West, whereas the LCA was primarily situated in the East and Midwest. If these characterizations are correct, then it is reasonable to claim that this major Lutheran denomination has involved transitions from classic sects to multiregional sects, to a multiregional denomination. Moreover, it is not unimportant that many of the smaller Lutheran groups that participated in the LCA, ALC, and, finally, the ELCA mergers at some time dropped ethnic labels from their names. Doing so at least gave the appearance of a more culturally normative motif (Americanization). Though the process may have been far less complex, because there were many fewer small sects at the outset, the same processes have characterized the Lutheran Church - Missouri Synod.

The United Church of Christ (UCC) represents a similar set of organizational processes, except that in this case regional differences between merger participants were accompanied by membership in very different theological families. The merger between New England Congregationalism, which by the twentieth century had been reduced to the status of a classic sect, and the Christian Church (1931) began a process of regional dispersion. The merger between the Reformed Church and the Evangelical Church in 1934 was based on regional (Midwest) and ethnic (German) commonality but theological differences (Lutheran and Calvinist). Both mergers, it may be argued, built the numeric and spatial reach of what formerly had been classic sects. The 1961 UCC merger joined a New England and Eastern religious group with a Midwestern one, forming a multiregional organization. Theological and ethnic traditions, if not blended, were, at least, by-passed to create this multiregional denomination.

With the American Baptist Churches in the U.S.A., a different process was involved. We already have seen (Chapter 1) that, in the early years of the republic, the new American nation possessed four "national churches," Episcopal, Presbyterian, Methodist, and Baptist. All four had connections to religious organizations in Europe, but actually had not carried their organizations with them to the North American continent. Rather, three of these, through early processes of merger would form distinct American organizations. They were the Protestant Episcopal Church (1784), the Methodist Episcopal Church (1784), and the merging of the Presbyterian Synods of New York and Philadelphia (1785). Ironically, all three of these early "national churches" would experience schism prior to the Civil War, and only one of these schisms would repair quickly to result in what we here have called a national denomination (the Episcopal Church). The Baptist situation was a bit different because of its adherence to congregational polity and the claim that there is no theological justification for a national organization.

Nevertheless, three national Baptist organizations had emerged by the early 1800s. They were the Baptist General Tract Society (1824), the General Missionary Convention (1814), and the American Baptist Home Missions Society (1832). Although there was no national denominational structure per se (i.e., between churches), to the extent that these three Baptist societies represented a national organization, it was split asunder by the formation in 1845 of the Southern Baptist Convention (Goen 1985, Sweet 1952). Thus, the slavery issue had disunited a potential national denomination before it had completed the process of organizational formation.

The merger in 1911 that created the American Baptist Convention marked a transition by a number of special societies (missionary, bible tract, etc.) as well as the union of Baptist societies from different regions (except the South) into a denomination. They surely cannot be characterized as sects because Baptism is a culturally normative form of Protestantism in the United States. Baptist theology represents an important segment of the American Protestant mainstream. At best, it may be argued that the formation of the American Baptist Convention (later American Baptist Churches in the U.S.A.), like the formation of two other multiregional denominations (the Christian Church [Disciples of Christ] and the Christian Churches and Churches of Christ), represents the transition from a widely dispersed religious movement to a religious organization. To the extent that the typology of organizations presented in this chapter focuses on organizations per se, movements—meaning religious faiths that are expressed locally but for which local communities have not joined to form "denominational" structures—stand outside these formal organizational processes.

From this standpoint, it is clear that religious movements may take organizational expression in any number of ways. Some, like the nineteenth-century movement known as Adventism, in a relatively short period of time led to the formation of classic sects, one of which by the close of the twentieth century grew to become a national sect (the Seventh-Day Adventists). Yet another organizational expression of that movement present in these data remains a classic sect (the Advent Christian Church). There is, then, no contradiction in recognizing that the American Baptist Churches as a normative religious movement attained their first organizational expression as a denomination. As we already have noted, two branches of the nineteenth-century Restoration Movement in American Protes-

tantism also do so (the Christian Church [Disciples of Christ] and the Christian Churches and Churches of Christ). Indeed, one branch of this movement, the Churches of Christ, is classified here as a national denomination. It is little accident that all three of these Restoration denominations are indigenous American expressions of the Baptist movement.

In summary, the classification system proposed here surely accounts for the fact that religious movements may configure their initial formal organizational expression in any number of ways. Many emerge organizationally as classic sects. However, within the Baptist family in the United States, it is clear that several widely dispersed culturally normative movements resisted formal organizational expression to a point where their first organizational structure can only be described as a denomination, not a sect.

Once an organizational form emerges, there are different pathways to national denominational status. The Assemblies of God, which at an earlier point in time might have been viewed as a multiregional or national sect, is classified as a national denomination because of its rapid growth as the result of evangelism throughout the twentieth century. In contrast, organizational mergers have characterized the twentieth-century experiences of the United Methodist Church and the Presbyterian Church (U.S.A.). The Catholic Church has accomplished national denominational status through adherent and spatial growth as the result of immigration and internal migration. Each of these organizations came to national denominational status via different pathways. These various processes are depicted in Figure 3-2 (p. 66) and are explored in greater depth as the individual religious sects and denominations are viewed in later chapters.

Figure 3-2 Organizational Processes Among Denominations and Sects

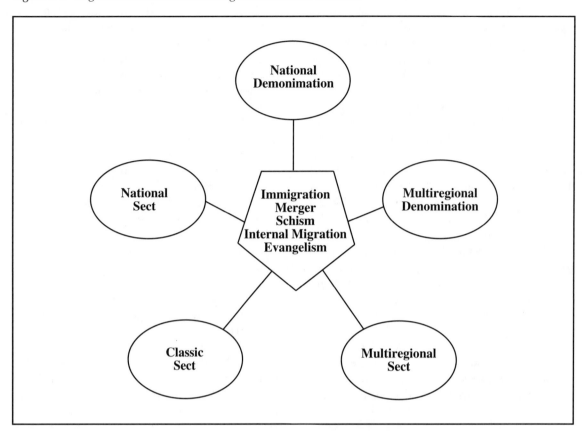

Chapter 4

The Denominations

Introduction

One of the *leitmotifs* of this atlas is that the religious organizational form known as the denomination is a social form that has been in the process of becoming over several hundred years in North America. The thirteen organizations described in this chapter all qualify as denominations because they may be viewed as carriers of mainstream religious and cultural values in the United States. This is not to suggest that there are not important differences in theology and religious practice among these organizations. Yet, the more important fact is what they share. When viewed in the context of the entire array of expressions of religion in American society, these organizations participate in what Will Herberg (1955) called America's "religion in general," or what sociologist Robert Bellah termed (1967) America's "civil religion." Stated simply, these thirteen organizations reflect widely held, normative, social, and religious values. Among these organizations, two types are distinguished, national denominations and multiregional denominations.

Seven national denominations are presented in this chapter. They are the Catholic Church, the Southern Baptist Convention, the United Methodist Church, the Presbyterian Church (U.S.A.), the Episcopal Church, the Assemblies of God, and the Churches of Christ. In what sense are these organizations "national?" As previously noted (Chapter 3), in certain regards, none of the religious organizations of the United States are "national." None are represented by nearly equal numbers of churches or adherents in all four regions of the country. Though several of these organizations (the Catholic Church and the United Methodist Church) are present in nearly all the nation's counties, it is more typical, even among these national denominations, for an organization to be present in as few as 60 percent or fewer of the counties in several regions (see Table 3-1, p. 58). However, national denominations are readily distinguished from both multiregional denominations and, for that matter, national sects, in two regards.

First, these seven religious organizations qualify as national not simply because they reflect mainstream religious values, but also because in all four regions of the nation, they are widely recognized as substantial components in the local religious culture. For example, few New Englanders are familiar with the beliefs of the Cumberland Presbyterian Church, and it is not likely that many Southerners have much awareness of the religious practices of the Church of the Brethren. However, most Americans, regardless of their region of residence, have some awareness of the Catholic Church, the Presbyterian Church (U.S.A.), and the United Methodist Church. Clearly, the latter three national denominations are national because they have a presence in the cultural life of all the nation's regions.

Second, these religious organizations provide clear statistical measures of their national status. As compared to the national sects (see Table 3-5, p. 59) and the multiregional denominations (see Table 3-2, p. 59), national denominations occupy, on average, twice as many counties. Similarly, national denominations never occupy fewer than 55 percent of the counties, even in their "weakest" regions. In contrast, multiregional denominations drop below 50 percent of the county units in nearly a third of all instances. Thus, although the national denominations surely are not equally present everywhere in the nation, they clearly have attained a distinctive presence in the cultural life of the nation's diverse regional settings.

Through what avenues of organizational development have these seven religious bodies arrived at national denominational status? First, five of these seven denominations trace their American origins to the Colonial era. Longevity, though not a requisite factor, obviously has promoted the geographic reach of these five organizations. Among these five, two of them, the United Methodist Church and the Presbyterian Church (U.S.A.), have re-established national status in the twentieth century by repairing earlier schisms. For that matter, the Episcopal Church, which also was divided by the Civil War conflict, also re-united, though in the immediate aftermath of the conflict rather than in the twentieth century.

Second, it is difficult to escape the conclusion that polity systems are important in supplying the organizational context for national status. The Catholic Church, of course, has implemented a hierarchical polity system (papal) that has held a diversity of many different ethnic Catholic communities within a single ecclesiastical organization. Indeed, it is widely recognized that Catholic parishes in the United States historically have been ethnically configured. Irish, French, Italian, German, Hispanic, and other ethnic Catholics have tended to worship in ethnically homogeneous churches. Even on a broad geographic scale (see Map 4-1, p. 71), it is clear that there are two distinct Catholic regional churches, with Euro-Catholicism dominant in the Northeast and Midwest, and Hispanic Catholicism more prevalent in the West and Southwest. Yet, the polity system has created one single national denomination.

Among the Protestant organizations in this grouping, connectional polity systems predominate. The Episcopal Church and the United Methodist Church both exhibit episcopal polity systems. The Presbyterian Church (U.S.A.) and the Assemblies of God both employ presbyterial polity systems. Though the Southern Baptist Convention might claim historically to adhere to a congregational polity system, in fact, the early formation of a connectional type system (1845) has distinguished the Southern Baptists from other organizations in the Baptist family. Sociologist Nancy Ammerman has documented (1990) the gradual emergence of connectional polity in this national denomination.

Finally, it is apparent that evangelism has been a factor in placing religious organizations into a national stature. Both the Baptist and Methodist traditions are widely recognized to have led the so-called Second Great Awakening of the nineteenth century. In the twentieth century, three of these organizations, the Southern Baptist Convention, the Assemblies of God, and the Churches of Christ, all have adopted the techniques of evangelism. In contrast, the two national denominations that least subscribe to these techniques, the Episcopal Church and the Presbyterian Church (U.S.A.), have experienced substantial declines in adherents in the latter half of the twentieth century. In this regard, it is again important to remember that organizational processes are dynamic, always changing, and that the positioning of organizations in a typology is, in a historical sense, momentary. Though these seven denominations are classified as national denominations based on their data for 1990, they are not all moving along the same paths of development. As we will demonstrate, several of the national denominations appear to be declining in adherent strength and spatial extent, whereas some have only recently arrived at a national status.

A second category of denominations is multiregional denominations. Although multiregional denominations may exhibit adherent levels as large as some national denominations, their spatial extent differs from that of the latter. Uniformly, they occupy fewer counties than national denominations and, consequently, evidence lower rates of counties occupied within the various regions, excepting, of course, those regions in which their historic core settlements are located. Ironically, two opposite organizational processes characterize this grouping of religious bodies. They are merger and schism.

Three of these organizations have attained the numeric strength and geographic breadth to qualify as multiregional denominations through mergers. The most diverse of these mergers, the United Church of Christ, amalgamated the predominantly New England-based Congregational Christian Churches with Midwestern branches of the Reformed and Evangelical traditions. Thus, regional, ethnic, and theological differences were brought under a common organizational umbrella to create a multiregional denomination.

Both of the Lutheran denominations in this grouping represent mergers among cousins within the same theological family. The Lutheran Church - Missouri Synod united various primarily Germanic synods into a single denomination in the nineteenth century. The Evangelical Lutheran Church in America (1985) represents the culmination of a long series of mergers, including those that formed the Lutheran Church in America (1962) and the American Lutheran Church (1930).

In contrast, the remaining three multiregional denominations reflect schismatic processes. The formation of the Northern Baptist Convention in 1907 essentially institutionalized the Civil War era division in the Baptist family. Given the near total absence of American Baptist churches in the southern region of the nation (see Map 4-21, p. 101) and failing a merger between the American Baptist Churches in the U.S.A. and the Southern Baptist Convention, the American Baptists are not likely to attain status as a national denomination.

Finally, the remaining two multiregional denominations, the Christian Church (Disciples of Christ), and the Christian Churches and Churches of Christ are two of the three organizations that have resulted from schisms within the Restoration Movement. If the fledgling national denomination the Churches of Christ was to be reunited with the other two multiregional denominations from which it is divided, then a national denomination of more than 3.5 million adherents would result (see Maps 4-13, p. 89; 4-14, p. 89; and 4-23, p. 104). Similarly, consider the effect of a merger between the two major Baptist denominations (see Maps 4-3, p. 74, and 4-21, p. 101). One cannot escape the conclusion that multiregional denominations often result either from national denominations not yet made, or national denominations in the process of decomposition.

National Denominations

Catholic Church

The American Revolution had the effect of severing ties to European-based ecclesiastical structures, and, thus, it created new independent organizations. For most religious communities, the sheer scale of North America's geography separated co-religionists into regional associations of congregations, a trend hastened by the North-South division of the Civil War. As a result, much of the story of religion in the United States has entailed the ebb and flow of the emergence of new distinct organizations on the one hand, and, on the other hand, the attempts to unify or re-unite these organizations. The genius of the Catholic Church in the United States is that its organizational structure made it largely immune to most of this type of activity. Accordingly, the Catholic Church's unified organizational structure, coupled with a seemingly unending stream of diverse immigrants, has produced the nation's largest religious body, accounting in 1990 for about one out of every five citizens.

The earliest Catholic presence in North America came from several different sources. Spanish colonists brought Catholicism to New Mexico and Florida in the sixteenth century. French Catholic settlers in Canada moved into the Great Lakes region early in the seventeenth century, and English Catholics seeking refuge from Cromwell's revolution found a safe haven in Maryland in the 1630s. Within the English seaboard colonies, Catholics generally were not welcome, thus, their churches were slow to develop. As revealed by Map 1-10 (p. 23), by 1776, there were only 56 Catholic churches in the colonies, with almost all of them located in Maryland and Delaware. Though estimates of the Catholic population at that time vary, none suggest more than 25,000, and our estimation procedure suggests an even smaller number. In short, on the eve of the nation's founding, the Catholic Church was a small and marginalized element in a religious culture dominated by Anglo-Protestantism. The "small" part of that description was to start changing very quickly, though the "marginalized" portion would take longer to change. Table 4-1 presents the available county, church, and adherents data for the Catholic Church.

For most of the new country's religious bodies, American independence brought new organizational developments. For Catholics, these developments focused on the organization of dioceses, the first of which was established in Baltimore in 1789. The creation of a diocesan organization in the United States paved the way for the arrival in the nineteenth century of millions of Catholic immigrants. That process began in earnest in the 1830s. Economic difficulties in Ireland precipitated a rapid exodus of Irish Catholics, many of whom ultimately migrated to the United States. Political unrest in Germany also triggered a substantial influx of German Catholics. Though both ethnic communities settled in many locations in North America, the Irish were more concentrated in Eastern Seaboard locations. German immigrants settled predominantly in the Midwest. Thus, for the Catholic Church, these arrivals meant both sizable growth and movement into new regions. By 1850, the *Baptist Almanac and Annual Register* reports 812 Catholic churches. Although adherents estimates for this date vary widely, our relatively conservative version suggests something on the order of 1.25 million adherents. Some of the uncertainty in

Table 4-1 Catholic Church

	1776	1850	1890	1952	1990
Number of counties	—	485	1,960	2,564	2,965
Number of churches	56	812	8,776	15,726	21,863
Total adherents	6,006	1,220,446*	9,037,129	29,689,148	53,108,015

* This number has been adjusted upward from that reported by the *Baptist Almanac and Annual Register* due to a substantial discrepancy in the church count in the *Almanac* (812 churches) as compared to the United States Census (1,227 churches).

those numbers, no doubt, can be attributed to the very sizable territorial acquisitions in the Southwest, Texas, and California on the eve of the 1850 Census. Nonetheless, even if this number were to be an undercount, the Catholic Church had grown very rapidly. Moreover, already at this early date, the Catholic Church contained substantial internal ethnic diversity. Map 4-2 shows that the approximately 500 counties with a Catholic presence were most concentrated in the Northeast, where they included Irish, German, and, in northern New England and New York, French Canadian Catholics. In the Midwest, especially in southern Ohio and Wisconsin, German Catholics were predominant. Outlying clusters of counties include the Cajun community in Louisiana, as well as new Hispanic communities in Texas and California. If these different ethnic populations with their different languages, located in such widely separated areas, had been Protestants, at least a half dozen separate religious organizations would have formed to meet their needs. The Catholic Church, with its multinational heritage, managed to keep them all under its single umbrella.

Although it may have seemed that large scale immigration was well under way by 1850, it really had only just begun. The years between 1850 and 1890 brought even greater numbers of immigrants, with progressively more of them from Central Europe and, after 1880, the beginnings of migration from both Eastern and Southern Europe. To the Irish and Germans were added more Germans and Austrians, Bohemians, Poles, and Italians. As shown in Map 4-2, by 1890, the Catholic presence blanketed the Northeast and Midwest, as well as the Pacific Coast. The number of counties occupied leaped from under 500 to almost 2,000, leaving only sparsely settled areas in the Mountain States, and scattered areas in the Southeast yet to be populated by Catholics. Additionally, the number of churches increased by a factor of 7 to almost 9,000. These increases were more than matched by a jump in adherent size to more than 9 million, making the Catholic Church the largest religious body in the nation. In little more than a century, what had been a small, and marginalized, almost cell-like presence had been completely transformed. It is a testament to the genius and organizational strength of the Catholic Church that in a century characterized by the proliferation of religious organizations based on ethnic differences, regionalism, and theological disputes, the Catholic Church managed these potentially divisive forces within a single unitary organizational structure. Though differences might exist between individual parishes or between dioceses, the overarching structure remained intact.

The years from 1890 to 1920, of course, involved the last great surge of European immigration. Among Catholics, Eastern Europeans, especially Poles, and Southern Europeans, primarily Italians, dominated the flow. Most of these ethnic communities moved into the developing industrial centers of the Northeast and Midwest and helped to complete the mosaic of a diverse European immigrant Catholicism in the nation's manufacturing and metropolitan areas. By 1952, the Catholic Church had again grown at a rate faster than that of the general population, reaching a total of just under 30 million adherents. Much of this growth served to strengthen existing Catholic communities, but along with this growth, by expanding into yet another 600 counties, the church also took the final steps toward becoming a national denomination.

Map 4-2 shows that most of these newly occupied counties were in the Mountain States and Southwest, where at least some of the churches probably serve a Mexican-American population. However, there also is the addition of substantial counties in the Southeast, most notably in Arkansas and Louisiana, and further to the East in Florida, the Carolinas, and Virginia. Thus, by 1952, the Catholic Church still may have been dominated by European immigrant groups in Northern metropolitan areas, but it clearly had become national in scope. Furthermore, with the passage of generations, the constituent groups of the church were becoming more Americanized. In the 1920s, the country may not yet have been ready for a Catholic president (Al Smith) but that, too, soon would change.

If by 1952, the Catholic Church had become truly national, the election of John F. Kennedy to the presidency in 1960 generally is recognized as signaling the transition of American Catholics into the cultural mainstream. Though clearly, they had "made it," new challenges were looming. The years between 1952 and 1990 brought whole new immigrant populations, including Puerto Ricans in the Northeast, Cubans in Florida, Mexicans in Texas and the Southwest, Mexicans and many other Central and South American groups in California, as well as Filipinos, Vietnamese, and other Asian Catholics in a variety of regional settings, but most particularly California. Confronted with this new diversity, the Church abandoned the Latin Mass, which had served to mask ethnic differences at the local level. By 1990, the Catholic Church had reached into 400 additional counties, largely in the Southeast and also had entered Mormon Utah. Located in 2,965 counties (only one fewer than the Methodists) and in at least 90 percent of the counties of each region (see Table 3-1, p. 58), the Catholic Church was literally

Map 4-1

CATHOLIC CHURCH

TOTAL ADHERENTS BY COUNTY 1990

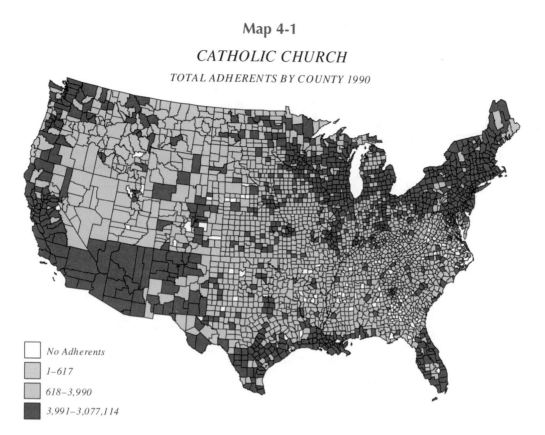

No Adherents
1–617
618–3,990
3,991–3,077,114

Map 4-2

CATHOLIC CHURCH

GEOGRAPHIC CHANGE BY COUNTY 1850, 1890, 1952, 1990

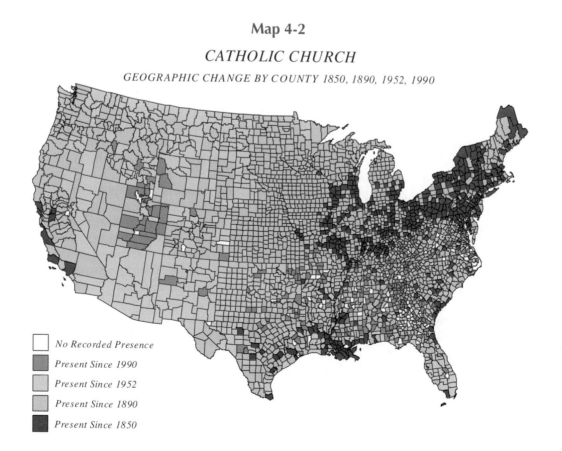

No Recorded Presence
Present Since 1990
Present Since 1952
Present Since 1890
Present Since 1850

everywhere. It built at least 6,000 new churches and reached an additional 23 million adherents nationwide. As had been true throughout this church's history, the number of adherents during the second half of the twentieth century increased even more rapidly. With more than 53 million adherents, in 1990, Catholics represented at least one of every five Americans. In both 1850 and 1890, the average parish had numbered around 1,000 persons. By 1952, that number had risen to almost 1,900, and by 1990 it grew to over 2,400. Catholic churches tend to be large and thus, clearly, are a visible element in local religious landscapes.

In 1990, the distribution of American Catholics, as portrayed on Map 4-1, was essentially bipolar. Counties with the greatest numbers of adherents were located in two large clusters. The more compact of these began in New England, stretched through New Jersey and reached as far as Minnesota. This cluster is the stronghold of European ethnic Catholics. County-level Catholic populations ranged in size from just below 4,000 adherents to more than a million. Contrasting with this more traditional locus of American Catholic settlement, was a more extended area stretching across the southern margin of the country from South Florida, along the Gulf Coast into Texas, and extending into California. The latter contained many more of the most recent Catholic immigrant populations from various Latin American and Asian nations. The apparent "core" of this second Catholic settlement zone is Los Angeles, which by 1990 had displaced Chicago (Cook County) as the largest single county for American Catholics. Clearly, where Catholics were numerous, they were very numerous, and those areas, by this point, were very widespread in regional terms. By comparison, in 1990, there were more Catholics than Mormons in the Mountain States and more Catholics than Methodists in the Southeastern states.

Conversely, it also is apparent from Map 4-1 (p. 71) that there were areas remaining where Catholics, while present, were not very prominent. The lower category of counties includes up to 617 adherents. Though this is a large number when compared to most religious organizations, it is below the more than 1,000-person limit for both the Southern Baptist Convention and the United Methodist Church. Catholics still had room for growth, particularly in the Southeast region north of the Gulf Coast and Florida. This region also contained a disproportionate share of those few counties where the Catholic Church was not yet present. Thus, this area of turf appears visually as sort of a geographical buffer between the two distinct zones of Catholic settlement.

The history of the Catholic Church in the United States is quite remarkable for its consistency. In spite of the anti-Catholic sentiment in the United States for much of the time encompassed by the data in this study, the last two centuries have been witness to uninterrupted growth and expansion for the Catholic Church. At the beginning of the twenty-first century, the Catholic Church has been accepted as part of the mainstream of American religious life and, therefore, almost certainly is one of the, if not the most, national denomination.

Southern Baptist Convention

The development of the Baptist movement in Europe dates to the period of the Reformation and to religionists who were called Anabaptists. The term *Anabaptists*, literally "re-baptizers," derives from the fact that this movement denies the validity of infant baptism and instead stresses the importance of adult baptism. The Anabaptists were received with hostility almost everywhere. Yet, they managed to develop followers in many different European nations, including England. By the first decades of the sixteenth century, at least three separate wings of the English Baptist movement had emerged and had dispatched adherents and missionaries to the American colonies.

The saga of the establishment of Baptist settlements in Rhode Island is well known. Although Rhode Island did, in fact, continue to serve as a Baptist stronghold, as can be seen on Map 1-4 (p. 20), Baptist churches spread throughout all the colonies. The data for 1776, derived from Paullin (1932) and displayed in Table 1-1 (p. 18), indicate that the Baptists, with nearly 500 churches, ranked fourth in size among immigrant churches in the colonies. Slightly more than half of these Baptist churches were located in the Southern colonies, though in declining numbers from Virginia southward. Table 4-2 presents the available county, church, and adherents data for the Southern Baptist Convention.

During just over a century in North America, Baptists moved from being a minor and persecuted community, to becoming a widely dispersed segment of the religious mainstream. The Baptist churches share a wide range of beliefs and practices with other Anglo-Protestant churches. Like the Presbyterians, the Baptists subscribe to the basic elements of Calvinist theology, and like the Congregationalists, most Baptists historically have emphasized the local autonomy inherent in a congregational polity system. Accordingly, Baptists initially did not create a national organizational structure and, at best, formed local and state associations among their churches. When

Table 4-2 Southern Baptist Convention

	1776	**1850**	**1890**	**1952**	**1990**
Number of counties		725	1,176	1,789	2,513
Number of churches	267*	5,622*	13,502	29,381	37,922
Total adherents	28,636**	580,834**	2,177,908	8,122,346	18,891,633

* These totals are generated by an arbitrary North-South division along the Mason-Dixon line.

** These statistics are based upon the southern proportion of "Regular Baptists" reported in the 1850 *Baptist Almanac and Annual Register.*

particular needs arose, they did create specialized national agencies, among them the General Missionary Convention of the Baptist Denomination in the United States of America for Foreign Missions (1814), a Baptist Home Missionary Society (1832), and the American Baptist Publication Society (1840). Interestingly, the latter would become the sponsor of the *Baptist Almanac and Annual Register,* data from which was used by the United States Census Bureau during the nineteenth century and which has been used here as a supplemental source for 1850 statistics (see Table 2-1, p. 39).

With impressive adherent growth during the first half of the nineteenth century, also came pressure for the creation of a more connectional ecclesiastical structure among the Baptists. Apparently, the Southern churches were the more strident advocates of this position, whereas the Northern congregations more staunchly defended the tradition of local autonomy. The issue came to a head in 1844, when the Northern wing suggested that the Southern churches might wish to form their own separate missionary society. Of course, the response came in 1845 with the formation not of a missionary society but of a new denomination, the Southern Baptist Convention. Obviously, the division between the two factions over the slavery issue was the larger precipitating force. However, it is worth noting that even before the protracted debate among the Baptists over slavery had resulted in this schism, the Southern churches already had expressed the desire for a more centralized denominational organization.

Several observations about these debates deserve mention. It is ironic that the Southern Baptists, while desiring a centralized organizational approach to religion, in contrast defended local autonomy and states' rights on the slavery issue. Conversely, the Northern Baptists supported the authority of the centralized federal government on the matter of slavery but opted for congregational autonomy among churches. More than 50 years would pass before the Northern Baptists would create the Northern Baptist Convention (1907). By the middle of the twentieth century, the well-organized Southern Baptist Convention would rank second in size among American Protestant

denominations, outnumbered only by the Methodist Church. In 1952, the more recently organized and less cohesively structured Northern (later called American) Baptist Convention would number only one quarter the size of the Southern Baptists. Finally, it is interesting that the *Baptist Almanac and Annual Register* published in Philadelphia in 1850, takes account of the organizational division of the Methodists but does not employ a regional division in the Baptist statistics. For that matter, in 1850, the United States Census also ignores all regional partitions among the nation's churches.

In the period from 1776 to 1850, the Baptist movement grew quite rapidly, expanding from 500 congregations to more than 9,000 nationally. From the 1850 United States Census, it is possible to identify as many as 5,600 of those congregations as being within the Southern states. When looking at the aggregate numbers of the Southern subset, it is obvious that the Baptists, like the Methodists in this same period, grew in remarkable fashion. The patterns on Map 4-4 (p, 74) for 1850 are a bit artificial because Baptist churches have been assigned to the Southern Baptist Convention based on state boundaries. Although this may not be entirely accurate, especially in Missouri and Maryland, it does create a base from which to proceed. The 1850 pattern shows Baptists to be almost everywhere in the Southeast north of Florida and east of Texas. The consistency of the distribution begins to decompose only on the then recently settled western margins in the Ozarks or eastern Texas. Though the largest single cluster of Baptist churches in 1850 was in Georgia, many of these Southern states had between 300 and 800 individual churches.

From these same numbers, it is apparent that even at its inception, the Southern Baptist Convention was in quite a strong position. To some degree at least, this view requires a bit of qualification. Unlike their frequent rivals, the Methodists, among the Baptists separate African-American organizations did not develop prior to 1845. This was not because of an absence of black Baptist congregations. In fact, it appears that nearly half the Baptist churches in the Southern states were composed in whole or in large

Map 4-3

SOUTHERN BAPTIST CONVENTION

TOTAL ADHERENTS BY COUNTY 1990

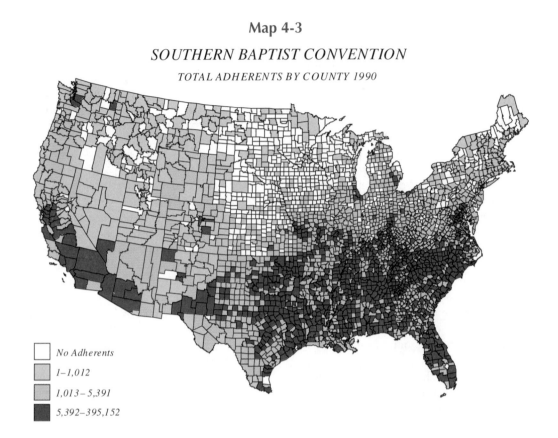

No Adherents

1–1,012

1,013–5,391

5,392–395,152

Map 4-4

SOUTHERN BAPTIST CONVENTION

GEOGRAPHIC CHANGE BY COUNTY 1850, 1890, 1952, 1990

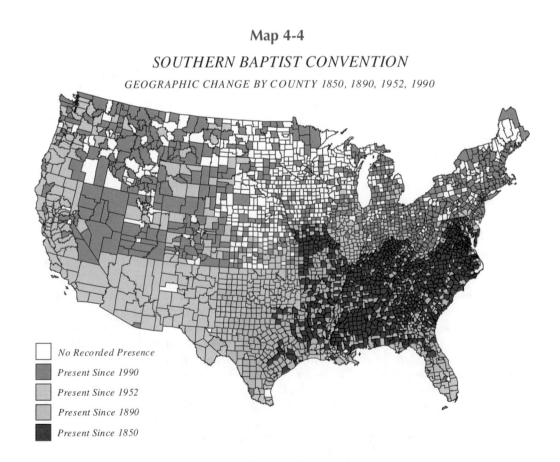

No Recorded Presence

Present Since 1990

Present Since 1952

Present Since 1890

Present Since 1850

part of African-Americans. In the era of the Civil War, these congregations developed their own organizations, separate from the Southern Baptist Convention. Unfortunately, African-American Baptist organizations have not participated in any of the private enumerations since 1952, and therefore it is not possible to trace their developments beyond the enumerations in the 1890 and 1916 United States Census reports. However, for the purpose of understanding the development of the Southern Baptist Convention, it is significant that their base of congregations and of adherents was to be reduced very substantially when the black Baptists formed their own organizations, first at the state level in the 1860s, and then with the formation of the National Baptist Convention in the 1880s (for additional details see the discussion of the African Methodist Episcopal Zion Church in Chapter 5).

Given the departure of the African-American Baptists during the years from 1850 to 1890, and the cataclysmic effects of the Civil War on the South, the status of the Southern Baptist Convention in 1890 is remarkable on two counts. First, its growth was substantial in spite of these departures. The body now was composed almost exclusively of whites, and the number of adherents had jumped to almost 2.2 million. Measured against the 1850 numbers that included the black Baptists, this represents a 374 percent increase, well ahead of the growth in the general population. Though accurate adjustments of the 1850 numbers are purely guesswork, if this expansion were measured against the number for white adherents only in 1850, it would probably represent a five- or sixfold increase. The same uncertainty clouds what already was a very substantial increase in the number of churches to just over 13,500. At the low end, this represents close to two and one-half times as many churches as reported in 1850. However, there easily may have been more than four times the number of white Southern Baptist churches than had existed only 40 years earlier. In either case, these growth rates represent impressive gains, especially given the very difficult social conditions in the South during and after the Civil War.

A second facet of the Southern Baptist Convention distribution in 1890 is that all of the growth has taken place within the pre-existing regional configuration. With more than 2 million adherents, only about 10,000 are outside the "Old South," in West Virginia, Kansas, and the Indian territory (later to become Oklahoma). Map 4-4 illustrates quite clearly that the organization in 1890 was still exclusively "Southern," with most newly appearing counties located on the western margins of the Confederacy. Therefore, between 1850 and 1890, the remarkable growth in churches and adherents for the Southern Baptist Convention occurred on their home turf. With an average of 11 churches and more than 1,800 adherents per county across the region, the Southern Baptists were clearly a cultural force in the region.

The twentieth century would see both the continuation of rapid Southern Baptist growth in their home region, as well as expansion into other regions of the country where the Southern Baptists had not previously been located. Between 1890 and 1952, the Southern Baptist Convention reached into more than 600 new counties. As shown on Map 4-4, though a few of these new counties were in the Northeast or Midwest, the vast majority were in the West, particularly in the Southwest from Oklahoma and Texas to California, and then northward along the Pacific Coast. The organization would have a very different spatial distribution in 1952 than in 1890, and also was positioned to benefit from the general population shift into the Sunbelt late in the twentieth century. Between 1890 and 1952, the number of Southern Baptist churches more than doubled to over 29,000, while adherents almost quadrupled yet again to more than 8 million. Again, these numbers indicate a continuation of growth in their home region, since the average congregation size increased by more than 100 persons to 276 adherents per church. The average number of churches per county also increased, from 11 to 16. Taken altogether, by 1952, the Southern Baptist Convention had grown well beyond its Old South core, to occupy more than half the nation's counties. Though still strongest in its original area of the South, it clearly was becoming national.

The almost 40 years from 1952 to 1990 extended these patterns. By 1990, the Southern Baptist Convention had moved into more than 700 new counties. It completed the transition to national status by establishing churches in the Northeast and Midwest, as well as the Mountain States of the western half of the nation. That national status is confirmed by Table 3-1 (p. 58), which shows the Southern Baptists to be located in no fewer than 60 percent of counties in the Midwest, and 71 percent of those in the Northeast, for a total of nearly 82 percent of counties nationally. This geographic expansion was accompanied by the creation of more than 8,500 additional churches. Even that remarkable increase was overshadowed by the increase in adherents, which more than doubled to almost 19 million persons. In 1990, about 7.5 percent of the American population were Southern Baptists.

The general pattern of Southern Baptist adherents in 1990 is strikingly apparent from Map 4-3 (p. 74). In the southern tier of the nation, from California to the Atlantic tidewater, many, if not most, counties fall into the highest category on the map. This indicates levels of at least 5,300 Southern Baptist adherents and probably many more. With an average congregation size of more than 500 adherents, each of these counties contained at least 10 and probably rather more Southern Baptist Convention churches. The area of their old core from Texas eastward still contained 85 percent of all Southern Baptist adherents. In this region, they certainly were a cultural force. The lower category of counties on the 1990 map of the Southern Baptist Convention is equally as revealing. The upper limit of these "smallest" Southern Baptist locations reached about 1,000 adherents. This is more than twice the comparable size limit for the largest Lutheran denomination, the Evangelical Lutheran Church in America, and almost identical to that of the United Methodists, who have been viewed as a national Protestant denomination for quite some time. Though these counties were largely found in the more recently entered northern tier of states, the track record of the Southern Baptists for producing growth within established churches hints toward future growth in these regions as well.

The Southern Baptist Convention is a very strong and dynamic organization. In the twentieth century, it has expanded from its original core area in the Southeast to become a national denomination. Its growth in adherents has placed it in a leadership position among Protestant bodies. Much of this success can be attributed to consistent and strong leadership from a central governing body with a clear sense of evangelism. It has served the organization well and moved these Southern Baptists across two centuries from the sidelines to the forefront.

United Methodist Church

The United Methodist Church at various points in its history appears to illustrate all of the organizational types employed in the present study. In their early years, the Methodists were a dissident evangelizing sect. However, within a century, their status had been transformed to that of the largest and most widely dispersed normative religious organization in the nation. At a number of points in their history, particularly in the nineteenth century, the Methodists experienced significant schisms, some of which prevail into the twenty-first century. On the other hand, especially in the twentieth century, the Methodists have been involved in a series of major organizational mergers. These have both repaired earlier

schisms and expanded the traditions encompassed by the United Methodists. Clearly, for most of the twentieth century, the Methodists have been a mainstream national denomination in the United States.

The origins of Methodism in England date to the meetings of a group of students at Oxford University led by John and Charles Wesley. The Wesleys themselves visited the North American colonies of Georgia and Pennsylvania in the 1730s before returning to England to formally organize their movement. Since the Methodists envisioned themselves as a movement within the Church of England, an autonomous Methodist organization did not emerge until after John Wesley's death in 1791. Though the impact of Methodist preachers, most notably George Whitefield, was immense throughout the colonies, there is scant evidence of this in terms of the measures used here: churches and adherents. The earliest Methodist Chapel was established in New York in the late 1760s, and by 1776, as seen on Map 1-9 (p. 23), there were 65 Methodist congregations, most of them between Maryland and New Jersey. The total number of Methodist adherents in 1776 is estimated at less than 7,000. Immediately following the Revolution, an autonomous American Methodist Church was established, thus setting the organizational framework for a movement that would sweep the country in the nineteenth century. Table 4-3 presents the available county, church, and adherents data for the United Methodist Church.

The combination of an evangelizing style and circuit riding clergy were ideal tools for reaching people across the rapidly expanding new nation. What had been only a series of small individual congregations in 1776 grew to become the nation's leading religious organization by 1850. This growth transpired despite a number of defections and at least one major schism. In the years immediately following the Revolution, African-Americans, first in Philadelphia and then in New York, formed separate congregations, with similar events later occurring elsewhere in the Northeast. In time, these congregations organized as the African Methodist Episcopal Church (1816) and the African Methodist Episcopal Zion Church (1821). Each would evolve into an organization with thousands of churches and more than a million adherents. Additionally, a sizable contingent of Methodist congregations withdrew from Methodism and created the Christian Church or Disciples of Christ. The Disciples and, eventually, two other related Restoration Movement organizations would constitute a major defection from the Methodist camp.

Finally, two additional schisms from within Methodism should be noted. The first of these led to

Table 4-3 United Methodist Church

	1776	1850	1890	1952	1990
Number of counties	—	1,336	2,573	2,890	2,966
Number of churches	65	13,338*	22,844	41,048	37,238
Total adherents	6,971	1,632,613**	6,243,337	9,509,418	11,077,728

* The number of churches in 1850 is drawn from the United States Census count of Methodist churches. This may be an overcount if it includes the African-American Methodist bodies.

** The 1850 total adherents statistic represents adjusted membership totals for the three Methodist bodies that were to merge in 1939. These data are drawn from the 1850 *Baptist Almanac and Annual Register*.

the creation in 1830 of the Methodist Protestant Church. This organization attempted to create more balance between the clergy and laity in church governance. The far greater schism was to occur over the issue of slavery. The Methodist Episcopal Church, South, was created in 1850 and accounted for approximately 40 percent of American Methodists. Both of these schisms remained unrepaired until 1939 with the creation of the Methodist Church.

The 1850 United States Census reports 13,338 Methodist churches, a total representing more than one-third of all the churches enumerated. For several reasons, this statistic may be viewed as an overcount relative to the twentieth century constituency of the United Methodist Church. However, it is nonetheless clear that Methodism enjoyed explosive growth during the nineteenth century. When the 1850 membership statistics for the three major Methodist organizations are combined, they total more than 1.6 million persons out of the nation's total religious adherents of 6 million. Thus, Methodism already constituted the dominant family in America's developing religious mosaic, and, as can be seen on Map 4-6 (p. 78), in 1850 they were present in virtually every part of the country that had been settled.

Between 1850 and 1890, Methodism attained organizational stability in the context of rapid geographic expansion and numeric growth. By 1890, the three primary Methodist organizations reached into more than 2,500 counties and planted 10,000 new churches. The 1890 distribution of Methodism, as seen on Map 4-6 (p. 78), is a close approximation of the general patterns of population settlement. In the 40 years from 1850 to 1890, Methodism occupied virtually all the counties in the Midwest, from the Canadian border in North Dakota to the Oklahoma Territory. In the West, Methodism reached into almost all areas of the three coastal states. However, with the exception of Colorado, this church did not much penetrate the Mountain States. The largest "blank" area in the 1890 pattern extends from Oklahoma and west Texas, across New Mexico to Arizona. With that exception, by 1890, the Method-

ists are already remarkably national in extent. Between 1850 and 1890, the average number of churches per county decreased from ten to nine. Yet, Methodism in 1890 had nearly twice as many county locations as it did in 1850! The key indicator of Methodist growth is its total adherents, which grew by almost fourfold to 6.25 million. In 1890, the average congregation among Methodists numbered more than 270 persons, and they averaged upward of 2,400 adherents per county.

If the nineteenth century was marked by organizational division contrasted with strong numerical growth, the twentieth century has seen the healing of some of the earlier divisions, contrasted with more modest growth. In 1939, the three largest white Methodist organizations—the Methodist Church (the northern church), the Methodist Church, South, and the Protestant Methodist Church (a more liberal wing founded in the 1820s)—reunited to create the Methodist Church. That organization was to be further enlarged by a merger with the Evangelical United Brethren (EUB) in 1968, creating the United Methodist Church. While it was not possible to create combined statistics for 1850 or 1890, it is possible to do so for 1952. At that date the EUB and Methodist organizations had expanded into more than 300 additional counties. As seen on Map 4-6 (p. 78), most of those counties were found in the western half of the nation, although there also was some modest expansion in the South, most notably in south Florida. Since the Methodists already had occupied most of the country prior to 1890, geographic expansion after that date must have been somewhat limited. In contrast, by 1952, the number of churches once again almost doubled to more than 41,000, a number far greater than that for any other American religious organization. On average, in 1952, there were 14 Methodist congregations per county, and only about 200 counties with only one Methodist church. The number of total adherents grew by a somewhat more modest 52 percent, which in absolute numbers represents a sizable increase of 3.25 million people. However, for the first time since the founding of the nation, the Methodist

Map 4-5

UNITED METHODIST CHURCH

TOTAL ADHERENTS BY COUNTY 1990

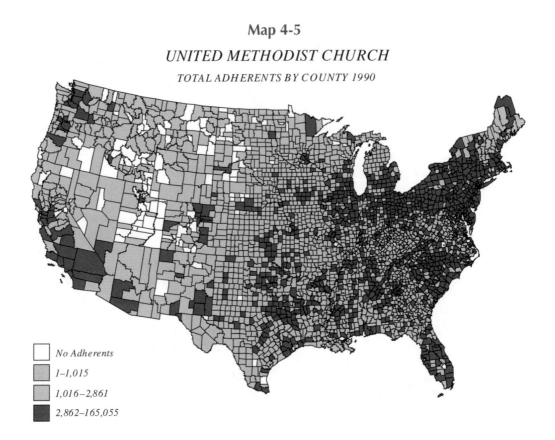

No Adherents

1–1,015

1,016–2,861

2,862–165,055

Map 4-6

UNITED METHODIST CHURCH

GEOGRAPHIC CHANGE BY COUNTY 1850, 1890, 1952, 1990

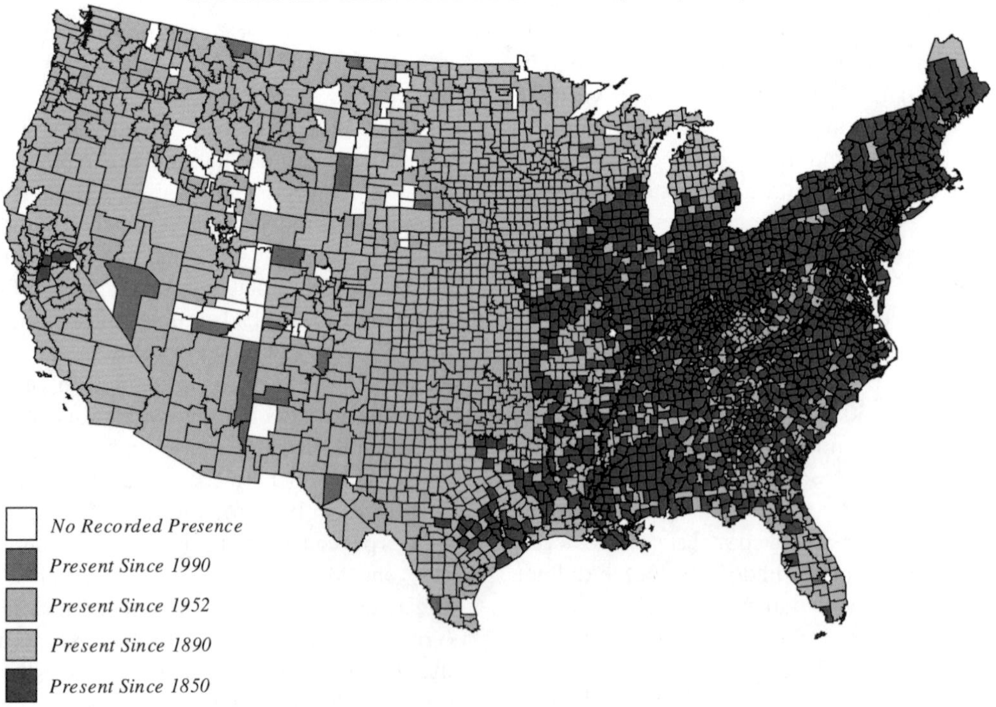

No Recorded Presence

Present Since 1990

Present Since 1952

Present Since 1890

Present Since 1850

growth rate fell behind that of the general population (62 percent).

Between 1952 and 1990, the various indicators of growth show still further moderation. With almost no counties left to be occupied, the Methodists still managed to push their total higher to a level of 2,966 out of the 48-state total of 3,073. They were present virtually everywhere and continued to lead all religious organizations in this regard. On the other hand, the number of individual churches declined to 37,238, a loss of almost 10 percent. This may have represented consolidation of smaller churches, as well as losses from EUB congregations not participating in the 1968 merger. Though these are plausible explanations, the new pattern of contraction is in sharp contrast to the rapid proliferation of churches in each of the preceding periods. The total adherents figure for the United Methodist Church was a bit more than 11 million, a number that represents a 16.6 percent increase from 1952. However, this is smaller than the totals reported in the 1971 (Johnson, Picard, & Quinn 1974) and 1980 (Quinn et al. 1982) studies *Churches and Church Membership in the United States*. Thus, Methodist growth in the second half of the twentieth century has not been linear and also has not kept pace with growth in the general population.

The United Methodist Church is a major element in the religious culture of the United States, and Map 4-5 shows this graphically, as there are so few counties without Methodists. In fact, Table 3-1 (p. 58) indicates that in 1990 only in the West did Methodists occupy fewer than 97 percent of counties. Moreover, the smallest Methodist counties may have contained as many as 1,000 adherents which, given a current average congregation size of just under 300, means that even counties with "small" Methodist populations may have had several churches. At the other end of the scale, using the same ratio, the almost 1,000 counties in the highest category contained 10 or more Methodist churches each, as well as several thousand Methodist adherents. The geographic concentration of those counties was strongest in the Northeast and central Midwest, but they also appeared in the Carolinas, Florida, and Texas, as well as in the major urban centers of the Western states.

The development of the United Methodist Church has involved a complex organizational history as well as a century of explosive growth followed by a century of moderate change. The end product of all this change is an impressively large and widespread denomination that is a major element in the nation's religious culture. Methodism is a prevailing national denomination.

Presbyterian Church (U.S.A.)

Church historians often refer to the English Reformation as if the transformation of religious life in the British Isles that took place in the sixteenth century was a thing completely apart from simultaneous events occurring on the European mainland. The pervasive influence of John Calvin upon Anglo-Protestantism belies that characterization, and, of course, his teachings were the foundation of the Presbyterian movement in the British Isles. Religious and political strife in both England and Scotland prompted many followers of this movement, in an attempt to find a safe haven, to emigrate to the American colonies. Once here, Presbyterianism developed rapidly but like many other American religious movements experienced organizational schisms resulting from social and theological controversies during the nineteenth century. During the twentieth century, however, a series of organizational mergers have attempted to reunify the movement in a process that is not entirely complete. Nonetheless, that process has advanced to a stage where the largest Presbyterian organization, the Presbyterian Church (U.S.A.), is truly national in scope and plainly denominational in stature. Although British Presbyterians had entered the colonies and established individual congregations by the mid-seventeenth century, the more sizable influx of Presbyterians occurred with the arrival of Scottish and Scotch-Irish immigrants at the turn of the eighteenth century. The latter resulted in the development of a series of regional synods, the first of which was organized in 1706 in Pennsylvania. By the end of the Colonial era, Presbyterian churches had become so common as to rank second in size only to the Congregationalists. With a total of 588 churches and an estimated 63,000 adherents, the Presbyterians were well positioned to become a leading national denomination. As shown in Map 1-2 (p. 19), the Presbyterian Churches could be found throughout the colonies, although they were more common in the mid-Atlantic area and relatively scarce in New England. Table 4-4 presents the available county, church, and adherents data for the Presbyterian Church (U.S.A.).

This early start notwithstanding, American Presbyterianism already was beginning to feel the effects of internal division. A division between "Old School" and "New School" Presbyterians arose during the Methodist revival movement of the mid-seventeenth century, with a formal split between the two camps occurring in 1837. Conditions on the new American frontier were not well suited for some of the more formal organizational and liturgical practices of Presbyterianism. Accordingly, in 1810, a schism resulted in the formation of the Cumberland

Table 4-4 Presbyterian Church (U.S.A.)

	1776	1850	1890	1952	1990
Number of counties	—	922	2,028	2,435	2,381
Number of churches	588	4,067*	9,784**	12,841**	11,433
Total adherents	63,063	478,546*	1,601,681**	3,415,837**	3,553,335

  * Represents totals of "Old School" and "New School" Presbyterians from *Baptist Almanac and Annual Register* of 1850.

** Represents totals of "Northern" and "Southern" Presbyterians as well as the United Presbyterians in the 1890 United States Census, and the United Presbyterian Church and the Presbyterian Church in the United States in the 1952 NCCC enumeration *Churches and Church Membership in the United States* (Whitman & Trimble 1956).

Presbyterian Church, the congregations of which were centered primarily in Kentucky and Tennessee. Thus, while the early years of the new nation saw considerable growth and expansion of Presbyterianism in general, this period also witnessed the fragmentation of the Presbyterian movement. The 1850 United States Census designated the Presbyterians as a single family, whereas the *Baptist Almanac and Annual Register* of 1850 documents the splitting of their ranks into four separate types of Presbyterians. Of those, the Old School was the largest, with more than 2,500 churches, while the New School reported more than 1,500. The Cumberland Presbyterian Church numbered more than 1,200 and would remain separate throughout the twentieth century. The other two large branches of Presbyterians, the Southern and Northern Presbyterians, ultimately would reunite. They have been recombined, therefore, in these statistics, yielding a total of more than 4,000 churches and close to a half million adherents.

As seen on Map 4-8, by 1850, these two main strands (Old School and New School) of Presbyterianism were solidly established in both the North and the South. The sweep of Presbyterian congregations from the Hudson Valley to the Mississippi is almost unbroken. Though the pattern is a bit less solid across the Southeast, with the exception of pockets in eastern Kentucky and in south Georgia, Presbyterians are reported in nearly every county. By the mid-nineteenth century then, Presbyterianism was one of the strongest and most widespread of America's faith communities. In both churches and adherent size, they had experienced more than a sixfold expansion since 1776. However, even further division within the ranks was looming on the horizon.

Although the Presbyterians were a bit slower to divide their churches in accordance with the battle lines of the Civil War, such a development was inevitable. An initial break occurred in 1857 between Northern and Southern New School churches and, in 1861, a further division emerged within the Old School churches. Each of the Southern factions originally formed a separate body, but at the conclusion of the Civil War, they joined to form the Presbyterian Church in the United States. This "Southern Presbyterian" organization would continue to exist until 1983. Similarly in the North, Old School and New School factions reunited by 1870, forming the Presbyterian Church in the U.S.A. Subsequently, this "Northern Presbyterian" organization would absorb a number of other smaller Presbyterian bodies. The United States Census of 1890 reflects these and other divisions in the ranks of Presbyterianism by reporting data on a dozen separate organizations. Again, these have been combined in the data presented here to reflect the contemporary merged organizational structure.

The several organizations that later would become the Presbyterian Church (U.S.A.) almost exactly kept pace with national patterns of growth and expansion during the nineteenth century. As Map 4-8 reveals, by 1890, they occupied all of the Great Plains from Texas to the Dakotas, as well as most of the Pacific Coastal fringe. There also had been a more limited in-filling of previously unoccupied spaces in the Southeast. For the most part, anywhere that there had been appreciable general population settlement by 1890, there also were Presbyterian churches. They had already reached into more than 2,000 counties and had established close to 10,000 local churches. Additionally, their adherent ranks had swelled to more than 1.6 million, an increase by a factor of three since 1850. Under their various organizational labels, Presbyterians were virtually everywhere in the United States. With an average congregation size of 143 persons and an average of almost five churches per county, in many areas Presbyterians constituted a significant element in the religious landscape.

The period from 1890 to 1952 was one of relative organizational stability within Presbyterian ranks. Though a group of congregations from the Cumberland Presbyterian Church and a separate Welsh body both joined the Northern Presbyterians, the three basic organizational building blocks of what would become the Presbyterian Church (U.S.A.) were still separate entities in 1952. Again, the 1952 data has

Map 4-7

PRESBYTERIAN CHURCH (U.S.A.)

TOTAL ADHERENTS BY COUNTY 1990

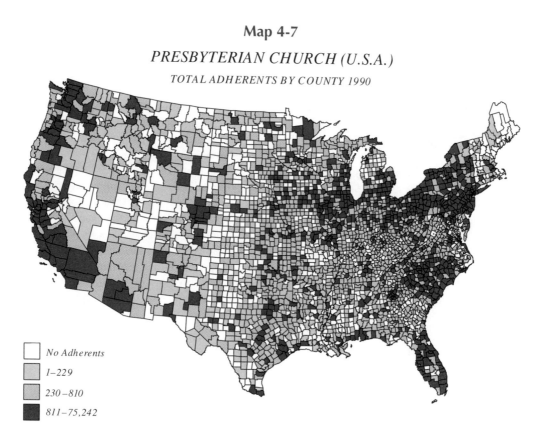

No Adherents
1–229
230–810
811–75,242

Map 4-8

PRESBYTERIAN CHURCH (U.S.A.)

GEOGRAPHIC CHANGE BY COUNTY 1850, 1890, 1952, 1990

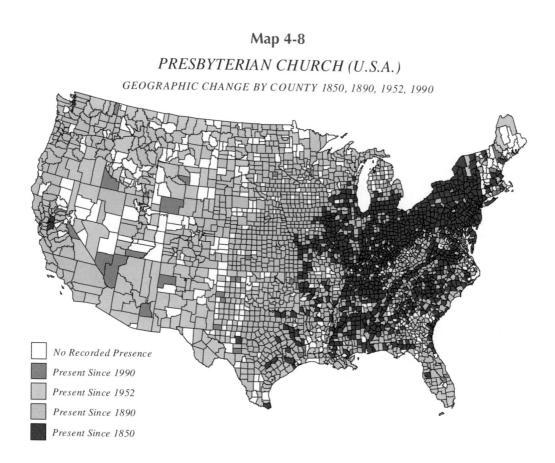

No Recorded Presence
Present Since 1990
Present Since 1952
Present Since 1890
Present Since 1850

been combined here to provide a comparable statistical base. By 1952, the Presbyterian Church had advanced, although at a somewhat slower rate than earlier. Presbyterianism added a bit more than 400 counties, largely in the West (see Map 4-8, p. 81), bringing its total to more than 2,400 counties and thus eliminating the major gaps in its national distribution pattern. They also developed more than 3,000 new churches, most of which obviously served to strengthen the presence of Presbyterianism in areas where it already had been present. The strongest growth took place in terms of adherents, which rose to 3.4 million, an increase of more than two times over the 1890 level, and a rate of growth almost exactly the same as that of the general population during this same period. Though a small part of these statistics may reflect some double counting of individual congregations that maintained dual affiliation with two of the three major denominational bodies, the general patterns are quite clear. The three major Presbyterian bodies had more than 12,000 individual congregations that were operating in three fourths of the nation's counties. The average congregation size was 266, which means that most congregations were sizable, and many counties had several such churches. In the aggregate, Presbyterian churches had become an important element in the nation's religious landscape.

Placed in the context of ongoing merger efforts in other religious families, it is not surprising that the Presbyterians would begin to undertake similar efforts. The period between 1952 and 1990 witnessed two mergers of substantial size. First, in 1958, the Northern Presbyterians (the Presbyterian Church in the U.S.A.), numbering about 2.5 million, joined with the quarter million strong United Presbyterian Church of North America to form the United Presbyterian Church (U.S.A.). The smaller of these two organizations was itself the product of a nineteenth century merger (1858) between two primarily Scotch churches, the Reformed Presbyterian Church and the Associate Presbyterian Church. The 1958 merger that created the United Presbyterian Church in the U.S.A. represented a reunion of Old School and New School branches, a further blending of ethnic communities, and also extended the reach of the Northern Presbyterians into the Ohio Valley and the West. Second, in 1983, the Civil War era split was healed by a merger between the Northern (United Presbyterian Church in the U.S.A.) and Southern (Presbyterian Church in the United States) wings of Presbyterianism, creating the Presbyterian Church (U.S.A.). Although a precise accounting is difficult since some congregations had maintained dual affiliation, the Northern body provided between two-thirds and three-quarters of the new organization's adherents. The Southern Presbyterian organization, the Presbyterian Church in the United States, had changed very little in its geography since the days of the Confederacy and so was clearly regional. Conversely, the Northern Presbyterians, while expanding through merger into the West, had penetrated the Southeast to only a limited degree. The 1958 and 1983 mergers created a truly national denomination. In contrast, prior to these mergers, there had been one regional group of uncertain status, one regional denomination, and a multiregional denomination. The success of these mergers in creating a national body is confirmed by Table 3-1 (p. 58), which shows that in 1990, the Presbyterian Church (U.S.A.) was found in between 72 and 82 percent of the counties of each of the nation's four regions.

Despite these very significant organizational strides, between 1952 and 1990, the newly configured body did not fare as well (see Map 4-7, p. 81). As measured by both its number of counties and number of churches, the organization was in a period of modest decline, some of which may reflect consolidation of churches flowing from the mergers. However, adherent numbers also showed only a modest increase of less than 140,000 in a period when the general population continued to surge. Moreover, Presbyterian decline in these years must be viewed in the context of sizable growth for some other religious organizations. Though this slowing of growth may be troubling, there can be no doubt that the Presbyterian Church (U.S.A.) enters the twenty-first century as a national denomination of considerable size and stature.

Episcopal Church

Anglicanism arrived in the American colonies as the "established" or state church of England. That status served to propel the church into a leading role during the Colonial era. However, the social position of the Episcopal Church was to shift dramatically during the period of the Revolution. Ever since that time, Episcopalianism has contended with both the advantages and the disadvantages of being identified as part of "the establishment" in American society. The major advantages have been that the Episcopal Church has developed parishes in virtually all parts of the country and is universally recognized as a carrier of the dominant values of the American religious community. In contrast, being identified with "the establishment" in a society characterized by religious innovation and pluralism may have constrained the ability of the Episcopal Church to grow as rapidly as some religious organizations. Nonetheless, its position generally within the society and its widespread distribution means that the Episcopal Church is numbered among America's national denominations, a position it has held for a long time.

As stated earlier, the Protestant Episcopal Church traces its origins to England. The widely known events of Henry VIII's severing ties with Roman Catholicism and establishing the Church of England occurred in the 1530s, nearly a century before England's initial colonization of North America. The sixteenth century was a period of great religious ferment throughout British society. Included are the emergence of the Baptist Movement and Puritanism in England, the adoption of Calvinism in Scotland, and continuing controversy within Roman Catholicism. Despite many rivals, the Church of England remained the established church of the state and, in time, became a primary export to the North American colonies. Regardless of the prevailing mythology about America as a haven for religious dissidents, the colonies also attracted substantial numbers of settlers affiliated with the Church of England. As seen in Table 1-1 (p. 18), by 1776, almost 500 Anglican churches had been planted, making it the third most numerous religious body in the thirteen colonies. Map 1-3 (p. 19) reveals that, while those churches were most numerous in Virginia, they also could be found in every colony. Although the American Revolution was to bring drastic change to this community, it is clear that at the creation of the new nation, the foundations of the Episcopal Church had been very well established. Table 4-5 presents the available county, church, and adherents data for the Episcopal Church.

The American Revolution was a traumatic period for what was to become the Episcopal Church. Anglican priests serving in parishes in the colonies had taken oaths of allegiance to both the church and the crown, and as such became Loyalist opponents to independence. At the end of the conflict, most Anglican parishes were left without clergy and some were depopulated in terms of parishioners as well. Protracted efforts by a small number of remaining clergy resulted in the establishment of an independent American version of the church headed by bishops who were enabled to ordain future clergy. This permitted both the resuscitation and the contin-

ued existence of the church, which was renamed the Protestant Episcopal Church (1783). From these precarious times, the new Episcopal Church began a process of rebuilding during the early years of the Republic. By 1850, the *Baptist Almanac and Annual Register* tallied 1,192 Episcopal churches. Though that number seems to reflect slow growth compared to the number in 1776, it must be remembered that this organization was close to extinction shortly after the War of Independence. On the other hand, the formalism of the Episcopal Church in liturgy and polity was not well suited to the American frontier, with the result that development lagged behind less established but more aggressive religious movements, most especially the Methodists and Baptists. The patterns on Map 4-10 (p. 84) show that in 1850, the Episcopal Church still was largely an East Coast organization, solidly blanketing counties along the seaboard from Virginia to Maine. Establishment of Episcopal churches further to the South or into the interior had been much more spotty, except in upstate New York. In fact, in 1850, more than half of the Episcopal churches were located in just five coastal states, New York, Virginia, Pennsylvania, Massachusetts, and Connecticut. It also is clear that many Episcopal churches were relatively small, with the average congregation size slightly larger than 60 persons.

Between 1850 and 1890, the Episcopal Church experienced substantial growth and expansion. The number of congregations tripled to more than 5,000, with churches located in half the nation's counties. As depicted on Map 4-10 (p. 84), that expansion reached into every region. The church experienced particularly strong development across the Midwest into the eastern edge of the Great Plains. Many areas of the Pacific margin had been entered, although much of the Mountain West, other than Colorado, had not. Development of Episcopal churches in the Old South had occurred in the Carolinas and Florida, with the greatest increases in Texas. Clearly, in the 40-year interval between 1850 and 1890, the Protestant Episcopal Church moved significantly toward a national geographic distribution. The number of adherents also reveals impressive growth, with an eightfold increase to just under 800,000. This number signals not only an increase in aggregate strength but also, of

Table 4-5 Episcopal Church

	1776	1850	1890	1952	1990
Number of counties	—	480	1,604	1,946	2,089
Number of churches	495	1,461	5,019	6,467	7,333
Total adherents	53,089	95,110	784,852	2,555,063	2,427,350

Map 4-9

EPISCOPAL CHURCH

TOTAL ADHERENTS BY COUNTY 1990

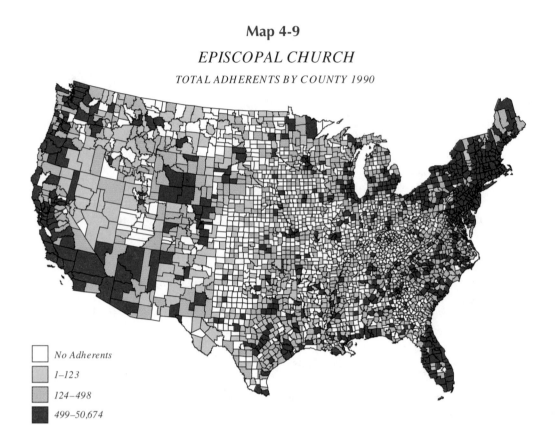

No Adherents
1–123
124–498
499–50,674

Map 4-10

EPISCOPAL CHURCH

GEOGRAPHIC CHANGE BY COUNTY 1850, 1890, 1952, 1990

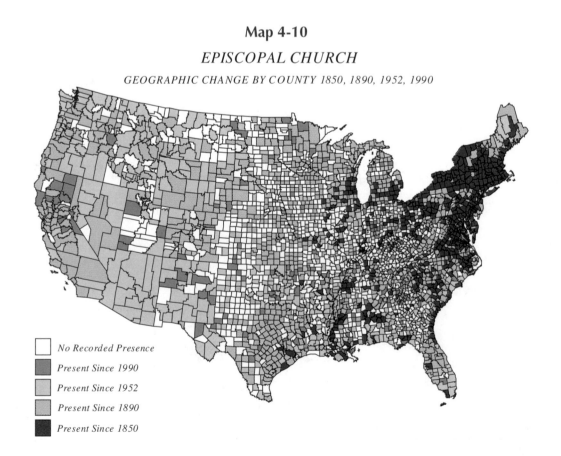

No Recorded Presence
Present Since 1990
Present Since 1952
Present Since 1890
Present Since 1850

equal importance, an increase in strength and stability on the local level. The average congregation size had grown to 156 persons, an increase of almost 100 persons per church in a period of 40 years.

In the years since 1890, growth and expansion patterns of the Protestant Episcopal Church have been mixed. Between 1890 and 1952, the increase in individual parishes and in geographic extent continued, as demonstrated by the addition of 1,448 churches and 342 counties. Map 4-10 shows that though some of this expansion took place in the Southeast, most occurred in areas from Oklahoma westward. If any doubt lingered as to whether the Protestant Episcopal Church was a national religious organization, this period of expansion eliminated it. Numerical growth continued, with the number of total adherents rising above 2.5 million, a number exceeded in 1952 by only four other religious communities: the Catholic Church, the Methodist Church, the Southern Baptist Convention, and the Jewish population. Average Episcopal parish size jumped yet again to just under 400 persons, and in many counties several Episcopal churches were present. Based on these several indicators, by 1952, the Protestant Episcopal Church was one of the leading religious bodies in the nation, with a valid claim to representing mainline American Protestantism.

However, the period from 1952 to 1990 was one of a relative decline in stature for this organization, which adopted the name Episcopal Church in 1967. It continued to expand in territory, as evidenced in 1990 by its presence in more than 2,000 counties and by the addition of 866 new parishes during those years. The national extent of the organization is corroborated by Table 3-1 (p. 58), which shows that the Episcopal Church was present in at least 60 percent of the counties in each of the four regions of the nation in 1990. Yet, the number of total adherents declined between 1952 and 1990 by over 100,000. In an era marked both by a number of sizable organizational mergers (Lutheran, Methodist, United Church of Christ, and Presbyterian) and explosive growth by various religious organizations, including the Southern Baptist Convention, the Church of Jesus Christ of Latter-Day Saints (Mormons), and several smaller bodies, the Episcopal Church has been less dynamic and robust. This characterization should not obscure several important points. Even a cursory glance at Map 4-9 shows that in 1990 the Episcopal Church was both widespread and sizable in adherents in a variety of areas. The largest third of counties with Episcopalians present reported 499 or more adherents each, and there were nearly 700 such counties nationwide. Clusters of these counties were

in areas as diverse as the Carolinas and Florida, Ohio and Michigan, Texas and Colorado, Washington and Arizona. Though Episcopalian strength may have been greatest in the Northeast, it was not confined to that region. By 1990, the countervailing trends of declines in adherents but increasing numbers of churches resulted in a thinning of the distribution. The average size of congregations declined sharply to 334 adherents, and, again, as seen on Map 4-9, one-third of all the organization's counties contained fewer than 125 adherents. The latter counties were most common in the Great Plains and into the interior portions of the Southeast. In these areas, while for historical reasons the Episcopal Church may be widely recognized, one must question whether it exerted much cultural influence.

The Episcopal Church has been a significant element in the religious culture of the United States since the Colonial era. Despite a brief period of very perilous times, by 1890, it had established a widespread geography and had grown impressively in numerical terms. Though these patterns continued into the first half of the twentieth century, this organization's experience in the latter half of the century has been somewhat less positive and has raised concern about its future. Those concerns notwithstanding, at the dawn of the twenty-first century, the Episcopal Church remains a widely recognized part of the mainstream of the American religious landscape in many parts of the nation and thus remains a national denomination in the United States.

Assemblies of God

The history of new American religious movements centers on two formative periods. The first is the early nineteenth century during which both the Mormons and the Disciples of Christ originated. The second large wave of new movements occurred between 1890 and 1920. That period often is characterized as involving revival movements, with the most prominent churches dating from this period being Pentecostal and Holiness organizations. By 1990, the Assemblies of God was the largest and most widespread of the religious organizations originating near the turn of the century. The revivals generated new individual congregations in a variety of different areas. In 1914, a group of those separate congregations banded together to organize the General Council of the Assemblies of God. This body often is described as fundamentalist, given its stress on a literal interpretation of the Bible and its belief in the presence of the Holy Spirit in such manifestations as divine healing and speaking in tongues. Having originated in 1914, the Assemblies of God first appears in the 1916 United States Census of Religious Bodies, in which it reports 118 churches, more than half of which were located in a band from Missouri southward through Arkansas and Oklahoma to Texas. At that date, the United States Census reported a total of fewer than 7,000 adherents for the Assemblies. Barely 70 years later, the 1990 enumeration tallied more than 11,000 churches in more than 2,500 counties, with more than 2 million adherents. This explosive growth has propelled the Assemblies of God from the status of a small regional sect to that of a bona fide national denomination, albeit one with somewhat non-mainline beliefs. Table 4-6 presents the available county, church, and adherents data for the Assemblies of God.

Table 4-6 Assemblies of God

	1952	**1990**
Number of counties	2,064	2,546
Number of churches	6,396	11,149
Total adherents	459,256	2,139,826

The founding of the Assemblies of God took place in Hot Springs, Arkansas, a location that appears to have approximated very closely the geographic center of the organization in its formative stage. Clearly, as illustrated by Map 4-12, that stage did not last very long. By 1952, less than 40 years after its founding, the Assemblies of God had organized more than 6,000 congregations in virtually every corner of the nation. The most solid area of development still was in that original core region, but Assemblies of God congregations had been developed across much of the Southwest into California, throughout the Pacific Coast region, across most of the Great Plains, and in much of the Midwest. The Assemblies even penetrated the Northeast in both Pennsylvania and New York. In 1952, the Assemblies of God, with close to a half million adherents and such a widespread geography, probably would have been classified as a national sect, rather than denomination, because of the small size of their individual congregations (averaging just over 70 adherents) and because of the non-normative status of Pentecostal theology and practices.

The period from 1952 to 1990 brought many types of growth and expansion to the Assemblies of God. As depicted on Map 4-12, the organization expanded throughout all the regions of the nation where it previously had been absent. Most notably, this involved the Southeast region, but also included New England and the largely Mormon area of Utah, Idaho, and Nevada. By 1990, the Assemblies of God

was present in more than 2,500 counties, and, as Table 3-1 (p. 58) shows, only in the West was the percentage of occupied counties less than 75 percent. This clearly represents a national distribution and an exceptional geographic expansion in less than a century.

The patterns of the Assemblies of God in 1990 reveal other dimensions of the organization's growing maturity. The average size of Assemblies of God congregations increased from 71 adherents in 1952 to 191 in 1990. This denotes a transformation from small socially marginal congregations to well-established and visible local religious organizations. Coupled with the fact that on average there were as many as four Assemblies congregations per county, these trends mean that the Assemblies of God has developed a considerable presence in many communities. The general dispersion of these locations is readily apparent on Map 4-11. Counties with the largest numbers of Assemblies of God adherents appeared in virtually every part of the nation, although they were least common in much of the Southeast and the Mountain States. In the Mountain States, sparse population is the most likely explanation for this pattern. In the Southeast, that weakness might be explained by their relatively recent entry into the region, as well as by strong competition from other fundamentalist organizations already active there. Though California and Texas contained the greatest numbers of Assemblies of God adherents, taken together they amount to less than a quarter of the total. Other sizable Assemblies populations were located in areas as widely dispersed as Florida, New York, Oklahoma, and Washington. In short, the Assemblies of God have not only become widespread but have grown to be relatively strong both in the aggregate and in a variety of regional settings.

As stated at the outset, when measured in many of the terms we are using in this study, the Assemblies of God stands as the most successful of the religious organizations arising out of the revival movements of the early twentieth century. It has become a large and very widely dispersed body that has blended fundamentalist teachings with a strong and well-organized evangelism. This blend has both strengthened existing congregations and promoted the rapid development of new churches in new locations to the point where this is clearly a national organization. Though their religious views might be thought of as somewhat outside the mainstream, the Assemblies of God has become so large and is so coherently organized that we have chosen to characterize it as a national denomination rather than a national sect. In so doing, it is presumed that this church's Pentecostal views are in step with local

Map 4-11

ASSEMBLIES OF GOD

TOTAL ADHERENTS BY COUNTY 1990

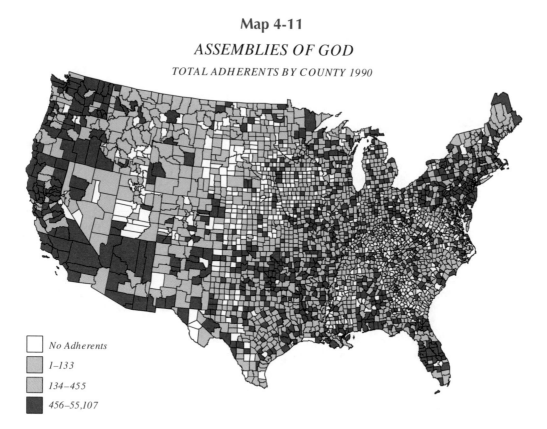

- ☐ *No Adherents*
- ▦ *1–133*
- ▨ *134–455*
- ▦ *456–55,107*

Map 4-12

ASSEMBLIES OF GOD

GEOGRAPHIC CHANGE BY COUNTY 1952, 1990

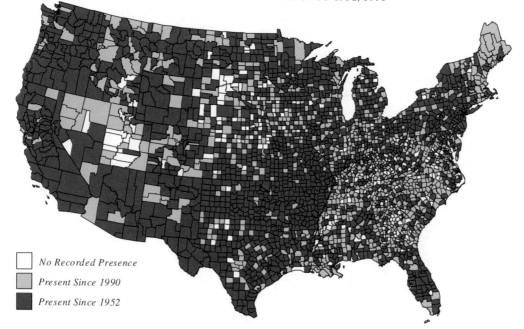

- ☐ *No Recorded Presence*
- ▨ *Present Since 1990*
- ▦ *Present Since 1952*

religious culture in their home turf of the Bible Belt and that outside that region, the system of local autonomy for local churches (actually a blend of congregational and presbyterial polity) has permitted Assemblies churches to arrive at some degree of accommodation with local religious cultures. With local congregations of such substantial size, distributed so widely, the Assemblies of God appear to be more of a denominational than sectarian event. Thus, in spite of the Assemblies of God's Pentecostal theology, we believe it to be a broadly influential body and one of the country's national denominations.

Churches of Christ

At the beginning of the nineteenth century along what was then the frontier in western Pennsylvania, Kentucky, and Ohio, a number of new religious movements developed and subsequently split away from the established organizations. This phenomenon is sometimes referred to as the Restoration Movement. Gradually what had been individual congregations coalesced to form a single body, which variously was called the Christian Church or the Disciples of Christ. The common bases for the movement were a commitment to congregational-level authority rather than hierarchical organization and a desire to return to the Bible as the source of teachings. The movement flourished during the nineteenth century, particularly in the years following the Civil War. By 1890, it had developed more than 5,000 congregations, largely in the midsection of the country (see Map 4-24, p. 104), and had a total of more than one million adherents. Two successive organizational ruptures, one early in the twentieth century and another in the 1960s, would divide the Disciples movement into three separate bodies.

The Christian Church (Disciples of Christ) (see p. 102) can be thought of as the source group since it has the longest continual history. Yet, by 1990, both of the denominations that had split away from it were larger than the Disciples in size, and one of these organizations, the Churches of Christ, was significantly more extensive in terms of its geographic dispersal. Unfortunately, the two younger organizations are too "new" to have been included in the 1890 United States Census study. The Churches of Christ first appeared in the 1906 United States Census of Religious Bodies, reporting more than 2,600 congregations. However, it is not included in the 1952 study *Churches and Church Membership in the United*

States (Whitman & Trimble 1956). The Christian Churches and Churches of Christ did not develop its separate identity, which incidentally it views as an association or fellowship of congregations rather than a denomination, until after 1968 when an additional 2,300 congregations split away. As a result, for both of these sizable religious bodies, only 1990 data and maps are available for discussion. Table 4-7 presents the available county, church, and adherents data for the Churches of Christ.

Table 4-7 Churches of Christ

	Churches of Christ 1990
Number of counties	2,397
Number of churches	13,097
Total adherents	1,677,711

The Churches of Christ has developed very strongly as an independent organization during the twentieth century. By 1990, it had organized more than 13,000 congregations and was present in almost three quarters of the nation's counties. The Churches of Christ originated early in the twentieth century largely as a Southern secession from the Disciples of Christ. A sizable number of congregations that held to more conservative or traditional positions, including their view that instrumental music is inappropriate in church services, created a separate association. As depicted on Map 4-13, in 1990, those Southern origins still were apparent. The highest category counties primarily were found in a large cluster from Tennessee to Texas. The 1990 enumeration shows that this seven-state core region contained more than 950,000 adherents or more than 57 percent of the organization's total. Secondary clusters also were apparent in California and Florida. The overall impression is of a very widespread association. That impression is confirmed by the data in Table 3-1 (p. 58), which shows that in 1990 between 55 and 76 percent of the counties in each of the nation's four regions contained congregations of the Churches of Christ. Across the northern tier of states, these counties contained relatively small numbers, mostly fewer than 100 adherents in what probably were single congregations. However, the denomination clearly has reached significantly into all regions, thereby earning its designation as a national denomination.

Map 4-13

CHURCHES OF CHRIST

TOTAL ADHERENTS BY COUNTY 1990

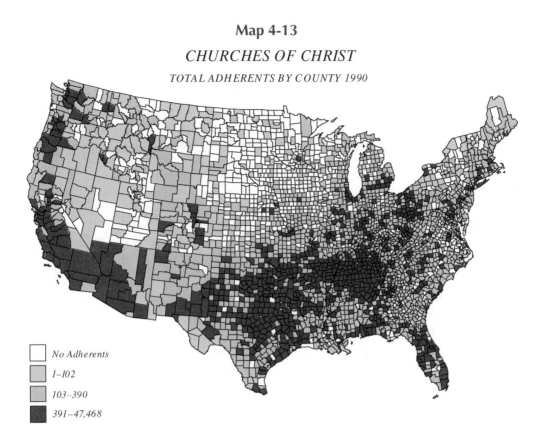

No Adherents

1–102

103–390

391–47,468

Map 4-14

CHRISTIAN CHURCHES AND CHURCHES OF CHRIST

TOTAL ADHERENTS BY COUNTY 1990

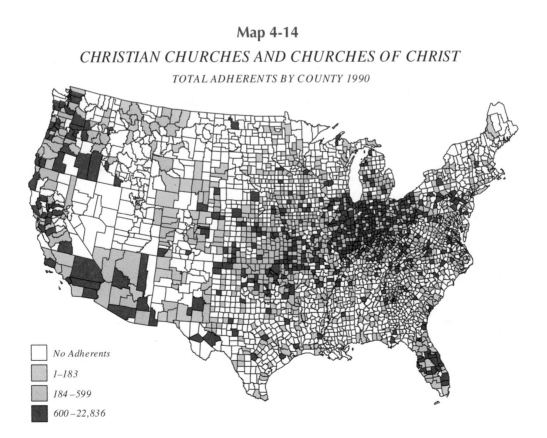

No Adherents

1–183

184–599

600–22,836

Multiregional Denominations

Evangelical Lutheran Church in America

The religious divisions that shook continental Europe in the 1500s took many forms, but the teachings of two men, Martin Luther in Germany and John Calvin in Switzerland, were to emerge as the most influential. Not surprisingly, movements following the teachings of Luther came to be dominant in many parts of Germany, as well as around the Baltic. This area, culturally and politically, was divided into a number of small states, and in many of them Lutheran churches supplanted Roman Catholic churches as the established or state church. Thus, it is not surprising that, when large numbers of immigrants from Central and Northern Europe began arriving in North America during the last half of the nineteenth century, one result was the creation of a dizzying array of Lutheran bodies (generally as synods) reflecting distinct language communities and ethnic origins, as well as their new regional settings in the United States. Earlier efforts to unify what had been primarily a German heritage group based in Pennsylvania, yielded to the flood of new and different Lutheran immigrants. The latter were destined for settlement in a variety of areas of the growing nation, and occasionally these emergent immigrant churches differed on doctrinal matters as well. These processes resulted in the creation of what has been estimated to be more than 150 different Lutheran organizations during the last half of the nineteenth century. For American Lutherans, much of the twentieth century has been focused on attempts to unify organizations that had become fragmented in the previous century. The organization most embodying that process is the Evangelical Lutheran Church in America (ELCA), which as a result of a series of mergers has become the largest American Lutheran body, with more than 5.2 million adherents in 1990.

There is no alternative to oversimplification in trying to briefly outline the process of mergers that culminated in the formation of the ELCA. In its most skeletal outline, the process has consisted of four stages or cycles of merger activity. Beginning with the most recent events, they are as follows. First,

in 1985, the Evangelical Lutheran Church in America was formed by a merger involving the American Lutheran Church (ALC), the Lutheran Church in America (LCA), and the Evangelical Lutheran Churches. Second, in 1962, the Lutheran Church in America was formed by a merger involving the American Evangelical Lutheran Church, the United Lutheran Church in America, the Augustana Evangelical Lutheran Church, and the Finnish Evangelical Lutheran Church. Further, the American Lutheran Church merged with the Lutheran Free Church, taking the former as its new name. In 1961, the American Lutheran Church was formed by a merger involving the United Evangelical Lutheran Church, the Evangelical Lutheran Church, and the American Lutheran Church.

Third, between 1917 and 1930, a series of mergers occurred. In 1930, the smaller (pre-1961) version of the American Lutheran Church was formed by a merger involving the Lutheran Synod of Buffalo, the Evangelical Synod of Iowa, and the Joint Evangelical Synod of Ohio. In 1918, the United Lutheran Church (see 1962 LCA merger) was formed by a merger involving the General Synod of Lutheran Churches, the General Council of Lutheran Churches, and the United Synod of the South. In 1917, the Evangelical Lutheran Church was formed by a merger involving the Hauge Norwegian Evangelical Synod and the Synod of Norwegian Evangelical Churches of America. Finally, in the years before the turn of the century, a large number of mergers took place that created the organizations just now described. Obviously, a great number of smaller or localized bodies were involved. This complicated and almost century-long process transformed what had been a sizable number of associations of Lutheran congregations based on ethnic origin or region of settlement in the United States into one of the nation's larger denominations. In part because of these mergers, the ELCA has become all but national in its geography. Table 4-8 presents the available county, church, and adherents data for the Evangelical Lutheran Church in America.

Table 4-8 Evangelical Lutheran Church in America

	1776*	1850*	1890	1952	1990
Number of counties	—	256	996	1,420	1,709
Number of churches	150	1,604	5,170	9,527	10,912
Total adherents	16,088	229,504	745,335	4,225,063	5,226,798

* Both the 1776 and 1850 data sources aggregate all Lutherans as a "family." With no sensible criteria for disaggregation, those family data in their entirety have been viewed as the antecedent of the ELCA.

The earliest data sets available for this analysis treat all Lutherans as a single family or religious category. From those data, it is apparent that as early as the Revolution, a Lutheran presence had been established in the colonies by the formation of 150 churches. As was true for other Germanic origin groups, Lutheran churches were most plentiful in the mid-Atlantic region, most especially in Pennsylvania. Although it is not entirely accurate to suggest that none of these churches later would become associated with organizations other than the ELCA, certainly most would have participated in the Pennsylvania-based body that became the first Lutheran Synod in America. Ultimately, it evolved into the General Synod (one of the constituents of the 1918 merger already noted).

By the middle of the nineteenth century, the Lutheran presence in the United States had expanded considerably. The large-scale immigration from Germany into the United States was bringing substantial numbers of Lutherans as well as Catholics to the country. By 1850, Lutherans had built more than 1,600 churches in 256 different county locations. As portrayed on Map 4-16 (p. 92), most of these counties were in a compact region from Pennsylvania westward through Ohio and into Indiana. There also were significant clusters of counties in Missouri and Wisconsin. Some of the latter, no doubt, were among those that had just organized the Lutheran Church - Missouri Synod. The small clusters of churches in the Carolinas were a remnant from Colonial era settlements and soon were to result in the Civil War era creation of a separate Lutheran body in the Southern states (the United Synod of the South). That body would not rejoin Northern Lutherans until after the First World War. The "newer" German immigrants settled in the urban areas of the lower Midwest, and along with their Catholic German neighbors, shaped a regional cultural mix that survives into the present century. That this influx was of considerable size is illustrated by an adherents estimate for 1850 of almost 230,000 Lutherans, a more than tenfold expansion since 1776.

However, that immigration wave had only just begun in 1850. The period from mid-century to 1890 was to see new groups of Lutherans, especially from Scandinavia, flock to the United States. The most frequent destinations for these new settlers were in the Midwest. Map 4-16 (p. 92) reinforces that impression strongly, with an almost solid pattern of "new" ELCA counties in 1890, from Michigan and Indiana, across the agricultural heartland into the Great Plains. Somewhat surprisingly, there also was a relatively sizable number of new ELCA counties across the Southeast. Those counties were located in

a scattered arc from the Colonial-period base in the Carolinas into Arkansas and into Texas. Clearly, in 1890, there were far more ELCA counties in the Southeast than in the West or the West Coast region. In this 40-year interval, the number of ELCA churches grew by a factor of more than three, while the total adherents also expanded by a factor of more than three. By 1890, the organizations identified by the United States Census that were antecedents to the ELCA included more than 745,000 adherents and had constructed a regional culture defined by Lutheranism, which during the 1990s was witnessed almost weekly by Garrison Keillor on *The Prairie Home Companion*.

In the early part of the twentieth century, substantial immigration of people from Lutheran areas of Europe diminished. Accordingly, between 1890 and 1952, the patterns of growth and change for the organizations that would become the ELCA were largely a result of natural increase and internal migration. As seen on Map 4-16 (p. 92), this period is characterized by a marked shift to the West. By 1952, the component organizations of the future ELCA had developed churches in almost every county from Lake Michigan to the Pacific Coast of Washington and Oregon, though not on the margins of the Mormon territory. Large areas of California, Colorado, and Arizona also were entered by Lutheran churches for the first time. Other significant territorial additions occurred in Texas and Florida, but the westward push appears dominant. Between 1890 and 1952, constituents of the ELCA had entered more than 500 new counties and built more than 4,000 additional churches. In short, despite the decrease in Lutheran immigration, growth in what would become ELCA churches was robust, as illustrated by the fact that adherent size increased more than five times to greater than 4.2 million.

The last half of the twentieth century brought considerably slower growth for the ELCA. The 1990 enumeration, the first after the 1985 merger that actually created the ELCA, found that the number of the organization's churches had grown by 14 percent, and the number of counties with ELCA churches had increased by more than 20 percent. These increases positioned the ELCA in more than 55 percent of the nation's counties. As depicted on Map 4-16 (p. 92), new counties in the 1952–1990 period most frequently were located in the West and Southeast. However, in both of these regions sizable numbers of counties have yet to be entered by the ELCA. Table 3-2 (p. 59) underscores this assessment, indicating that the ELCA was present in half of the counties in the Western region, and only 31 percent of counties in the Southeast.

Map 4-15

EVANGELICAL LUTHERAN CHURCH IN AMERICA

TOTAL ADHERENTS BY COUNTY 1990

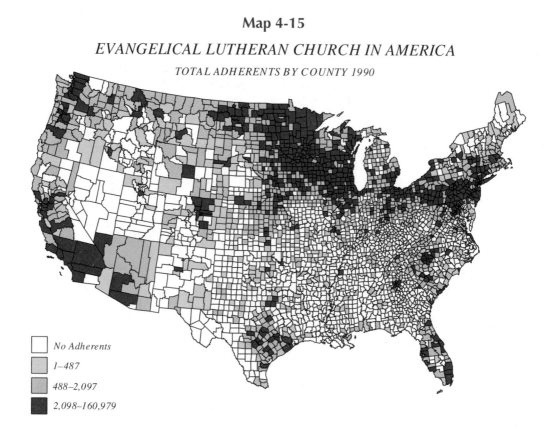

No Adherents
1–487
488–2,097
2,098–160,979

Map 4-16

EVANGELICAL LUTHERAN CHURCH IN AMERICA

GEOGRAPHIC CHANGE BY COUNTY 1850, 1890, 1952, 1990

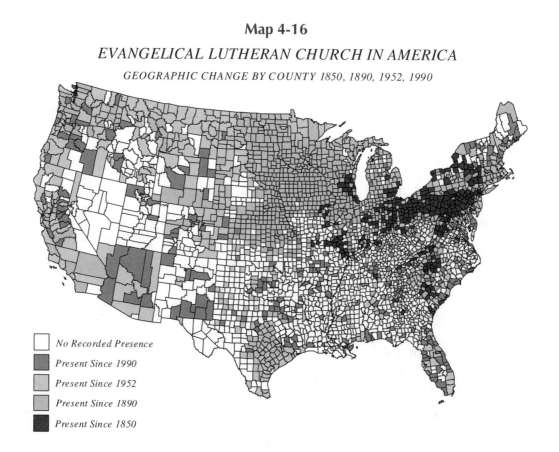

No Recorded Presence
Present Since 1990
Present Since 1952
Present Since 1890
Present Since 1850

This picture of an uneven distribution is strongly reinforced by Map 4-15, which shows the 1990 distribution of ELCA adherents. The solid wedge of counties from Lake Michigan into the Dakotas outlines what most people would think of as America's Lutheran region. Most counties in that region, which covers parts or all of six states, had more than 2,000 ELCA adherents, with some Lutheran populations ranging considerably higher. The earlier regions of Lutheran immigration in Pennsylvania and Ohio were both clearly evident and distinctly smaller than the region west of Lake Michigan. Elsewhere, the largest ELCA county populations were found in much smaller clusters. Indeed, entering the 1990s the Southeast and West regions each contained only about 10 percent of ELCA adherents, even though this represented about a half million persons in each case.

The ELCA is a large organization with more than 5.2 million adherents and thus ranks fifth among the organizations in this study. At the same time, it is found in comparatively few counties for an organization of its size and primarily is concentrated in two of the nation's four regions. This means that where the ELCA is present, it is likely to be relatively large and, therefore, likely to exert significant cultural influence. Average congregation size in 1990 was almost 500 persons, and average number of adherents per county was more than 3,000. These statistics attest to the strength of the ELCA distribution, which, however, is multiregional rather than national in character.

The twentieth-century organizational history of the ELCA represents a masterful case of institution building through merger. In this case, mergers have brought together people of different national heritage and regional location, all of whom share a common theological tradition. These mergers have absorbed most of the potential Lutheran partners, given that the Missouri and Wisconsin Lutheran synods both maintain somewhat conservative postures and are not disposed to merge. Thus, if the ELCA is to grow in the future, it must do so through different mechanisms, including outreach to new populations in regions where the ELCA traditionally has not been strong. Stagnation in adherent size during the last

half of the twentieth century has not been a good omen. It suggests that the ELCA is likely to remain a multiregional denomination rather than become a national denomination.

Lutheran Church - Missouri Synod

The history of Lutherans in the United States is lengthy and extremely complex. Lutherans were among the earliest colonists in both New York and Pennsylvania and were present in large enough numbers to have formed 150 congregations by 1776. However, early efforts to develop a cohesive national organization were frustrated by the dynamic events of the nineteenth century.

Large numbers of new Lutheran immigrants from a diverse array of European origins arrived and then scattered widely across the United States. The result was the proliferation of a large number of associations of Lutheran congregations, generally identified as synods. Most of these were united by some combination of ethnic origins and region of settlement in the United States. More than 150 different Lutheran organizations have existed in the United States at one time or another. In 1847, three associations totaling 12 German Lutheran congregations located in the Midwest organized under the name German Evangelical Lutheran Synod of Missouri, Ohio, and Other States. From that modest beginning has emerged a denomination that, in 1990, ranks as the second largest Lutheran body in the United States, containing 2.6 million adherents.

Throughout its history the Lutheran Church - Missouri Synod has remained steadfast in its conservative stance on both theological and social matters. Accordingly, rather than participating in mergers or other Lutheran unification efforts, the Lutheran Church - Missouri Synod has grown in size through the building of new churches as it has "followed its flock" of German Lutherans across the country. Table 4-9 presents the available county, church, and adherents data for the Lutheran Church - Missouri Synod.

The initial formation of the synod that would evolve into the Lutheran Church - Missouri Synod occurred in 1847. Both the 1850 United States

Table 4-9 Lutheran Church - Missouri Synod

	1890	1952	1990
Number of counties	645	1,423	1,779
Number of churches	1,531	4,651	6,020
Total adherents	357,153	1,856,638	2,603,725

Note: The 1850 data would be best described as identifying only the Lutheran "family." We have chosen to match that data with the Evangelical Lutheran Church in America and thus no data are presented here for that year.

Census and the *Baptist Almanac and Annual Register* of 1850 report Lutherans as a single family, with the result that individual data for the Missouri Synod is not available for that date. By 1890, the situation had changed drastically owing to the very sizable Lutheran immigration that occurred between 1850 and 1890. As stated previously, individual congregations of Lutherans banded together, sometimes based on theological commonality, though more often based on ethnic background, state, and regional settlement. Slowly, these synods began to develop connections to one another. By 1890, three larger synods and one smaller one located in the South had developed to the point where the census of that year described them as "General Bodies." One of these was named the Evangelical Lutheran Synodical Conference of America, which was composed of as many as a half dozen separate synods, the Missouri Synod being the largest. This body was to change in membership over the years but formed the nucleus from which the modern era Lutheran Church - Missouri Synod was to develop.

In 1890, the Evangelical Lutheran Synodical Conference contained 1,531 individual churches or almost 23 percent of all Lutheran churches nationwide. The Synodical Conference contained an even greater proportion of total Lutheran adherents, comprising 29 percent. Not surprisingly, as can be seen in Map 4-18, in 1890, this organization had a strong Midwestern flavor, centered in the Great Lakes region. In terms of adherents, the two largest states were Wisconsin and Illinois, which together contained 42 percent of the total. Outside of the Midwestern core, the Synodical Conference had established beachheads in a variety of locations such as southern New England, some of the Gulf Coast states, and Texas. The only sizable cluster of churches outside of the Midwest was in New York.

Between 1890 and 1952, the Lutheran Church - Missouri Synod grew quite rapidly. Its number of churches tripled to more than 4,600, and its total adherents grew by a factor of five to almost 1.9 million persons. Though the 1952 enumeration still included a dozen different Lutheran organizations, the Missouri Synod ranked first in the number of churches and second in adherents. Map 4-18 shows that the Missouri Lutherans had stabilized their geographic distribution by 1952. They were present in more than 1,400 counties, almost half of the nation's total number of counties. Although the Midwestern roots of the organization still were in evidence, the organization was almost as widely represented in the Northeastern and Pacific Coast states. While the denomination was not as well represented in the Southeast as in the other regions, it was far from

absent. Missouri Lutherans were present in substantial numbers of counties in the Carolinas and Tennessee, in Florida, and in Texas. By 1952, the Lutheran Church - Missouri Synod already was a multiregional denomination of considerable size.

Between 1952 and 1990, while much of the rest of American Lutheranism underwent a process of unification through merger, the Missouri Synod held fast to its separate and largely conservative identity. Therefore, although it has continued to grow and expand, the degree and direction of change appears more incremental than dramatic. In 1990, the number of counties in which the Missouri Lutherans were found increased to a total of 1,779, representing a gain of 25 percent. As seen on Map 4-18, most of those new counties were in the Southeast or the Mountain States. This is hardly surprising given the fact that by 1952, this organization had covered most of the other regions rather completely. As was also true for the other major Lutheran denomination (the ELCA), the only region in which the Missouri Synod was not broadly present was the Southeast, where, as shown in Table 3-2 (p. 59), by 1990, the Missouri Lutherans occupied only 30 percent of all counties. Indeed, it would appear that fewer than 10 percent of the denomination's adherents were in that region. This relative "hole" in their distribution is what characterizes the Missouri Lutherans as a multiregional rather than national denomination.

In terms of numerical expansion, the years from 1952 to 1990 saw the Missouri Synod grow to a total of just over 2.6 million persons. This represents an increase of more than 40 percent, and since the organization both had participated in only one merger with a very small group in 1964 and had experienced a schism in which a small group split away from the denomination, it is clear that this growth in members is not artificial. This appreciable growth rate was significantly higher than that reported by the Evangelical Lutheran Church of America but was significantly below the 65 percent increase in the United States population.

Map 4-17 portrays a denomination that still is rooted in the upper Midwest. Counties in the highest category contained at least 900 Missouri Lutherans and appeared to number well into the thousands. Such counties were numerous in upstate New York and appeared as far west as Iowa and the eastern Dakotas. They also were present in a series of smaller clusters in the Northeastern metropolitan corridor from Boston to Washington, in Florida and east Texas, from central Arizona through California, and north to the Canadian border in the West. With 2.6 million adherents in only 6,000 churches, some Missouri Synod congregations were apparently quite

Map 4-17

LUTHERAN CHURCH - MISSOURI SYNOD

TOTAL ADHERENTS BY COUNTY 1990

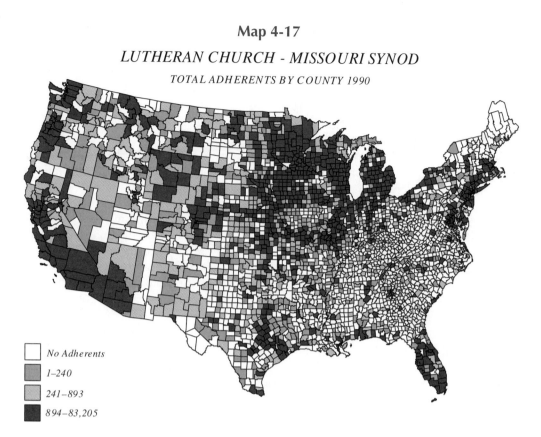

No Adherents
1–240
241–893
894–83,205

Map 4-18

LUTHERAN CHURCH - MISSOURI SYNOD

GEOGRAPHIC CHANGE BY COUNTY 1890, 1952, 1990

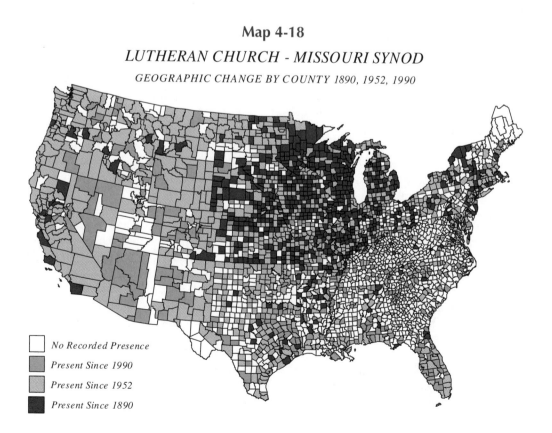

No Recorded Presence
Present Since 1990
Present Since 1952
Present Since 1890

large. Map 4-17 indicates that in 1990 even the smallest communities of Missouri Lutherans might have numbered more than 100 members.

The overall picture for the Lutheran Church - Missouri Synod then is one of a large denomination that, despite continuing growth and expansion, has not quite reached a truly national distribution. Clearly, in its home turf in the upper Midwest, and other parts of the country as well, the Missouri Synod has become a very recognizable part of the religious landscape. Because its developmental pattern in the twentieth century has been mixed in nature, it is difficult to predict what the twenty-first century will bring. The impressive growth up to mid-century has been tempered by a schism and a thinning of the organization's adherents at the county level (i.e., somewhat fewer adherents in more counties). Neither immigration nor merger appear to be likely mechanisms for future adherent growth.

The United Church of Christ

The United Church of Christ traces its origins to a number of religious movements with long histories in the United States. However, the key to understanding the nature of the modern-day organization is not continuity, but change and accommodation between people of different traditions. If organizational change is a key characteristic of American religious movements in the twentieth century, there is no better illustration of this than the United Church of Christ. Built upon a complex series of mergers much like the Evangelical Lutheran Church in America (ELCA), the United Church of Christ is a multiregional denomination assembled from a diverse assortment of individual religious bodies. Unlike the ELCA mergers, which basically unified coreligionists within a single faith family, the United Church of Christ is an assemblage of organizations of different religious and cultural traditions.

In brief, that merger process involved a three-stage sequence, originating in the early nineteenth century. First, between 1820 and 1850, the two movements known as the Congregational Churches and the Christian Church had developed some degree of formal organization. Similarly, the German Reformed Church in the United States and a composite Reformed and Lutheran body named the Evangelical Synod of North America also had organized. These four groups each had occupied separate "turfs"—New England, the Kentucky–Ohio Valley region, Pennsylvania, and the central Midwest, respectively. Second, between 1931 and 1934, these groups moved to an intermediate stage through two mergers. In 1931, a merger of these first two groups

created the Congregational Christian Churches, and in 1934 a merger of the second pair created the Evangelical and Reformed Church, with each merged organization retaining its former identity in the new body's name. The first of these represented an Anglo-Protestant constituency and historically adhered to local autonomy (i.e., congregational polity), whereas the second had its roots in German Calvinism and a more connectional (i.e., hierarchical) system of church government. Third, by the late 1950s, discussions had begun that culminated in 1961 with the merger of the Congregational Christian Churches and the Evangelical and Reformed Church, thus creating the United Church of Christ. This new organization transcended different regional and ethnic origins, as well as the theological traditions of the several constituent organizations.

Congregational churches, of course, were the most numerous of any group of churches at the time of the American Revolution. Almost entirely confined to New England, they numbered 668 and had more than 70,000 adherents (see Map 1-1, p. 19). The primacy of the Congregationalism was to be short-lived, and yet, its imprint on New England remains. Among the other antecedents of the United Church of Christ, the German Reformed churches also had become firmly established by 1776, as they had developed more than 150 churches largely in Pennsylvania (see Map 1-6, p. 21). Individually, the two bodies represented significant elements in the emerging cultures of their separate regions. Although it would be almost two centuries before the two organizations were to merge, in 1776, together, they would have comprised the largest American religious body by an appreciable margin and would have claimed a geographic distribution extending beyond the New England base of the Congregationalists well into the mid-Atlantic region. Table 4-10 presents the available county, church, and adherents data for the United Church of Christ.

Between the nation's founding in 1776 and 1850, the organizational and geographic elements of what would become the United Church of Christ would be expanded by the development of the two organizations. Although the movements that coalesced to form the Christian Church can be traced to several different locations, from an early date its greatest strength was in the Ohio Valley. By the 1850 United States Census, it reported 868 churches nationally, more than half of which were located in Kentucky, Ohio, Indiana, and Illinois. In contrast, though the Congregationalists had twice as many total churches, only 21 percent of their congregations were located west or south of Pennsylvania. In short, Congregationalism had not really been able to

Table 4-10 United Church of Christ

	1776	**1850**	**1890**	**1952**	**1990**
Number of counties	—	160	1,347	1,401	1,270
Number of churches	827*	2,832**	7,968	8,005	6,260
Total adherents	88,696*	398,388**	1,473,458	2,009,642	1,993,459

* These figures represent a combination of Congregational and German Reformed.

** This figure represents a combination of Congregational, German Reformed, and German Evangelical from the 1850 *Baptist Almanac and Annual Register*.

spread much beyond its Northeastern origins (see our discussion, p. 27). As a consequence, the 1929 merger between the Congregational Churches and the Christian Church entailed little if any geographic overlapping.

A somewhat similar fate was to befall the Reformed Church in the United States. Composed primarily of Germanic, but also several other immigrant churches, by 1850, it had doubled in size, with the United States Census reporting 344 churches. However, despite that growth, the Reformed Church remained concentrated in Pennsylvania, which accounted for 60 percent of its total adherents. Only Ohio immediately to the west had any appreciable number of churches, with 20 percent of its congregations. For the German Reformed Church in the United States, further expansion into the West was slowed by the emergence of a competitor from a series of state-level Evangelical Synods. As the mid-nineteenth century wave of new Germanic immigrants began to arrive in the central Midwest, these Evangelical churches were able to take root quickly. Though they are not identified in the 1850 Census, the *Baptist Almanac and Annual Register* of 1850 reports 600 Evangelical congregations. The eventual merger (1934) between the Evangelical Synod of North America and the Reformed Church in the United States would unite an older, more established, Northeastern religious organization with a newer Midwestern one. Taken individually in 1850, only the Congregationalists would have been viewed as something more than a minor regional organization. Taken together (as they were not to be for a century more), with more than 3,000 churches all across the northern half of the country, even though dwarfed by the Methodists and Baptists, these four religious organizations would have cast a far greater shadow in terms of both religious tradition and secular culture.

The years between 1850 and 1890 were, in the aggregate, good times for these four organizations. From approximately 3,000 churches, they expanded to 7,968 and their combined adherents grew to close to 1.5 million. Since each of the 1850 counts was "missing" one of the four bodies, it is impossible to measure rates of change precisely. However, data from both the 1850 and 1890 United States Census and the *Baptist Almanac and Annual Register* suggest a doubling of adherents, which also means that these organizations kept pace with the general demographic expansion of the country between 1850 and 1890. Map 4-20 (p. 98) shows that these several organizations also were able to expand geographically, although in very particular directions. From their various cultural and regional bases in the Northeast and Midwest, expansion into the Great Plains and across the mountains to the Pacific Coast was a natural outcome of the internal migration patterns of the time. A far more limited entry into the Southeast also occurred during this period and, thus, established the general outlines of the future organization's geographic shape for the next century. By 1890, the several components of the future United Church of Christ had reached into more than 1,300 counties, largely in the Northeast and Midwest.

The period from 1890 to 1952 was one of considerable expansion of the general population, as well as a time of significant growth for many religious organizations. That it was not such a time for these four organizations may, in some part, explain their willingness to enter into the series of mergers that were to take place in 1931, 1934, and 1961. The 1952 enumeration reveals that the combined constituencies from Congregational Christian Churches and the Evangelical and Reformed Church had fewer than 50 more churches than in 1890. It is true that some consolidation of congregations may have occurred as a result of the two mergers that already had transpired. However, other measures of growth also reveal only modest change. These organizations were in only 54 more counties in 1952 than in 1890, and although they had added 500,000 adherents, this represents growth of 36 percent during a period when the national population more than doubled. Map 4-20 (p. 98) depicts the geographic dispersion of new counties as being largely in the Mountain States and the Southeast, and to be quite limited in

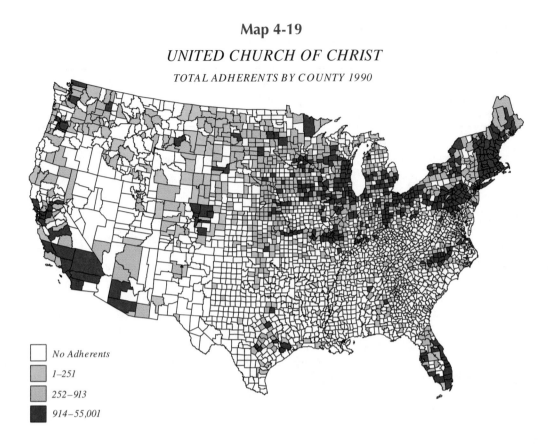

Map 4-19

UNITED CHURCH OF CHRIST

TOTAL ADHERENTS BY COUNTY 1990

No Adherents
1–251
252–913
914–55,001

Map 4-20

UNITED CHURCH OF CHRIST

GEOGRAPHIC CHANGE BY COUNTY 1850, 1890, 1952, 1990

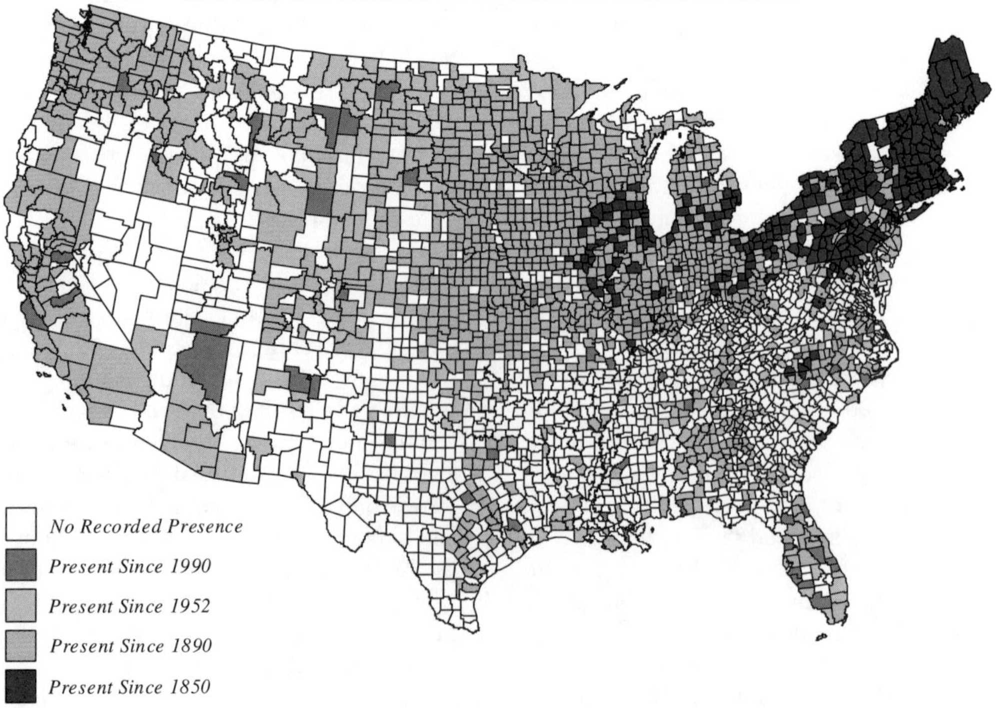

No Recorded Presence
Present Since 1990
Present Since 1952
Present Since 1890
Present Since 1850

both regions. It is difficult to escape the conclusion that for these two organizations, the Congregational Christian Churches and the Evangelical and Reformed Church, most growth probably was within existing churches and in their home turfs.

If the years from 1890 to 1952 were a period of only modest growth, the 1952–1990 period was even less favorable. From the pre-merger organizations' high point in 1952 of 1,401 counties and 8,005 churches, the United Church of Christ declined by 1990 to 1,270 counties and 6,260 churches. Some of these losses no doubt resulted as defections from the 1961 merger, which attempted to unite different theologies, organizational polities, and ethnic cultures. Indeed, even the number of total adherents was also smaller in 1990 than in 1952, although by a relatively small amount as compared to the decrease in the number of congregations. The geographic pattern of the United Church of Christ in 1990, as portrayed by Map 4-19, holds few surprises. This merged religious organization tended to be concentrated in a relatively limited number of regional settings, most especially in New England, and in a band of counties reaching from Pennsylvania through Ohio and Michigan into Illinois and Wisconsin. A significant number of counties in those areas contained 1,000 or more United Church of Christ adherents. By comparison, only a few isolated pockets in the Carolinas, Florida, and Texas interrupted a pattern of relative absence across the southern part of the nation east of Arizona. The basic picture of concentration in the Northeast and Midwest is confirmed by Table 3-2 (p. 59), which indicates that the United Church of Christ was present in only 17 percent of counties in the Southeast, and only 29 percent of those in the West.

In the first half of the nineteenth century four different religious organizations established their religious turfs in both theological and geographic terms. As the four organizations, through a series of mergers, formed the United Church of Christ, they have managed to transcend their historical differences in theology, ethnic culture, and organizational polity, but they have not managed to reach far beyond their original geographic boundaries. Their lengthy history and general cultural position in those regions ensures that they are within the mainline community. Consequently, the United Church of Christ surely should be classified as a denomination. However, the United Church of Christ's spatial distribution is multiregional rather than national. Furthermore, the general trends in adherent size and numbers of churches seem to indicate that there is little prospect that the United Church of Christ will alter its position as a multiregional denomination in the near future. Regardless of whether the organiza-

tion remains stable in numbers, shrinks further, or even begins to grow, it most likely will do so within its historic core areas.

American Baptist Churches in the U.S.A.

Some of the denominations that are classified as multiregional (the ELCA and UCC most notably) have attained that status in part through organizational mergers that broadened their geographic reach. The American Baptist Churches stands in sharp contrast since its existence is the result of a schism more than any other single factor—a schism that, although it occurred in the mid-nineteenth century, continues into the twenty-first century to partition dramatically Baptist ranks in the United States.

Though many Baptists would cite Biblical era precedents for the beginnings of their churches, most American Baptists trace their origins to the period of the English Reformation in the late sixteenth century. As was the case with other English religious dissidents, Baptists were among the earliest immigrants to the new colonies in North America. Although the earliest Baptist settlers were sometimes persecuted for their beliefs, the movement prospered and spread widely throughout the colonies. By 1776, almost 500 Baptist churches had been established, and, as seen on Map 1-4 (p. 20), they could be found in almost every part of the colonies, with the heaviest concentrations in Rhode Island and New Jersey in the North, and Virginia and North Carolina in the South. With more than 50,000 estimated adherents, Baptists were one of the four most common religious bodies, poised to become a national denomination in the new nation.

During the period from 1776 to 1850, the Baptist movement flourished, and, according to the *Baptist Almanac and Annual Register,* expanded from about 500 churches to more than 8,400. During much of this period, the Baptists were organized into regional associations of individual churches. Baptists did not develop strong centralized, formal organizational structures. Although this was conducive to much of the growth that occurred during this period, it also permitted the individual churches to drift apart with regard to certain practices and issues. The most pressing of these was the building controversy regarding slavery, although a number of theological questions also fostered some divisions among the Baptists. A major division among the Baptists occurred with the formation of the Southern Baptist Convention in 1845. Curiously, that split was not recognized in 1850 either by the United States Census or the *Baptist Almanac and Annual Register.* However, this division would be the most abiding of the religious schisms related to the issue of slavery and the Civil War. Baptists outside of the South continued for quite some time without any significant central organization, although they generally were known as Northern Baptists to differentiate themselves from their counterparts south of the Mason-Dixon line. There were, of course, certain national associations among Baptist congregations even before the formation of the Southern Baptist Convention in 1845. These associations—among them the Baptist Home Missions Society, the Baptist Sunday School Board, and the Baptist Foreign Missions Society—allowed local churches to cooperate for specified activities and purposes. However, these associations did not constitute a denominational-type organization for local churches. The Northern Baptist Convention became a formal organization in 1907 and, subsequently, in 1950, became the American Baptist Convention. Thus, the American Baptist Churches in the U.S.A. is directly descended from the 1845 cleavage of the Baptist movement into northern and southern branches. Table 4-11 presents the available county, church, and adherents data for the American Baptist Churches in the U.S.A.

As already noted, Baptists were well established by the end of the Colonial era. Although their distribution was a bit slanted toward the Southern colonies, there were more than 200 Baptist churches north of the Potomac by that time. When the Southern Baptist Convention was formed in 1845, based on a state by state count of Baptist churches as tallied by the United States Census in 1850, the Southern organization accounted for 58 percent of what were then termed "Regular Baptists." However, with nearly 4,000 churches in 1850, the "Northern" Baptists still were a very formidable religious community, outnumbering all other groupings except for the Methodists and Presbyterians, both of whom were soon to have their own North-South divisions. As can be seen on Map 4-22, Northern Baptists were found in virtually every county from Maine to the Mississippi River north of the Mason-Dixon. With almost 400,000 adherents and nearly 4,000 churches, they were a very appreciable presence almost everywhere in the North.

Between 1850 and 1890, the Northern Baptists grew in patterns that one might expect in the immediate aftermath of the Civil War. Map 4-22 shows an expansion that was almost exclusively westward, into both the Great Plains as well as the Pacific Coast. The area from Arizona east to the Atlantic shows only a small handful of counties entered, and most of those are either in the border states or along the Mississippi River. The number of new counties is a hint of the strong growth in local congregations, which increased to nearly 4,000, and in adherent strength, which more than tripled to more than 1.3 million. Clearly, even though these Northern Baptists were not making any appreciable in-roads in the Southeast, they were growing rapidly and expanding spatially in most other regions.

The period from 1890 to 1952 is an interesting one for this organization. During this time, the American Baptist Churches developed a more formalized central organization and also adopted the name "American" Baptist. These changes might seem to augur a significant push toward national status, but this was not the case. In fact, the American Baptists had fewer churches in fewer counties in 1952 than they had in 1890. This probably reflected the closing of small churches in declining rural areas, although many of the new counties shown on Map 4-22 for 1952 were found in lightly populated areas of the Mountain States. Strikingly, the Southeast still had not been entered to any appreciable degree. Offsetting this apparent geographic shrinkage was a modest expansion in adherents as the American Baptist Churches in the U.S.A. grew by 20 percent. That rate can be described as modest, since it occurred in a period when the general population more than doubled and when the Southern Baptist Convention grew by almost 6 million adherents.

The pattern of slow or modest growth established early in the century continued during the years from 1952 to 1990. The number of churches declined slightly, though the organization added 75 counties. Map 4-22 reveals that for the first time, more of those new counties were found in the Southeast than in the other regions. Nonetheless, the general avoidance of that region is overwhelmingly clear.

Table 4-11 American Baptist Churches in the U.S.A.

	1776	1850	1890	1952	1990
Number of counties	—	500	1,307	1,152	1,227
Number of churches	227*	3,957*	7,066	5,871	5,801
Total adherents	24,346*	391,661*	1,310,799	1,577,977	1,870,923

* Data sources for 1776 and 1850 do not divide Baptists into Northern and Southern branches. We have done so based on state boundaries to provide more comparable data.

Map 4-21

AMERICAN BAPTIST CHURCHES IN THE U.S.A.

TOTAL ADHERENTS BY COUNTY 1990

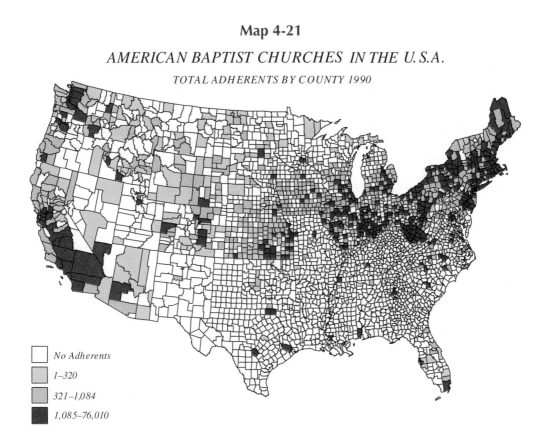

□	*No Adherents*
▨	*1–320*
▨	*321–1,084*
■	*1,085–76,010*

Map 4-22

AMERICAN BAPTIST CHURCHES IN THE U.S.A.

GEOGRAPHIC CHANGE BY COUNTY 1850, 1890, 1952, 1990

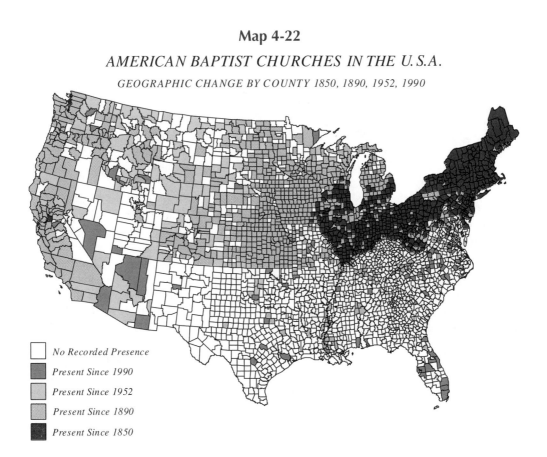

□	*No Recorded Presence*
▨	*Present Since 1990*
▨	*Present Since 1952*
▨	*Present Since 1890*
■	*Present Since 1850*

By 1990, the American Baptist Churches in the U.S.A. was present in only 12 percent of the counties in the Southeast (see Table 3-2, p. 59) in what remains one of the most sharply defined regional patterns among the larger organizations under study here. Though cut off from parts of the country that experienced the most rapid growth in population during these years, the American Baptist Churches in the U.S.A. still managed to grow by close to 300,000 adherents, which amounts to an almost 20 percent growth rate (see Map 4-21, p. 101). As in the preceding period, that growth seems more modest when compared to the population growth for the nation (more than 60 percent), and to the spectacular addition of more than 10 million adherents by the Southern Baptist Convention.

The American Baptist Churches in the U.S.A. provides a very striking case indeed. With a strong base established relatively early in the nineteenth century, this organization has grown only gradually during the twentieth century. Either by design or default, the American Baptist Churches in the U.S.A. has not competed successfully with the Southern Baptist Convention in its home turf in the Old South. Even more telling is the fact that by 1990, the Southern Baptist Convention outnumbered the American Baptist Churches in the U.S.A. in every region except the Northeast. As a result, despite a total of nearly 2 million adherents and a long history in North America, the American Baptist Churches in the U.S.A. does not convey the image of a robust or aggressive organization. The organization's geographic distribution appears to have been fixed during the nineteenth century in a pattern that did not include the Southeast. Moreover, there is little to indicate that this pattern will change anytime soon. As a result, though the American Baptist Churches in the U.S.A. is a well-recognized component in the religious community in many parts of the country, it remains a multiregional rather than a national denomination.

Christian Church (Disciples of Christ)

The early years of the new nation were a period of great ferment in American religion. Having rejected the established government and created a new and different form of political organization, it is not surprising that established religious bodies, particularly those associated with England, should find themselves challenged by new and different approaches to theology or religious organization. In the process, a wide array of new movements took root, especially in the parts of the country that were then on the frontier, where formal organizations were more difficult to maintain. Though many of these movements were to be short-lived, oth-

ers flourished and became significant elements in the religious culture and geography of the United States. One of the more important of these is the Christian Church (Disciples of Christ), hereafter referred to as the Disciples. During the first decades of the nineteenth century, the Disciples emerged as part of what is generally called the Restoration Movement, an effort to open established churches, in this case particularly Presbyterian churches, to a more inclusionary policy. The individual leaders of this effort were located in western Pennsylvania and Kentucky. Although one of those movements adopted the name "Christian," the other preferred the name "Disciples." When the two movements merged their efforts in 1832, both names were retained. By 1839, the movement had become strong enough to begin organizing at the level of several state organizations, and, in 1849, a first national convention was held. Given that these highly localized movements coalesced into a national organization only a bit before the 1850 United States Census enumeration, it is not surprising that the Disciples were collapsed into the category of minor sects, where they are listed as "Campbellites," after the name of two of the founding leaders. From those origins in the Ohio River region, the Disciples grew and expanded rapidly in the post–Civil War period. Subsequently, two major schisms were to divide the movement into three separate bodies—the Disciples, with an adherents total in 1990 of 1 million; the Churches of Christ, with total adherents in 1990 of almost 1.7 million; and the Christian Churches and Churches of Christ, which reported total adherents of 1.2 million in 1990. The Disciples emerged from this process as the smallest of the three bodies. Table 4-12 presents the available county, church, and adherents data for the Christian Church (Disciples of Christ).

Although, it is not possible to map the Disciples as of 1850 from the available data in the United States Census reports, two things are clear. First, for a relatively young organization, it had enjoyed a degree of success as evidenced by the 1850 *Baptist Almanac and Annual Register,* which reports more than 1,800 churches and total adherents of more than 160,000. Second, the early development of the organization was focused in the greater Ohio River Valley, encompassing the states of Ohio, Indiana, Kentucky, and Tennessee. In those earlier decades, the Disciples implemented a congregational-type polity system, in which the organization was held together by state conferences and occasional national conventions.

The latter half of the nineteenth century witnessed both numeric and spatial expansion among the Disciples. Their number of local churches almost tripled between 1850 and 1890, while their adherents base increased by a factor of 6 to more than one

Table 4-12 Christian Church (Disciples of Christ)

	1850	1890	1952	1990
Number of counties	—	1,500	**	1,379
Number of churches	1,848*	5,324	7,559	4,035
Total adherents	167,014*	1,020,541	1,836,104	1,037,757

  * 1850 data from the *Baptist Almanac and Annual Register* listing for "Campbellites." The United States Census grouped them as part of a miscellaneous category labelled "Minor Sects."

** County-level data were not reported.

million. As seen in Map 4-24 (p. 104), the Disciples blanketed the midsection of America from the southern Great Lakes to the Gulf of Mexico, and from the Appalachians into the Great Plains. By 1890, they occupied half of the nation's counties and, having made in-roads into the West and Southeast, seemed to be positioned to evolve into a national denomination. In areas where they already were present by 1890, the Disciples had become a significant influence, with churches averaging almost 200 adherents and with an average of more than three churches per county.

However, a major schism within the movement was already brewing, and by the time of the United States Census of Religious Bodies in 1906, a new organization, the Churches of Christ, had separated from the main Disciples organization. As of 1906, that group reported 2,649 churches (a number that would later be described as an undercount). Such a total would have represented nearly a 40 percent loss in the ranks of the Disciples. Clearly, this was a very significant schism. The Churches of Christ, being more conservative in theology, was composed largely of congregations that were located in the southern tier of states. Thus, this organizational schism was regional as well as theological. Between 1890 and 1952, the Disciples added 800,000 adherents and 2,000 churches. However, apparently predicated on the spatial aspect of the schism, its geographic orientation shifted to the North. Although the Disciples organization was included in the study *Churches and Church Membership in the United States, 1952* (Whitman & Trimble 1956), its data were not automated. Therefore, a 1952 map of the organization's distribution cannot be presented.

Between 1952 and 1990 yet another schism divided the Disciples. During the 1960s, a movement emerged to create a stronger national organization closer to the original model of presbyterial polity from which the movement had emerged. This movement contradicted greatly the Disciples' lengthy history of congregational polity and resulted in a major defection of congregations. In 1968, the dissenting congregations assembled themselves into a new association called the Christian Churches and Churches of Christ. This new association initially was composed of 2,300 congregations, which represents approximately 30 percent of the parent body. Thus, the net effect of the two post-1890 schisms was that the Disciples of Christ entered the 1990s with virtually the same number of adherents as it had a century earlier and with fewer churches located in fewer counties.

The geographic distribution of the Disciples in 1990 is portrayed on Map 4-23 (p. 104). The first, and perhaps most striking, aspect is the comparison with the 1890 pre-schism pattern of county coverage shown on Map 4-24 (p. 104). The denomination's loss of territory, as well as its shift to the North both are quite clear. Further comparisons between the Disciples and both the Churches of Christ (Map 4-13, p. 89) and the Christian Churches and Churches of Christ (Map 4-14, p. 89) reveal both the geographic losses by the Disciples, but also the aggregate numerical strength of these three Restoration Movement organizations. The Disciples has come to be a predominantly Midwestern phenomenon. The counties in which it was strongest all contain more than 600 Disciples adherents and, in most cases, several Disciples congregations. Such counties primarily were located in an area from Ohio westward into Kansas, where six states contained more than 40 percent of the denomination's adherents. Outside of this core, there were isolated clusters of strength in the Northwest, around both Los Angeles and San Francisco, and in eastern North Carolina. As seen in Table 3-2 (p. 59), in 1990, the denomination was present in between 42 and 52 percent of the counties of three of the nation's regions, although it was significantly weaker in the Northeast. Despite its twentieth-century losses, the Disciples was a denomination of more than one million adherents, found in more than 40 percent of the nation's counties, most often reporting fairly appreciable numbers of adherents.

The Christian Church (Disciples of Christ) has had an organizational history marked by an initial

Map 4-23

CHRISTIAN CHURCH (DISCIPLES OF CHRIST)

TOTAL ADHERENTS BY COUNTY 1990

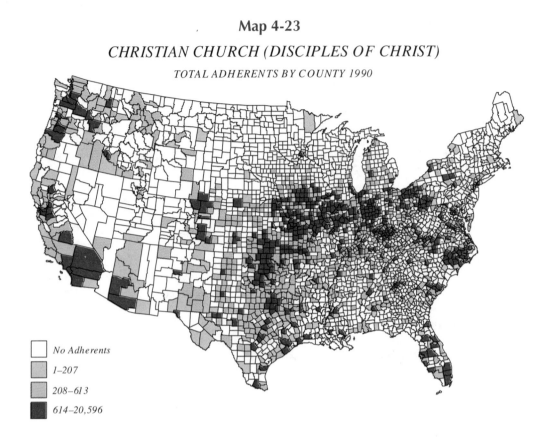

No Adherents
1–207
208–613
614–20,596

Map 4-24

CHRISTIAN CHURCH (DISCIPLES OF CHRIST)

GEOGRAPHIC CHANGE BY COUNTY 1890, 1990

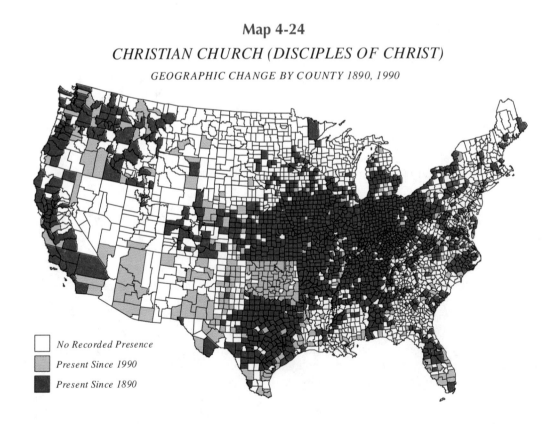

No Recorded Presence
Present Since 1990
Present Since 1890

phase of impressive growth, followed by divisions that have fractured the movement, leaving the Disciples in a state of relative decline. In particular, in the twentieth century, the denomination has retreated toward its Midwestern agricultural core area and has declined in adherents. Extrapolating from those trends and the denomination's location in a demographically stable region, it seems likely that the organization will remain static or possibly decline somewhat. A larger question involves the possibility of organizational shifts within the various Restoration Movement denominations. If the passage of time were to soften the issues that fractured the movement into three parts, the twenty-first century might well see a process of reunification mergers, creating a significantly larger and more national denomination. Though such a development would now seem wild conjecture, the experiences of other religious organizations in the United States during the twentieth century are at least suggestive of that possibility. For the moment, however, the Disciples remains the smallest of the three Restoration Movement churches and is classified as a multiregional rather than national denomination.

Christian Churches and Churches of Christ

The Christian Churches and Churches of Christ is the most recently formed of the three Restoration Movement organizations (see historical discussions of Churches of Christ and Disciples of Christ, p. 88 and p. 104). During the late 1960s, the Christian Church (Disciples of Christ) decided to move back toward its Presbyterian origins by developing a stronger centralized polity structure. Many of the Disciples' individual churches remained focused on the local autonomy of a more congregational polity. These congregations dissented from that new direction, instead forming their own association of congregations devoid of any significant central organization. Map 4-14 (p. 89) shows these congregations to be concentrated in Ohio, Kentucky, Indiana, and Illinois, which together contained 40 percent of the movement's total adherents. Secondary clusters of counties appeared along the West Coast and in Florida. By 1990, more than 5,000 congrega-

tions had joined the new association. These congregations contained more than 1.2 million adherents and were located in 1,300 counties. Table 3-2 (p. 59) shows them in 1990 to be concentrated in the Midwest, where they populated more than 60 percent of the region's counties. In contrast, they did not reach the 50 percent threshold in the other three regions. Nonetheless, with proportions ranging from 38 to 45 percent in those other regions, the Christian Churches and Churches of Christ was quite widespread and was present to some degree in many parts of the country. Table 4-13 presents the available county, church, and adherents data for the Christian Churches and Churches of Christ.

Table 4-13 Christian Churches and Churches of Christ

	Christian Churches and Churches of Christ 1990
Number of counties	1,300
Number of churches	5,238
Total adherents	1,210,319

During the twentieth century, both the Churches of Christ and the Christian Churches and Churches of Christ have experienced strong growth and expansion. Maps 4-13 and 4-14 (p. 89) to some degree depict the sections of a jigsaw puzzle along a seam in the Ohio Valley. This sense of a partition of territory can be further seen by comparing both of these patterns with that of the Christian Church (Disciples of Christ) (see Map 4-23). The Disciples core region lies a bit to the north and west of these two younger organizations. When those visual impressions are combined with statistical data for the three bodies, it is clear that the combined Restoration Movement denominations have become a national phenomenon of considerable dimension. Should the twenty-first century bring any significant reunification of these organizations, it is easy to see that their combined role and scope as a national denomination will be considerable.

Chapter 5

The Sects

Introduction

There is, of course, a certain contradiction in the distinction between denominations and sects. All religions exhibit particularism. The adherents of each and every faith system claim to have found the one right way, the one correct path. In this sense, all religions view their followers as a chosen and distinct flock. Every religious community thrives on its sense of distinctiveness. Indeed, if the path chosen is not special, then why follow it at all?

Yet, from the sociological point of view, there is no denying that each society views certain religious paths as normative and others as deviant. Moreover, societies differ in terms of the latitude that is allowed in degrees of normativeness and departure from those norms, especially where religious matters are concerned. For most of human history and thus, in most societies, religious pathways are configured quite narrowly. The chosen and the infidel are sharply distinguished. In contrast, we have dubbed the period encompassed by this study the Denominational Era because, in American society, religious faiths seem to have evolved into a great pluralism of formal organizational expressions. Stated differently, in the American social experiment, there are wide degrees of variation among both normative and deviant forms of religious belief and practice. Moreover, there are a great many more deviant than normative forms of religion on the American landscape. Of the 39 organizations that are the focus of this text, only 13 are denominations, whereas 26 are sects. Additionally, the 39 organizations studied here are drawn from a much larger universe of cases, of which clearly, most are understood socially as diversions from the more traveled religious paths.

As we've already seen, the typology employed here provides for three distinct categories of sect: classic sects, multiregional sects, and national sects. This chapter begins with the classic sects, of which there are nine. Because all of them are sects rather than denominations, it might be assumed that uniqueness of theology is their key feature. However,

this is not entirely so. The North American Baptist Conference, for example, seems to have focused its organizational separateness upon ethnic (German) distinctiveness in a regional setting where the latter historically are not so populous. Yet, there is no denying that for the rest of this grouping of organizations, some combination of distinct theology, combined with ethnic closure, and in several cases, a resulting distinct culture or way of life (Mennonites, Brethren, and Moravians) create sect status. Additionally, for at least four of these sects (the Cumberland Presbyterians, the Advent Christians, the Free Methodists, and the Evangelical Congregational Church), organizational schism has been the specific mechanism giving them organizational life.

The classic sects most resemble our common sense or everyday conceptions about what sects are like. Each is socially non-normative. They are small—only one of them has more than 100,000 adherents (the Mennonite Church). They tend to be contained in a single, or at best, a very small number of core clusters of counties. Finally, classic sects exhibit very little regional dispersion. Of these nine organizations, only two (the Mennonites and the Free Methodists) seem to depart from the general pattern of regional concentration (see Table 3-4, p. 59).

With regard to the history of the classic sects, it is useful to remember that not all religious movements begin small. Again, four of these organizations emerged from schisms within major American faith communities: Presbyterian, Methodist, Baptist, and Adventist. One of these, the Cumberland Presbyterian Church, was substantial in size at the time of its formation and, for a time, was viewed as a major expression of American Presbyterianism. For that matter, as we already have seen (pgs. 26–27, 96–99), Congregationalism was a major faith in the Colonial period and, had it not later been merged into the United Church of Christ, might not continue to occupy denominational status. By the close of the nineteenth century, New England Congregationalism already had become a regional sect.

A host of factors may affect the longevity of an organization's position as a classic sect. Clearly, the extent to which a religious community departs from the central values of the host society, the extent to which it opts for a different lifestyle, is important. When the latter is combined with a high degree of social enclosure—physical separateness from the host society—there is little impetus for change. It is not surprising that several Amish-type organizations are found among these classic sects (the Brethren in Christ Church and the Mennonite Church).

The second category of sects is the multiregional sect. Data are available for ten organizations in this category. They are the Wisconsin Evangelical Lutheran Synod, the Reformed Church in America, the International Church of the Foursquare Gospel, the Christian Reformed Church, the Church of the Brethren, the Unitarian-Universalist Association, the Baptist General Conference, the Pentecostal Holiness Church, Int., the Friends, and the Salvation Army. Like all sectarian organizations, their religious and/or social views are understood to be outside of the mainstream. In this sense, they are viewed sociologically as non-normative. However, unlike the classic sects, these multiregional sects have extended their geographical reach beyond a single regional pocket or core area. To be sure, as Table 3-3 demonstrates (p. 59), they do not occupy equal proportions of the counties in the various regions. Most, though not all, exhibit a single dominant regional setting either in terms of the percentage of counties occupied in a region or the proportion of the organization's adherents in a single region. Nonetheless, as we will show, the spatial patterns of these organizations contrast substantially with those of both the classic sects and the national sects.

The ten organizations classified here as multiregional sects as a group demonstrate the theological diversity of sectarian forms of religion in the United States. They differ in their historical origins, their theological and social characteristics, and in the processes that have brought them to multiregional sect status.

First, in terms of historical origins, four of these, the Reformed Church in America, the Christian Reformed Church, the Church of the Brethren, and the Friends all trace their American beginnings to the Colonial period. The two Reformed bodies stem from the Dutch Reformed Church, which migrated to North America in the 1600s. The Friends are the descendants of the Quakers that found refuge in the colony of Pennsylvania, and the Church of the Brethren descends from Pietists who settled in the Amish enclave in Pennsylvania in the 1700s. A fifth organization, the Unitarian-Universalist Association claims late eighteenth and early nineteenth century roots in the United States. The presence of these five organizations having either a Colonial or early Federal period heritage demonstrates that time alone does not ensure growth to denominational status.

Three of the organizations included here, the Wisconsin Evangelical Lutheran Synod, the Baptist General Conference, and the Salvation Army represent late arriving (mid- to late nineteenth century) immigrant movements. Finally, two of these ten organizations, the International Church of the Foursquare Gospel and the Pentecostal Holiness Church, International, represent native American brands of Protestantism emerging from the Pentecostal and Holiness movements late in the nineteenth century and early in the twentieth.

Second, the social and theological features that distinguish these organizations as sects also are highly diverse. Ethnicity has played a key role in the history of the Baptist General Conference (Swedish), the Reformed Church in America and the Christian Reformed Church (both Dutch), and the Wisconsin Evangelical Lutheran Synod (German). Both the International Church of the Foursquare Gospel and the Pentecostal Holiness Church, Int., are brands of "born again" Protestantism, which, though growing throughout the twentieth century, and surely identified with the regional setting called the "Bible Belt," are not yet viewed as normative. The Church of the Brethren and the Friends have translated their theologies into total lifestyles, as have the uniformed members of the Salvation Army. Finally, the Unitarian-Universalists seem to represent a far "left" theology that contrasts with both mainstream Protestantism, as well as with the more theologically conservative ("right") views of most other sects.

The third manner in which these sects differ is the diverse pathways they have followed to multiregional sect status. Organizational schism has resulted in the contemporary organizations of the Reformed Church in America and the Christian Reformed Church. The Baptist General Conference and the Wisconsin Evangelical Lutheran Synod, if not the products of schisms per se, have at least remained aloof from larger organizational cousins that have amalgamated and merged. Both organizations explicitly have disavowed connections with their mainstream counterparts. However, organizational merger also has produced multiregional sects, among them the Unitarian-Universalist Association and the Pentecostal Holiness Church, Int. Of course, a substantial number of these sects, as the designation implies, simply have walked a "different path" from the time of their arrival in the United States. The very beliefs and practices that initially marked them as different continue to do so in the modern era. Here, the Friends, the Brethren, and the Salvation Army provide examples.

Given that the various types in the classification scheme employed here are to be viewed as stop-over points in the life history of these organizations, it is useful to consider the direction of movement of the organizations designated here as multiregional sects. Clearly, for some, such as the Pentecostal Holiness Church, Int. and the International Church of the Foursquare Gospel, arrival at this status suggests the possibility of continued expansion both spatially and numerically. These relative newcomers may be advancing toward national sect or national denomination status in the twenty-first century. In contrast, for organizations with Colonial and Federal period origins, one wonders whether their twentieth century status as multiregional sects is a prelude to more restricted positions as classic sects. As we have noted in our previous work with these kinds of organizational statistics, processes of organizational change are slow and best are viewed not in terms of decades but across centuries. This is not possible with the most recently formed organizations examined here, as they are not yet a century old.

A third category of sect examined here is national sects. These organizations are so named because like all sects, they appear to stand theologically outside the American religious mainstream. Yet, they claim adherent populations that are as large, and sometimes even larger, than some national denominations. Obviously, they are designated as sects precisely because, in spite of their large adherent numbers, these organizations still represent non-normative religious motifs in American society. Again, to say that they fulfill the sociological category of "non-normativeness" simply means that they are different somehow from what the culture defines as the religious mainstream. With regard to their national status, it is useful to repeat here what already has been said about national denominations. Strictly speaking, no American religious organizations are national because none are found virtually everywhere, and none are found everywhere in the same relative pattern of numeric strength. All American religious organizations evidence core areas of original founding and settlement. Even the very largest of them, Catholics, Southern Baptists, and United Methodists have distinct pockets of adherent strength in their spatial distribution

patterns. Though found in all regions, they are not equally represented in all regions. The same may be said of the national sects. They too, are found in all regions, and as can be seen clearly by comparing Table 3-5 with Tables 3-2 and 3-3 (p. 59), national sects are more evenly distributed across regions than are either multiregional sects or multiregional denominations. Seven national sects are described in this chapter. They are the Jewish population, the Church of Jesus Christ of Latter Day Saints (Mormons), the African Methodist Episcopal Zion Church, the Seventh-Day Adventists, the Church of the Nazarene, the Church of God (Cleveland, Tennessee), and the Church of God (Anderson, Indiana).

What factors provide avenues to national sect status? First, it is noteworthy that five of these seven cases represent "new" theological departures with origins in the nineteenth century. In this sense, it is little surprise that they are viewed as sects, for in one way or another they intended to improve upon, reform, or depart from several different mainstream or normative branches of American religion. Adventism, the Nazarenes, and both Churches of God emerged from established traditions, primarily Methodist and Baptist. The Mormons, of course, claim an entirely new testamental revelation, the Book of Mormon. Additionally, though it may be argued that the Church of the Nazarene attained national status through organizational mergers, it is undeniable that the Mormons, Seventh-Day Adventists, and the Church of God (Cleveland, Tennessee) are doing so through evangelism, with the Church of God (Anderson, Indiana) exemplifying perhaps a lesser case of this.

Two of these national sects present instances where minority social status owing to imputed racial and/or ethnic traits results in separate religious organizations. Both American Jews and African-Americans are "minority groups" in the sociological sense of possessing social traits that the host society defines as "different." As such, their religious organizations also are viewed as outside the mainstream. Interestingly, though under very different circumstances, both blacks and Jews also were immigrant populations, and in this sense also were viewed as "outsiders." How long it may take for such social labels to be modified and what factors promote the assimilation of minority religious communities into the mainstream are questions beyond the scope of the present work.

Classic Sects

Mennonite Church

If any religious body in the country may be said to typify the concept of a sect for most Americans, it is probably the Mennonites. Despite having been here for a very long time (this church was first organized in 1683 in Germantown, Pennsylvania), they have remained resolutely separate and distinct from the mainstream, although not as sharply so as their theologically and culturally more conservative cousins, the Amish. The Mennonite Church exemplifies classic sectarian processes, as it is an ethnically and theologically closed enclave. As a traditionally agriculture-based community, several patterns have prevailed and can be observed in both the numerical and geographic data that lead to the classification of this religious organization, despite its relatively large total numbers and wide spatial distribution, as a classic sect. Table 5-1 presents the available county, church, and adherents data for the Mennonite Church.

The Mennonites were present in sufficient numbers to be recognized in the compilation of data for 1776. At that point, 16 congregations could be identified, of which 13 were in the southeastern section of Pennsylvania. The latter, of course, long has been identified as Pennsylvania Dutch country. The number of adherents in that small number of congregations (16) is, at best, estimated to have represented approximately 2,000 adherents. Nonetheless, the Mennonites clearly were "present and accounted for" by 1776. Between 1776 and 1850, the numbers and maps tell a story of growth, though primarily within that established culture hearth area. These agricultural populations tended to have large families, and, as their numbers grew, out of concern for cultural solidarity and connectedness, they expanded into surrounding available agricultural areas rather than opting for long-distance migration. Only when an established area had been filled did they expand to new more distant areas. When that saturation level was reached, they frequently established a new area that would then begin to develop in the same strongly clustered pattern.

Consequently, by 1850, the populations identified as Mennonites (which is probably a more inclusive grouping than simply the Mennonite Church) had grown to nearly 82,000 adherents. This growth transpired largely without the benefit of new arrivals from abroad. Nonetheless, by 1850, their 400 congregations or communities were found in only 19 counties. One of these was located throughout the Great Valley, a widely recognized path of settlement expansion from Pennsylvania, while several more Mennonite communities appeared across the mountains in Ohio. Both areas were destined to become secondary core areas or pockets of Mennonite and Amish settlement, especially the one in northeastern Ohio. However, the primary core clearly was established in Pennsylvania (see Map 5-2).

Between the 1850 and 1890 United States Censuses, the development by the Census Bureau of a more discrete approach to the identification of the various religious organizations resulted in some apparent anomalies. By the later enumeration, as might be expected, this classic sect had expanded in both the number of churches, which almost doubled, and in the number of counties in which they were found. The latter expanded by a factor of more than seven. Despite this pattern of sharp increase, the number of reported adherents in 1890 was only 41,000. These patterns seem to be an accurate reflection of the social process that gave rise to the Mennonite Church. Though Mennonites do not observe the strictest level of adherence to the traditional elements of the "plain life," nonetheless, they have maintained their separate Mennonite identity outside the mainstream of religious practice. This element of religious and social distinctiveness is, of course, the key factor in our understanding of the Mennonite Church as a sect, and as a classic sect.

The geographic distribution in 1890 followed the same general patterns already described. First, the sect expanded into counties immediately adjacent to the existing core settlement areas. This

Table 5-1 Mennonite Church

	1776	1850	1890	1952	1990
Number of counties	—	19*	137	230	445
Number of churches	16	400*	198	544	1,242
Estimated adherents	1,716	81,664*	41,496	66,652	154,259

* 1850 *Baptist Almanac and Annual Register* data apparently places all Mennonites including Amish into one category. The United States Census of 1850 reports only 112 churches.

Map 5-1

MENNONITE CHURCH

TOTAL ADHERENTS BY COUNTY 1990

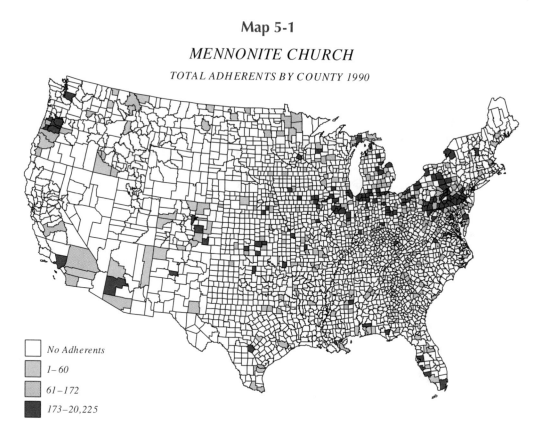

No Adherents

1– 60

61 – 172

173 – 20,225

Map 5-2

MENNONITE CHURCH

GEOGRAPHIC CHANGE BY COUNTY 1850, 1890, 1952, 1990

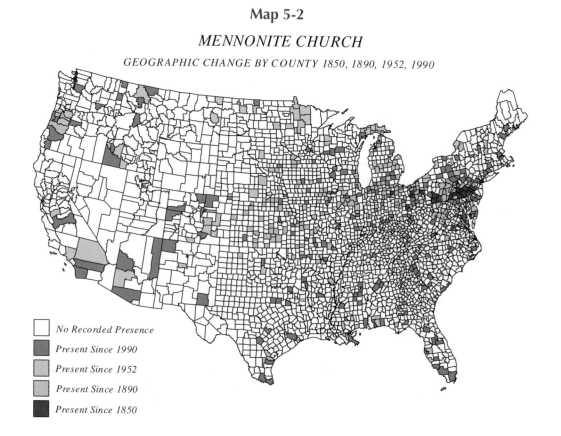

No Recorded Presence

Present Since 1990

Present Since 1952

Present Since 1890

Present Since 1850

pattern occurred in central Pennsylvania as well as in both Ohio and Virginia. The second pattern involved expansion across the rural agricultural areas of the Midwest in a generally east to west progression into the Great Plains. By 1890, only a limited number of isolated settlements appeared in the South, in the northernmost tier of states, or as far west as Oregon. Although the pattern was considerably more scattered than earlier, it still was characterized by the dominance of rural areas and the presence of bundles of contiguous counties. However, it is worth remembering that with only 41,000 adherents in 198 churches, the average congregation or community in 1890 numbered only a bit over 200 (207), and with 198 churches scattered across 137 counties, the characteristic pattern was one of a single church with probably fewer than 200 people in any given county. Clearly, these were not likely to be a dominant influence in defining the culture of most counties where Mennonites were present.

Between 1890 and 1952, the patterns of change continued to reflect the same sorts of thinning, albeit in a slightly different fashion. The number of adherents had grown from 41,000 to 67,000, which is relatively modest given that the general population more than doubled over that period. For the Mennonite Church, this process of thinning did not so much occur in terms of its presence in counties, the number of which grew proportionally to the church's growth in adherents, but rather in terms of the numbers and size of individual congregations. The number of congregations grew by a factor of 2.75 to well over 500, with the result that the average congregation size dropped sharply to 123. Though the average county in 1952 may have had two congregations, it is likely that most of the newly added counties contained relatively small churches. Geographically, these new areas in 1952 were fairly widespread, including a few areas in New England and a substantial entry into the Southeast and into the area from Colorado to the Pacific Coast. Significantly, the largest number of these new counties added to the pattern by 1952 were located in a broad band from the mid-Atlantic hearth into the eastern margin of the Great Plains. This reinforces the general characterization of the sect as agriculture based and as growing primarily in places adjacent to previously occupied core locations.

Toward the close of the twentieth century, the patterns established over the previous century appeared to be holding. In some ways, this has been a relatively good period for the Mennonite Church. By 1990, the number of adherents rose significantly to more than 150,000, a growth rate well above doubling and significantly greater than the 1.73 percent

increase in the general population. The number of churches or congregations rose by a very similar rate to more than 1,200. The number of counties also increased, but not as sharply (445). As a result, the overall pattern changed very little. Individual congregations numbered about 125 adherents, which is relatively small, but the average number of churches per county continued to increase, and in 1990, approached three per county. The average number of adherents per county rose to well above 300. Though this would seem to indicate a move toward a new pattern, these averages are somewhat misleading. As revealed by Map 5-1 (p. 111), fully a third of all the counties of this classic sect had fewer than 60 adherents, whereas the second third of the sect's counties each had fewer than 173 adherents. The largest single county had more than 20,000 adherents and thus, about one eighth of the entire national adherence total. These numbers place in sharp relief the fact that in most parts of the country, the Mennonite Church casts a very small shadow in the landscape of religious diversity. As shown clearly on Map 5-1 (p. 111), the Mennonite Church's core area remained sharply defined in a relatively small area centered in eastern and southern Pennsylvania. Thus, despite a substantial size in both total adherents and in the number of counties occupied, the Mennonite Church still is best classified as a classic sect. Consistent with the criteria of classification employed here, by 1990, the Mennonite Church claimed just over 150,000 adherents and was present in fewer than 20 percent of the nation's counties. Its religious and cultural distinctiveness was reflected in a spatial pattern that, from the 1770s to 1990, consistently remained focused on a readily identifiable core cluster of county locations with similar, though smaller, pockets of believers gradually dispersing into other geographic regions. In 1990, the Mennonite Church appeared to be a growing religious community, but still exhibited the key features of a classic sect. Indeed, perhaps more than most religious sects, this classic sect has encapsulated ethnic and theological distinctiveness into a way of life.

Cumberland Presbyterian Church

The Cumberland Presbyterian Church has had a long and relatively unique history among the organizations whose histories are portrayed here. The church was founded in 1810 as part of the process of religious transformation associated with the American frontier. This development represented a split within Presbyterianism in large part over the requirements for ordaining the clergy. Having enjoyed relatively solid growth during the nineteenth century, in the twentieth century the Cumberland Presbyterian Church has been characterized by shrinkage in both numbers and geographic extent. It is this more recent history of decline and retreat into a single regional core that has prompted us to designate it a classic sect. Table 5-2 presents the available county, church, and adherents data for the Cumberland Presbyterian Church.

As noted earlier, Presbyterians were among the earliest and most numerous arrivals during the Colonial era. By 1776, they were the second largest religious community in terms of the number of churches, with almost 600 congregations. At that time, they were widely distributed in the colonies especially outside of New England (see Map 1-2, p. 19). As was common for the more established religious organizations, migration to the frontier in the early nineteenth century brought strains that led to schisms and new organizations. The emergence of the Cumberland Presbyterians is typical of these processes and involved some of the usual mixture of doctrinal as well as organizational differences. Unlike many religious organizations emerging from schism, the Cumberlands retained a clear identification with their parent group. As was common for these religious organizations formed on the American middle frontier in the early nineteenth century, the Cumberland Presbyterians prospered in the nineteenth century. By 1850, the *Baptist Almanac and Annual Register* reported 1,250 churches and an estimated 70,000 adherents. Though a mapping of their geographic distribution is not possible due to the lack of county level Census Bureau data, the origin in and long-term association with Tennessee by the Cumberland Presbyterians suggests a core location in the middle South.

The Census enumeration of 1890 provides a picture of the Cumberland Presbyterians essentially at their organizational zenith. From 1850 to 1890, this religious organization expanded to more than 2,000 congregations and almost 300,000 adherents, an expansion that outpaced the growth of the general population. Their general spatial distribution in 1890 is shown in Map 5-4 (p. 114). Clearly, by that date, the Cumberland Presbyterians were solidly

entrenched in an area extending from Illinois and Missouri southward along the Mississippi to the northern border of Louisiana, and from the western margin of the Alleghenies in Tennessee and Kentucky westward into central Texas. Outside of this core area, there were a number of counties in California and the Pacific Northwest, as well as in Colorado and western Pennsylvania. The rapid growth in geographic extent and adherents made it appear that the group was poised to become at least a multiregional organization, and perhaps something more (a denomination rather than a sect) both organizationally and geographically.

The future, however, was to be somewhat different. In 1906, discussions with the Presbyterian Church (U.S.A.) resulted in both a merger and a schism. Many Cumberland Presbyterian congregations rejoined their larger and more mainline cousins, while a significant number of congregations, to use the language of Mead, "perpetuated the Cumberland Presbyterian Church as a separate denomination" (1975, 228). In this process, the group was sharply reduced in both size and extent. By 1952, the Cumberland Presbyterians were found in fewer than half as many counties as in 1890 and clearly were shrinking in toward their original core area in Tennessee. The churches more on the margins of the 1890 distribution clearly and understandably had been those most likely to join the more mainline organization, the Presbyterian Church (U.S.A.). This process of contraction by merger and schism is one that is encountered infrequently in these organizational histories, but has clearly marked the twentieth century as a period of shrinkage for the Cumberland Presbyterians.

The last half of the twentieth century has seen the continuation of the 1890–1952 trends, although less dramatically so. Between 1952 and 1990, the number of Cumberland Presbyterian churches dropped by another 173, representing almost 20 percent of the 1952 total. The number of counties where the organization is present declined by 10 percent, and the number of adherents also declined, although by only a small amount. Though there is no clear evidence for this, it may well be that some of these "lost"

Table 5-2 Cumberland Presbyterian Church

	1850	1890	1952	1990
Number of counties	—	649	307	275
Number of churches	1,250*	2,024	910	737
Total adherents	70,400*	293,671	92,656	91,040

* The 1850 Census did not differentiate among Presbyterians, but the *Baptist Almanac and Annual Register* does provide statistics on churches and membership.

Map 5-3

CUMBERLAND PRESBYTERIAN CHURCH

TOTAL ADHERENTS BY COUNTY 1990

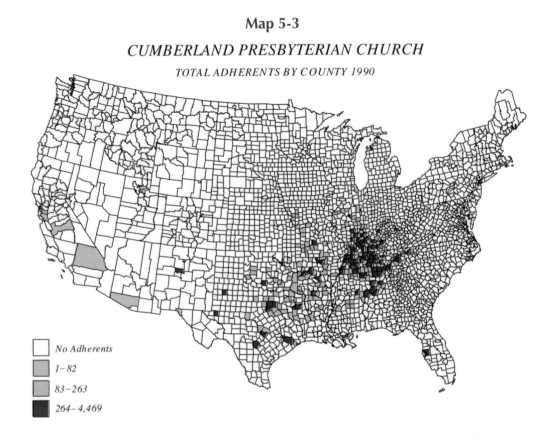

No Adherents
1– 82
83–263
264– 4,469

Map 5-4

CUMBERLAND PRESBYTERIAN CHURCH

GEOGRAPHIC CHANGE BY COUNTY 1890, 1952, 1990

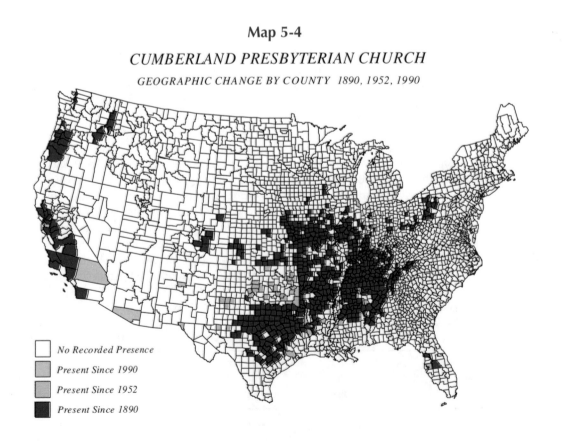

No Recorded Presence

Present Since 1990

Present Since 1952

Present Since 1890

congregations opted to join the merger of the two larger Presbyterian bodies (Presbyterian Church in the United States and United Presbyterian Church in the U.S.A.) when they reunited in 1983.

By 1990, the general distribution pattern was clearly focused on the middle South in a band of counties extending from western Kentucky south through Tennessee into central Alabama. Most of the highest third of counties were found in that area, with that category having a size range of 264 to 4,469 adherents. For an organization with an average church size of 123 adherents and one-third of its counties containing 82 or fewer adherents, this region was clearly the core area. Yet, even here, with what in most instances were probably two or three churches per county, the organization remained only a secondary element in the local mix of faiths in its core region. Outside of this core region, many of the isolated high category counties were metropolitan areas, particularly in Texas, where once again a small handful of Cumberland Presbyterian congregations were not likely to be defining elements in the local culture widely recognized to be Methodist and Baptist dominated.

The case of the Cumberland Presbyterians provides a unique cartographic comparison among these various organizations. Here, one must inspect the two maps in a different fashion than is typical, because the mapping convention adopted to show change over time is designed for organizations where growth and expansion are the norm, and this case definitely does not conform to that scheme. The 1890 distribution pattern in Map 5-4 is far more extensive than the 1990 pattern shown in Map 5-3. Additionally, in 1990, there were only one-third as many congregations as there were in 1890. Thus, this classic sect has been retreating inward over this hundred-year period. It remains to be seen whether this remnant organization will retain the energy to sustain a separate identity over the long term.

In summary, if it is reasonable to classify the Cumberland Presbyterian Church as a classic sect, it has arrived at this category through a very different route than most other such organizations. Here, a branch of a mainstream denomination has retreated into sectarian status through schism, and has furthered the process of sectarian withdrawal through numeric contraction and spatial limitation during the twentieth century. This case, like all "non-normative" cases, underscores a basic point about religious organizational processes and about our attempt to classify organizations into types. These processes constantly are unfolding, and organizations fulfill typological criteria differently at different points in time. In this particular case, the most recent emergent organizational pattern is sectarian, not denominational. Once a component in a larger denominational pattern, at the dawn of the twenty-first century, the Cumberland Presbyterian Church registers a double-digit county-level percentage in only two regions (Southeast and West) and is present in fewer than 10 percent of the nation's counties. It has shrunk to fewer than 100,000 adherents and likely will become smaller. Regardless of its status in earlier times, in 1990 it is a classic sect.

Free Methodist Church of North America

The Free Methodist Church of North America was created in 1860, in part, as a manifestation of abolitionist politics on the eve of the Civil War and also as a classic schismatic movement to purify and return to the original roots of the Methodist movement. Unlike many of the church divisions that partially or wholly were prompted by the issue of slavery in the United States, this organization has survived, but in a configuration of size and distribution that mark it as a classic sect.

Obviously, statistical records begin with the organization's founding in upstate New York in 1860. By the time of the 1890 Census, the organization had grown and dispersed significantly, with more than 600 churches located in 463 counties. As an organization originally formed by a dissident clergyman, it may be assumed that a significant portion of these congregations represented either entire established Methodist congregations or perhaps even more likely, segments dividing off from such congregations. Table 5-3 presents the available county, church, and adherents data for the Free Methodist Church of North America.

The schismatic character of this organization in 1890 is demonstrated by an average congregation size of only 55 persons, with an average of only 1.3 churches per county. Thus, in the most likely occurrence, one would have encountered a single congregation consisting of approximately 10 or 12 families in a county. As seen on Map 5-6 (p. 116), the 1890 distribution was anchored in the upstate New York area of the organization's founding and extends from there, across the Midwest into Michigan, Illinois, Wisconsin, and beyond into the Great Plains. As

Table 5-3 Free Methodist Church of North America

	1890	1952	1990
Number of counties	463	577	515
Number of churches	620	1,117	1,038
Total adherents	34,260	49,052	70,394

Map 5-5

FREE METHODIST CHURCH OF NORTH AMERICA

TOTAL ADHERENTS BY COUNTY 1990

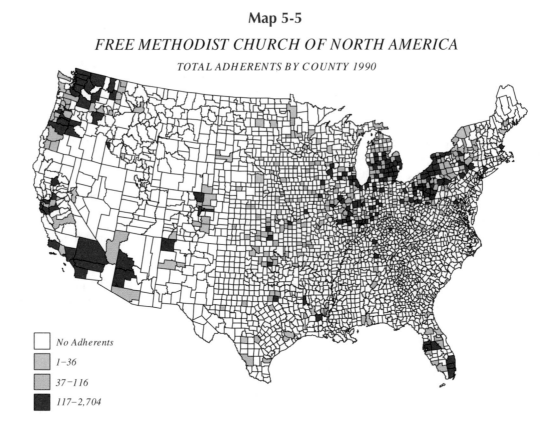

No Adherents
1–36
37–116
117–2,704

Map 5-6

FREE METHODIST CHURCH OF NORTH AMERICA

GEOGRAPHIC CHANGE BY COUNTY 1890, 1952, 1990

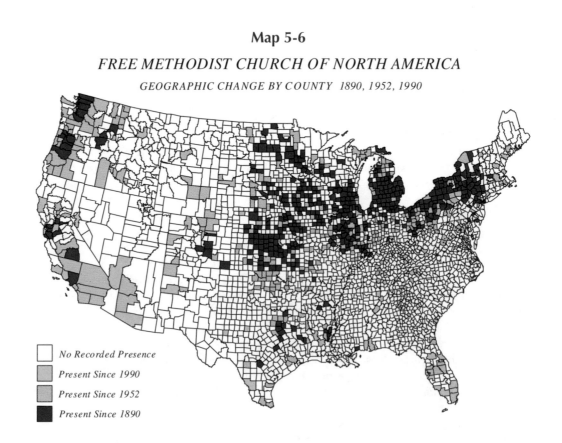

No Recorded Presence
Present Since 1990
Present Since 1952
Present Since 1890

might be expected for an organization with abolition-ist roots, by 1890, there had been little or no movement into the southern portion of the country. In contrast, movement to the West Coast was apparent, especially in Washington and Oregon. In short, in only 30 years' time, the movement had spread from coast to coast in the northern tier of states, but almost always in the form of single, quite small congregations.

Between 1890 and 1952, the Free Methodists continued to expand in terms of the number of congregations, increasing to 1,117, or almost doubling over the period. Once again, a glance at Map 5-6 reveals a clear pattern. The original areas in New York, Pennsylvania, and Michigan largely had been settled by the Free Methodists prior to 1890, so the areas of new growth by 1952 were primarily in the Great Plains, the Mountain States, and the West Coast. Although the Southeast still appeared to be the weakest area for this organization, a scattering of counties were located across the Southeast and even more clearly appeared in Oklahoma and Texas. The rate of geographic expansion, however, slowed considerably, as only 114 new counties were added in the more than 60-year period between 1890 and 1952. As a result of these two somewhat divergent growth patterns, though the average number of adherents per county had increased by 1952, the average size of congregations had declined to only 44 persons, demonstrating even more clearly the sectarian character of the Free Methodist Church of North America.

The period from 1952 to 1990 involved still different sorts of changes for this small organization. On one front, the alliance with the Holiness Movement in Canada (with whom the Free Methodists previously had jointly undertaken an overseas missionary effort) was a significant positive development. Such a missionary effort seems ambitious for such small organizations. On the domestic front, the evidence was a bit more mixed. The number of counties in which the Free Methodists were present has dropped to a level about halfway between that of 1952 and 1890, with a loss of more than 60 counties. This shrinkage was mirrored by the loss of 79 congregations. Given the small average congregation size in 1952, some church failures or closures might well have been expected. Thus, it is not entirely surprising to find such losses. However, offsetting those declines has been a continuation of growth in adherents. That number increased by more than 20,000 to a total of 70,394, meaning that individual congregations became somewhat larger and, therefore, probably more viable in the long term.

Despite this relatively good news concerning the Free Methodist Church, an inspection of Map 5-5, as well as the data for 1990, reveals several less encouraging trends. First, the Free Methodist Church had significantly fewer than 100,000 members nationally, with most of them found in relatively small communities. One-third of the more than 500 counties containing Free Methodist churches had no more than 36 adherents, a number including both adults and children. Two-thirds of the counties contained fewer than 117 adherents, and the largest single county contained only 2,704 adherents. Plainly, this religious organization, despite having grown, has done so as a communion of very small individual churches, meaning that it seldom, if ever, can play a strong role in determining or defining local or regional culture. As a consequence, though the Free Methodist Church of North America has been an enduring phenomenon, it appears to be almost resolutely configured as a classic sect.

Clearly, Methodism is one of the largest and most widely dispersed American religious communities. The character of the Free Methodists as a classic sect is demonstrated not simply by its formation through the process of schism, but also through its remaining organizationally separate during a period when the greater body of American Methodists joined through mergers to form the United Methodist Church. In this regard, the Free Methodist's sectarian position among Methodists is similar to that of the Cumberland Presbyterian Church. Both classic sects were formed through schism and both remain distinct from the mainstream organization in their faith community.

North American Baptist Conference

The North American Baptist Conference presents one of the most distinct examples in these data of a classic sect that has retained its separate organizational status because of ethnic distinctiveness. Theologically, it does not depart significantly from the beliefs of mainstream Baptist denominations such as the Southern Baptist Convention, the American Baptist Churches in the U.S.A., and the nation's largest black Baptist organization, the National Baptist Convention USA, Inc. Moreover, it does not subscribe to the conservative views of other German Baptist sects such as the various Dunkers or Brethren organizations. Yet, having been shaped by the migration of small groups of German Baptists to the United States in the mid-nineteenth century, it has retained organizational distinctiveness focused on its Germanic origins. According to Frank Mead, these churches, located primarily in New Jersey and more so in Pennsylvania, organized a conference that by 1851, consisted of "8 churches and 405 members" (1975, 56). Apparently, so small an organization was not recognized or recognizable by any of the mid-nineteenth century enumerations. In fact, it also eluded mention in the 1890 United States Census, by which time it had apparently grown in both size and geographic spread, moving with German heritage migrants into the Great Plains. The earliest date for which clearly matching data is available is from the NCCC 1952 enumeration (Whitman & Trimble 1956). Table 5-4 presents the available county, church, and adherents data for the North American Baptist Conference.

Table 5-4 North American Baptist Conference

	1952	1990
Number of counties	146	163
Number of churches	210	267
Total adherents	35,431	54,010

As is depicted clearly on Map 5-8, by 1952, this small sect had shifted location from the area of its mid-Atlantic origins, to the upper Midwest and Great Plains, with a fairly obvious cluster of local churches in the Dakotas. By that date, there also were a few counties still further west in Washington, Oregon, and California, but the area from Lake Michigan to the Dakotas appears to have become the core region. Here it is wise to remember that the group numbered only 35,000 adherents nationally and was present in fewer than 5 percent of the nation's counties. Furthermore, most of those counties represent only a single congregation, with an average congregation numbering just 169 persons.

Between 1952 and 1990, the North American Baptist Conference grew in adherent size by more than 52 percent, with a 27 percent increase in the number of churches. The rate of adherent growth for this classic sect was relatively close to that of the general population, almost 65 percent. A clear suggestion of the general pattern of this growth emerges from the comparison of the data and Maps 5-7 and 5-8. First, only 17 new counties were added to the distribution in these years, significantly fewer than the 57 new congregations. Thus, it would appear that most new church growth took place in the vicinity of existing churches. This impression is reinforced by Map 5-8, which reveals that most new counties in 1990 were adjacent to counties already reporting churches and members in 1952. By 1990, average congregation size had increased to more than 200 persons, which again indicates a pattern of growth and expansion close to home. Thus, in both 1952 and 1990, this organization was characterized by limited size and modest spatial reach, in just over 5 percent of the nation's counties.

Therefore, while it may be true that the North American Baptist Conference has shifted dramatically away from its mid-Atlantic origins to parts of the Midwest and West Coast, it has not developed strongly enough to be thought of as something other than a classic sect. In 1990, it was present in fewer than 200 counties across the nation, one-third of which contained no more than 115 adherents (see Map 5-7). The combination of limited size and limited county-level occurrence surely are among the definitive characteristics of a classic sect.

Moravian Church in America (Unitas Fratum)

The Moravian Church, or Unitas Fratum (literally, "Unity of Brethren"), can lay claim to being the oldest of the "Protestant" churches to have survived to the modern day. The movement dates from almost 100 years before the Lutheran and Calvinist Reformation of the early 1500s and originated in the regions of Bohemia and Moravia from which the organization has taken its American name. During the religious wars that followed the Reformation, the movement was almost eradicated. Small surviving groups were dispersed into other parts of Europe, and in time, a small Moravian community embarked for North America arriving in Georgia in 1734. In one of the more interesting coincidences in the history of American religion, they traveled to North America on the same ship that brought John Wesley and, thus, Methodism to North America. The divergence in the development patterns of these two religious movements since that beginning in terms of their growth and cultural or societal roles could hardly be greater. Methodism, of course, became one of the strongest families of religious organizations in the United States, with the United Methodist Church ranking in 1990 as the nation's third largest national denomination. In contrast, the Moravian Church, though active in missionary work in a wide array of locations globally, and though classified as evangelical (i.e., reaching out), grew only modestly within a series of small clusters in a fashion characteristic of a classic sect. Table 5-5 (p. 120) presents the available county, church, and adherents data for the Moravian Church in America (Unitas Fratum).

The Moravians remained in Georgia for only a few years before shifting to Pennsylvania, which ever since has remained one of their primary centers. In the almost 40 years leading up to the Revolution, the Moravians became an established organization and had a presence in their core area with 31 churches and an estimated 3,300 adherents. Thus, though not one of the larger factors in the religious matrix of Colonial America, they had more churches

Map 5-7

NORTH AMERICAN BAPTIST CONFERENCE

TOTAL ADHERENTS BY COUNTY 1990

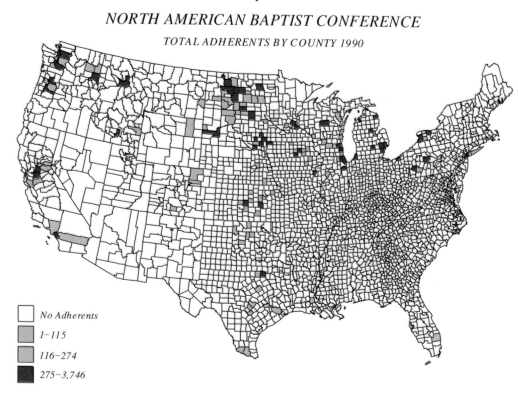

No Adherents

1–115

116–274

275–3,746

Map 5-8

NORTH AMERICAN BAPTIST CONFERENCE

GEOGRAPHIC CHANGE BY COUNTY 1952, 1990

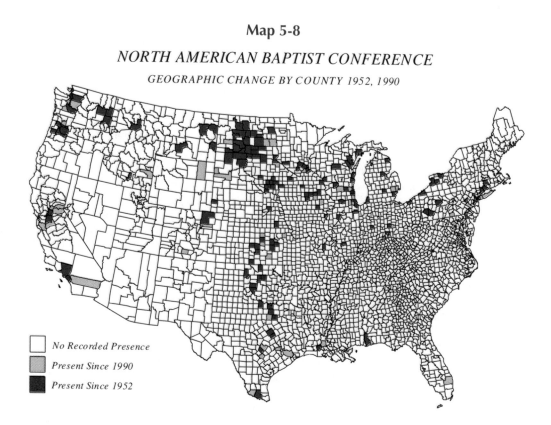

No Recorded Presence

Present Since 1990

Present Since 1952

Table 5-5 Moravian Church in America (Unitas Fratum)

	1776	1850	1890	1952	1990
Number of counties	—	12	42	50	64
Number of churches	31	331*	114	139	153
Estimated adherents	3,324	8,448	18,137	46,618	52,519

* This number reported by the Census Bureau seems highly unlikely, since half of that number of churches is reported in Ohio, never a real stronghold of the group. The *Baptist Almanac and Annual Register* reports only 22 churches, which may be a bit of an undercount.

and probably more adherents than did the Mennonites with which they shared a home turf. Together with the Mennonites and other German origin religious organizations, the Moravians created a geographic niche and a place in America's cultural mosaic that has proven to be very enduring.

By 1850, their initial patterns appear to have changed very little. Map 5-10 reveals Moravian communities located in a small handful of counties in eastern Pennsylvania. Elsewhere, the distribution is limited to isolated individual counties in North Carolina, Ohio, and Indiana. By this relatively early date, they not only had "fallen behind" many of the mainline religious organizations in geographic expansion, but a comparison with Map 5-2 (the Mennonite Church, p. 111) reveals that they had not even equaled the expansion of one of the other organizations sharing their general cultural and regional origins. The estimated number of adherents in 1850 was well below what might have been expected by simple demographic expansion. From 1776 to 1850, this sect grew by a factor of only 2.5, while the national population grew by a factor of 5.9. It would appear that even by this early date, the organization was losing potential members to more mainstream religious organizations and, most likely, to mainstream culture.

This trend of modest growth might also be thought of as relative slippage and has continued to be a dominant pattern for the Moravian Church for the ensuing almost 150 years. Between 1850 and 1890, the Moravians almost kept pace with general population growth by more than doubling in size (2.1) during a period when the general population grew by a factor of 2.7. As is displayed on Map 5-10, that growth transported the Moravian Church into a scatter of counties largely in areas of the Midwest, especially in Wisconsin, Minnesota, and Iowa. Only a few counties show up on the Carolina-Virginia border in what would become the second core region for this organization. It must be assumed that with only 114 churches nationally, most of these new counties represented the creation of a single church or community. This pattern leads to the conclusion that the

role of the Moravians in influencing local or even regional culture was minor, excepting, of course, in conjunction with other groups of similar heritage in eastern Pennsylvania.

In the period from 1890 to 1952, the Moravian Church continued growing, with the number of adherents more than doubling, climbing at a rate approaching that of the general population (2.5 vs. 2.4). This growth took place largely "at home," with only 8 new counties and 25 additional churches added. As a result, the size of the average individual congregation grew from 160 to more than 330. This indicates a second facet of this sect's development. They tend to settle and remain together! The relatively few new counties that appeared by 1952, as portrayed on Map 5-10, were mostly adjacent to counties previously occupied and were more notable in the Carolinas and the Pennsylvania–New Jersey cores than elsewhere in the nation. Though the Moravian Church grew in this period, it appears to have done so in two primary small core regions and in a number of smaller clusters.

After two and a half centuries in North America, by 1990, the Moravian Church had grown to only 52,519 adherents and 153 churches nationwide. As shown on Map 5-9, Moravians were located in only 64 counties, in a pattern dominated by two clusters, one centered on Pennsylvania and the other on the Carolinas. More than one-third of these counties represented fewer than 200 Moravians, whereas the middle third of county locations had Moravian populations in the 200 to 500 range. While some counties, in fact, had fairly large populations, there were only 20 such counties in the entire nation. This combination of small total numbers and very limited geographic distribution, dominated by pockets of numerical strength, are hallmarks of a classic sect's long-term organization profile. Indeed, statistics ranging from 1776 to 1990 revealed no significant change in the relative status of this classic sect. Very much like its neighbor the Mennonite Church, the Moravian Church exemplifies the processes through which ethnic and theological distinctiveness combine to form and sustain a socioreligious enclave.

Map 5-9

MORAVIAN CHURCH IN AMERICA (UF)

TOTAL ADHERENTS BY COUNTY 1990

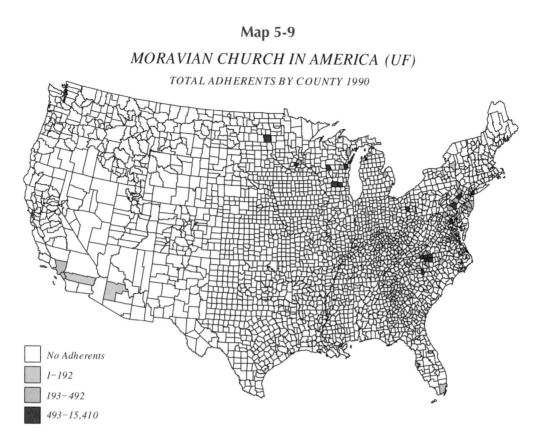

No Adherents
1–192
193–492
493–15,410

Map 5-10

MORAVIAN CHURCH IN AMERICA (UF)

GEOGRAPHIC CHANGE BY COUNTY 1850, 1890, 1952, 1990

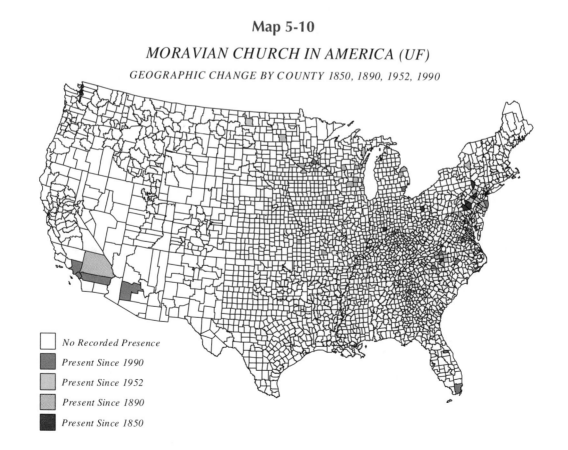

No Recorded Presence

Present Since 1990

Present Since 1952

Present Since 1890

Present Since 1850

Evangelical Congregational Church

The historical evolution of this organization is one defined by a series of schisms in which progressively smaller bodies split from larger ones. The origins of the Evangelical Congregational Church can be traced to the nineteenth-century emergence of the Evangelical Church. That body primarily was composed of Continental Protestants from both Lutheran and Calvinist traditions who settled largely in the mid-Atlantic and Midwestern regions. As these Evangelicals grew both in numbers and geographic extent, a more formalized organizational structure, including a hierarchy of leadership, developed. Many in the church resisted this development, preferring instead to retain local autonomy or a congregational model of organizational authority. In 1894, this issue led to a schism resulting in the formation of the United Evangelical Church. A generation later, an effort at reunification with the parent organization was only partially successful and resulted in a minority of United Evangelical congregations forming the Evangelical Congregational Church (1922). As a schismatic organization formed from yet an earlier splinter movement, the Evangelical Congregational Church has twice moved in the direction of becoming smaller. This propensity to emphasize theological distinctiveness and organizational separateness typifies classic sects. Moreover, like both the Cumberland Presbyterians and the Free Methodists, these Evangelical Congregationalists represent a sectarian branch of a larger faith community that was formed through schism and has retained sectarian status. Table 5-6 presents the available county, church, and adherents data for the Evangelical Congregational Church.

Table 5-6 Evangelical Congregational Church

	1952	1990
Number of counties	34	36
Number of churches	167	159
Total adherents	28,596	33,166

Since the present-day organization dates only from 1922, the first date for which there is mapped data is 1952. A glance at Map 5-12 reveals a sharply defined pattern stretching from Pennsylvania and New Jersey to Illinois, primarily in three clusters. One of these is in eastern Pennsylvania, one in western Pennsylvania and northeastern Ohio, and one in northern Illinois. As the organization was located in only 34 counties nationwide, it is not surprising that only one of these clusters, the one in eastern Pennsylvania, consisted of more than 10 counties. The number of churches reported was only 167, meaning that although the organization was not very widespread, in at least some localities it was represented by multiple congregations. With an average of almost five churches per county, a few counties probably contained more than a half dozen of these churches. In that very small number of counties, with an average congregation numbering more than 170 persons, this organization may have begun to be a recognizable and perhaps a significant cultural element.

As seen in Map 5-12, between 1952 and 1990, the picture changed only marginally. The organization increased in adherents by almost 5,000, representing a modest expansion of about 16 percent. It also added eight new counties. However, organizational losses, as revealed by a decline of an equal number of churches, offset these apparent gains, with the result that the net change in the number of counties is an addition of only two, with a total of only 36 counties nationwide in 1990.

These trends reflect a continuation of the organization's earlier pattern. As shown graphically on Map 5-11, the spatial core of the organization remained in eastern Pennsylvania, which included all but one of the largest counties in terms of numbers of adherents. Indeed, in that region, one single county held more than 20 percent (almost 7,000) of the organization's total adherents. By comparison, the counties west of Ohio included only two instances with more than 140 adherents and thus probably contained either single congregations of modest size or a small number of tiny congregations.

The distribution of this organization typifies that of a classic sect. It is extremely small in total adherence and spatially is highly concentrated in roughly a dozen counties in a section of only one state (eastern Pennsylvania). In many of the counties outside this small enclave, where the organization can be found it is characterized by either isolated congregations or very small ones. In all of these ways, it is sect like. In terms of organizational behavior it is noteworthy that even in such a small body, there is a division between the Eastern and Midwestern regions, which are recognized as separate districts. This, in part, reflects structural features of the polity system that the organization employs.

Advent Christian Church

Adventism, meaning a belief in the second coming of Christ as an impending event, began early in the nineteenth century as a movement among established churches. It generally is associated with the ideas of William Miller and his followers, and its largest present-day organizational manifestation is the

Map 5-11

EVANGELICAL CONGREGATIONAL CHURCH

TOTAL ADHERENTS BY COUNTY 1990

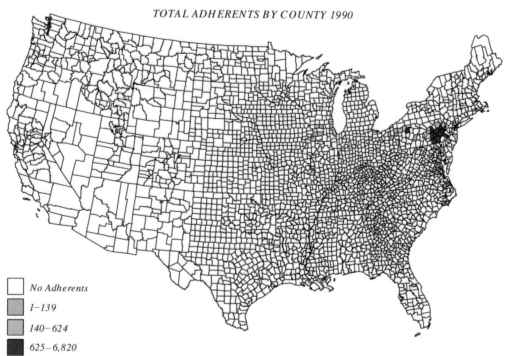

No Adherents

1–139

140–624

625–6,820

Map 5-12

EVANGELICAL CONGREGATIONAL CHURCH

GEOGRAPHIC CHANGE BY COUNTY 1952, 1990

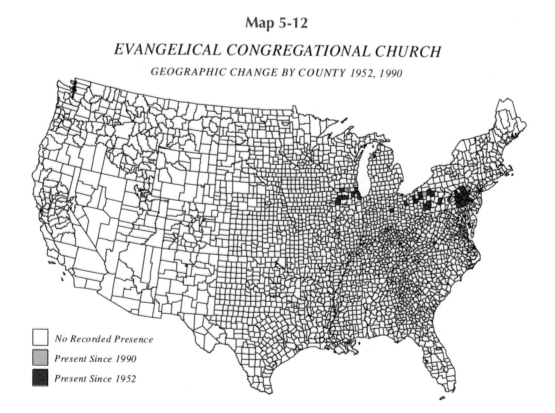

No Recorded Presence

Present Since 1990

Present Since 1952

Seventh-Day Adventist Church. In actuality, when the second coming of Christ did not occur as predicted by Miller in 1844, the movement split into a number of factions. Among these was the Advent Christian Church, which was founded in 1860–61 in Massachusetts.

As has already been suggested, all forms of Adventism in American society are best understood as sectarian because of their theology. However, the Advent Christian Church adds to the element of theological departure, formation through schism. Thus, it exemplifies two simultaneous paths toward classic sect status. The parent organization from which the Advent Christian Church divided, the Seventh-Day Adventist Church, has grown to the status of a national sect. In contrast, the Advent Christian Church enjoyed a modest degree of success in the late nineteenth century, but during the twentieth century experienced decline. Table 5-7 presents the available county, church, and adherents data for the Advent Christian Church.

Table 5-7 Advent Christian Church

	1890	1952	1990
Number of counties	281	—	185
Number of churches	294	396*	329
Total adherents	39,061	30,765*	23,794

* The 1952 data are not included in the computerized data file and are drawn directly from the NCCC 1952 reports (Whitman & Trimble 1956), which is why the county count is not available.

Comparison between Maps 5-13 and 5-14 is most instructive because the most recent distribution represents a considerable shrinkage from earlier times, a trend that is strongly counter to general population change. As can be seen in Map 5-14, by 1890, this organization not only virtually blanketed New England, but also was located in a significant number of counties stretching from New York to Iowa. One of the interesting characteristics of the 1890 distribution is its dispersion pattern, which is virtually even given that there were 294 churches occupying 281 counties. With an average congregation size of 132 adherents, these numbers suggest a very thinly spread organization lacking any area where it might have been present in sufficient strength to influence even the local culture. Nonetheless, a strong regional bias to the Northeastern quadrant of the nation is fairly apparent.

Between 1890 and 1952, the characteristic of "thinness" was extended. The number of total adherents declined by more than a fifth to only a bit over

30,000, while the number of churches expanded by more than a third to almost 400. The net result is a sharp reduction in the size of the average congregation to less than 80 persons including children, clearly a very small number.

By 1990, the Advent Christian Church had become further reduced in size. The organization reported fewer than 25,000 adherents nationally and was present in fewer than 200 counties. The number of congregations declined by almost 70 from the 1952 total, and the average congregation size declined to only 72. As depicted in Map 5-13, in 1990, fully a third of the organization's counties contained no more than 40 adherents, whereas counties with the strongest representation may have contained as few as 120 adherents. Only in New England was any cluster of multiple adjacent counties apparent, and, even there, the Advent Christians would have to be characterized as a trace element. Nowhere did the organization report more than 1,600 persons in a single county. By all measures, this is a shrinking classic sect that was a minor presence within a very small number of somewhat scattered areas of the nation. That enduring pattern confirms the characterization of the Advent Christian Church as a classic sect. Clearly, this case invites comparison with the organizational processes that have characterized its former parent body, the Seventh-Day Adventist Church. The latter, of course, emerged in the twentieth century as a national sect. In contrast with the Advent Christian Church, the Seventh-Day Adventists have carried the theology of Adventism into larger and more widely dispersed locales and into growing local congregations. The comparison between these two organizations demonstrates that sectarian beliefs do not automatically limit a religious organization to either spatial confinement or statistical marginality in terms of adherent size.

Brethren in Christ Church

The Brethren in Christ Church traces its origins to religious conflict and persecution in Central Europe in the aftermath of the Protestant Reformation. Many of the targeted groups fled to the American colonies, especially to Pennsylvania. Among these was a community of German Pietists that became known as the River Brethren. During the Civil War period, they became more formally organized in order to provide legal recognition for their conscientious objections to military conscription. They adopted the name Brethren in Christ Church. The combination of pacifism and nonconformity to general societal standards explains why these Brethren have remained generally quite localized and quite small in size.

Map 5-13

ADVENT CHRISTIAN CHURCH

TOTAL ADHERENTS BY COUNTY 1990

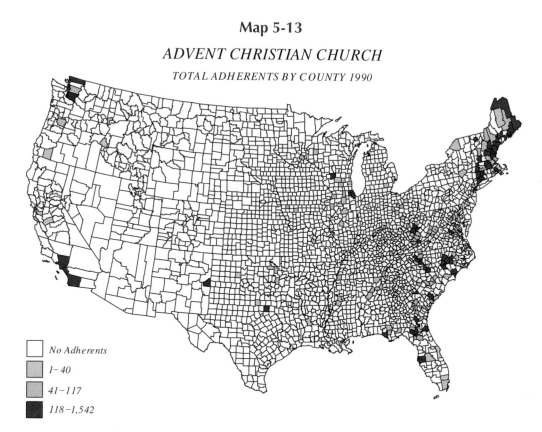

No Adherents
1– 40
41 – 117
118 –1,542

Map 5-14

ADVENT CHRISTIAN CHURCH

GEOGRAPHIC CHANGE BY COUNTY 1890, 1990

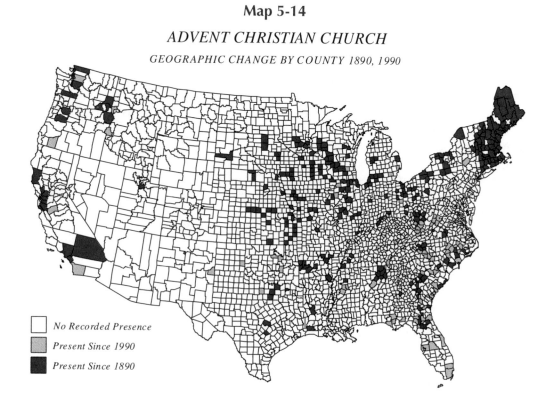

No Recorded Presence
Present Since 1990
Present Since 1890

The Brethren in Christ Church provides an unmistakable instance of sectarian social position created through central theological beliefs that result in general social nonconformity. Its theological ideals conflict with fundamental social norms of the host society. In this sense, the degree of tension with the host culture that the Brethren experience is greater than that of either the Seventh Day Baptists, Advent Christians, or other classic sects. This is because their departure from prevailing norms is viewed as both religious and secular in nature. Table 5-8 presents the available county, church, and adherents data for the Brethren in Christ Church.

Table 5-8 Brethren in Christ Church

	1890	1952	1990
Number of counties	—	57	90
Number of churches	45*	113	188
Total adherents	2,688*	6,007	19,769

* Data were reported for churches and adherents but were aggregated into a larger category for mapping and so we have chosen not to include these figures in our discussion.

As stated earlier, the people from whom the Brethren in Christ Church descend first arrived in Pennsylvania prior to the American Revolution. In their early years, they did not become formally organized. However, they subsequently became divided into the more organized United Brethren and the less structured River Brethren, with the latter the direct antecedents of the Brethren in Christ Church. The Brethren in Christ became formally organized in 1863. Obviously, because of this founding date, the organization was not among those enumerated in the earliest census counts. Nonetheless, two very generalized assumptions can be made. First, the organization was centered in Pennsylvania (the name River Brethren was derived from their location along the Susquehanna River). Second, the organization was quite small, as it was formed by a schism leaving this body and the United Brethren (from whom they divided) so small that both were aggregated with many other small religious organizations in the minor sect category of the 1850 United States Census.

In the following century, these Brethren became somewhat more dispersed, as can be seen on Map 5-16. Although the original core area in eastern Pennsylvania still was clearly visible, a scattering of counties appeared elsewhere. By 1952, the only clusters of growth were in Ohio and Michigan, but a limited number of counties across the plains and in the West also had been established. It is worth noting that the county total in 1952 was only 57, or less than

2 percent of the national total, and these counties held only 113 Brethren churches and just over 6,000 adherents.

Between 1952 and 1990, the Brethren in Christ Church actually experienced relatively substantial growth. The number of counties grew by 57 percent, the number of congregations by 66 percent, and the total adherents number more than tripled. This expansion appears to have involved three sorts of growth, as revealed by Map 5-16. First, many of the new counties appeared in and around the long-term core area in Pennsylvania. Second, a number of more isolated communities were established in what appear to be other more rural or small town locations in the country's agricultural interior. Finally, there also were a new group of Sunbelt locations in California, Texas, and especially Florida. For a mainline denomination, this might be expected to represent retirement locations. However, this seems not quite so for a culturally marginal sect.

Nonetheless, in the final analysis, this picture is dominated by limited size and cultural impact. With fewer than 20,000 total adherents found in fewer than 200 counties, the Brethren in Christ Church is not a major cultural influence in a national sense. As shown by Map 5-15, in one-third of its counties, fewer than 50 adherents are present, whereas the largest communities might have included as few as 150 adherents. The only real cluster of "larger" counties continued to be in eastern Pennsylvania, where, in conjunction with other more numerous German heritage groups such as the Amish, these Brethren contribute to the "Pennsylvania Dutch" identity. However, even here, the Brethren in Christ Church is a secondary rather than primary element. Indeed, one is left to marvel at the longevity of such a small sect over several centuries of American history. However, as a result of internal cohesion and social solidarity, this persistence also may be viewed as one of the defining characteristics of the classic sect.

Seventh Day Baptist General Conference

The Seventh Day Baptist General Conference is a very small, but nonetheless, interesting religious organization, in large part because of its combination of small size and longevity. The English Reformation is frequently thought of strictly in terms of Henry the VIII's establishment of the Church of England. However, other influences and organizations, both Calvinist and Baptist, were present and active during the sixteenth century. By 1600, the Baptists had become divided into three components, consisting of one mainline and two schismatic organizations— the Free Will Baptists and the Seventh Day or

Map 5-15

BRETHREN IN CHRIST CHURCH

TOTAL ADHERENTS BY COUNTY 1990

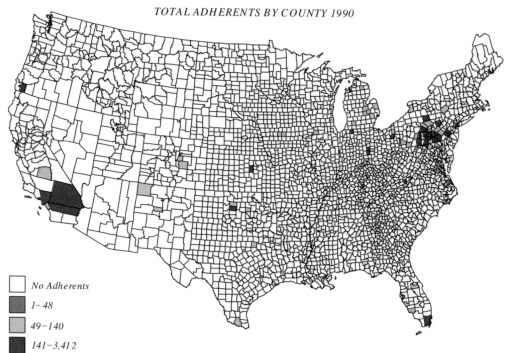

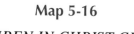

No Adherents
1– 48
49– 140
141– 3,412

Map 5-16

BRETHREN IN CHRIST CHURCH

GEOGRAPHIC CHANGE BY COUNTY 1952, 1990

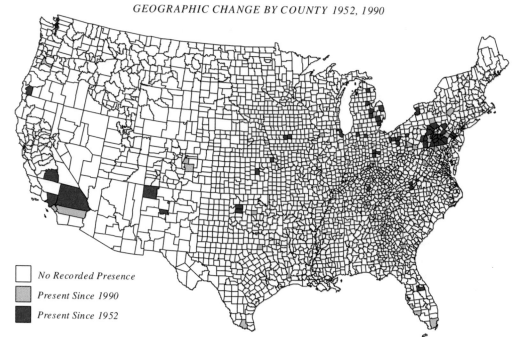

No Recorded Presence

Present Since 1990

Present Since 1952

Sabbatarian Baptists. All three branches ultimately would appear in the English colonies, with the Seventh Day Baptists tracing their American founding to 1672 in Rhode Island. Despite this early settlement in North America, the organization has remained very small. Yet, it also has become rather widely dispersed. This combination of limited size and substantial geographic dispersion is typical of several of the classic sects encountered in these data. Table 5-9 presents the available county, church, and adherents data for the Seventh Day Baptist General Conference.

As is clear from most historical treatments, this organization was established in southern New England well before the American Revolution. However, since the 1776 data combine all Baptist churches together, it is not possible to determine how widespread the Sabbatarian Baptists had become by that date. The 1850 edition of the *Baptist Almanac and Annual Register,* however, does identify this organization separately as consisting of 52 churches with more than 6,000 members (or 8,790 adherents when adjusted). This small number of churches stands in sharp contrast to the 8,400 regular Baptist churches or even to the 1,252 Free Will Baptist churches enumerated in this 1850 source. It is particularly striking that during a period of dramatic expansion among all organizations based in the Baptist heritage and movement, this one Baptist organization did not prosper. It would seem that its identity as a sect already had been established.

The 1850 and 1890 data do not permit an early geographic portrait of the Seventh Day Baptists. Between 1850 and 1890 this sect added churches at a decent rate, but gained only a few hundred adherents. The longer range changes from 1850 to 1952 were even less positive and reinforce the characterization of this organization as a classic sect removed from mainstream trends. In a century that saw the total population increase from 23 million to more than 150 million, this organization lost adherents and gained only nine congregations, resulting in 6,425 adherents in 61 churches in 1952. This reflects an average congregational size of just over 100 persons, and, since the number of counties was quite close to the number of churches (46 versus 61), meaning that most counties have one church of 100 or fewer persons. This presence was hardly noticeable, especially given the very widely dispersed pattern shown on Map 5-18. The more typical pattern for small sects showing a regional core area does not occur here. Rather, the map displays only a small handful of two or three county clusters and many individual counties almost randomly scattered from coast to coast.

Between 1952 and 1990, these patterns only became more accentuated. The Seventh Day Baptists experienced a 50 percent growth in the number of counties and a 36 percent expansion in the number of churches, while their total adherents grew by just 14 persons. Clearly, the impact was a thinning of the general distribution pattern. By 1990, average congregation size fell from more than 100 to only 77 adherents, and actually, as shown on Map 5-17, two-thirds of their counties had fewer than 67 adherents. Furthermore, the geographic pattern of new locations was highly dispersed. As can be seen on Map 5-18, only six of the new counties were adjacent to counties containing congregations prior to 1952. Thus, not only was the distribution thinning, but it also was becoming more dispersed. Clearly, these are the patterns of a "remnant" classic sect. Both the Seventh Day Baptists and the Brethren in Christ Church are remnant bands in the sense that both are numerically diminutive and geographically dispersed. Their shared status appears to be an end-state position for classic sects that over long periods of time do not grow to occupy other sectarian positions, namely multiregional or national sect forms.

Table 5-9 Seventh Day Baptist General Conference

	1850	1890	1952	1990
Number of counties	—	—**	46	69
Number of churches	52*	78**	61	83
Total adherents	8,790*	9,143**	6,425	6,439

* Data are from the *Baptist Almanac and Annual Register*. Therefore, county-level 1850 United States Census data are not available.

** This organization was not included in the automated version of the 1890 United States Census enumeration but aggregate totals of churches and adherents are available.

Map 5-17

SEVENTH DAY BAPTIST GENERAL CONFERENCE

TOTAL ADHERENTS BY COUNTY 1990

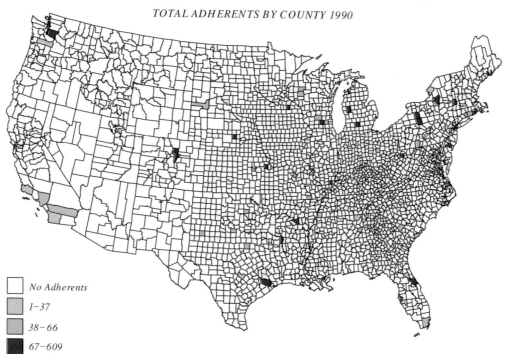

No Adherents
1–37
38–66
67–609

Map 5-18

SEVENTH DAY BAPTIST GENERAL CONFERENCE

GEOGRAPHIC CHANGE BY COUNTY 1952, 1990

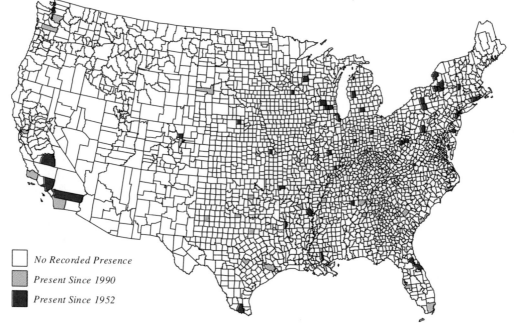

No Recorded Presence
Present Since 1990
Present Since 1952

Multiregional Sects

Wisconsin Evangelical Lutheran Synod

The history of Lutheranism in the Unites States is marked by a period of extreme fragmentation during the nineteenth century followed in the twentieth century by protracted and largely successful efforts at integration through organizational mergers. That process of consolidation has resulted in the development of two quite large organizations, the Evangelical Lutheran Church in America (ELCA) and the Lutheran Church - Missouri Synod. Additionally, one middle-sized organization, the Wisconsin Evangelical Lutheran Synod, also plays a role in the Lutheran family in the United States. The 1990 *Churches and Church Membership in the United States* (Bradley et al. 1992) contains another nine smaller Lutheran organizations that have resisted Lutheran unification efforts. Like most American Lutheran organizations, the Wisconsin Lutherans trace their origins to both a particular ethnic (i.e., European national) origin and a well-defined area of settlement in the United States. In this instance, the organization originally was composed of German immigrants settling in the Midwest in the 1840s. By 1850, one of these associations of local congregations had organized as the German Lutheran Synod of Wisconsin. In 1918, that organization merged with two other primarily German synods based respectively in Minnesota and Michigan. They adopted the name "Joint Synod of Wisconsin and Other States." Since that date, the organization has strongly objected to efforts at further unification. As a result, both doctrinally and organizationally, the Wisconsin Lutherans generally have been characterized as a component in the conservative wing of American Lutheranism. Table 5-10 presents the available county, church, and adherents data for the Wisconsin Evangelical Lutheran Synod.

Table 5-10 Wisconsin Evangelical Lutheran Synod

	1952	1990
Number of counties	248	503
Number of churches	831	1,228
Total adherents	316,692	418,820

Note: The 1850 data from both the United States Census and the *Baptist Almanac and Annual Register* are reported only for one all encompassing category of Lutherans, and despite the inclusion in the 1890 Census of 16 different "brands" of Lutherans, none can be clearly identified as the constituent organizations in the 1918 merger. Thus no data are reported here for 1850 or 1890.

As previously noted, Lutheran churches in some number had been founded in the colonies prior to the American Revolution, mostly in the mid-Atlantic region and mostly involving emigrants from Germany. Nineteenth-century political upheaval in Central Europe and economic stress in the Scandinavian countries triggered far greater Lutheran migration to the United States, primarily in the period from 1840 to 1890. These migrants brought with them ethnically based (sometimes European state church) versions of Lutheranism that then became even more fractionated into state or regional synods as those immigrant groups became dispersed across the extensive geography of the United States. Mead (1976) estimates that at one time there may have been as many as 150 Lutheran organizations in the United States. It is unfortunate that earlier data sources utilize names and labels for Lutheran bodies that are not easily connected to present-day Lutheran organizations. Thus, though we know that the Wisconsin Evangelical Lutheran Synod has its origins in the 1850s, available data sources for this organization only begin in 1952.

By 1952, the Wisconsin Lutherans had become one of the more sizable Lutheran organizations in the country, with more than 800 congregations and 300,000 adherents. The original core area in Wisconsin, Michigan, and Minnesota is easily discerned on Map 5-20. The organization was not particularly widespread beyond that initial base, occupying only 248 counties nationally. By 1952, the earliest date for which county-level data are available for them, outlying pockets of Wisconsin Lutherans had developed in the Dakotas and Nebraska, as well as in Colorado, Arizona, and Washington. With more than three times as many congregations as counties, it is apparent that areas populated by Wisconsin Lutherans were densely populated by them. They registered an average county adherent level of more than 1,200 persons. In 1952, this degree of concentration was far more prevalent in the three original core states, Wisconsin, Michigan, and Minnesota, than elsewhere.

The period from 1952 to 1990 evidenced significant changes in the shape of American Lutheranism, most especially because of the organizational mergers, which culminated in the formation of the Evangelical Lutheran Church in America in 1985. Despite their resistance to overtures for merger with other Lutheran organizations, the Wisconsin

Map 5-19

WISCONSIN EVANGELICAL LUTHERAN SYNOD

TOTAL ADHERENTS BY COUNTY 1990

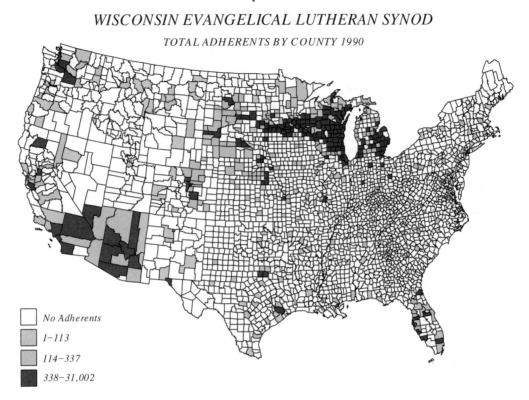

No Adherents
1–113
114–337
338–31,002

Map 5-20

WISCONSIN EVANGELICAL LUTHERAN SYNOD

GEOGRAPHIC CHANGE BY COUNTY 1952, 1990

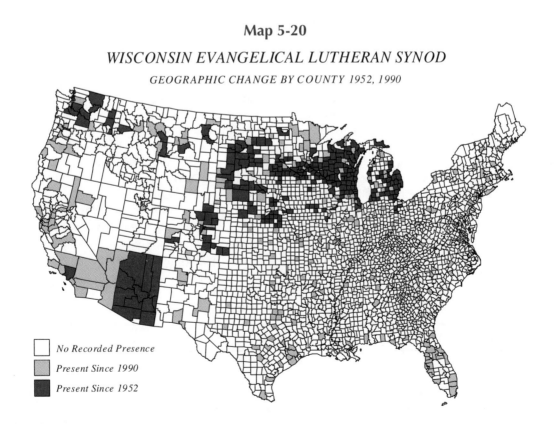

No Recorded Presence
Present Since 1990
Present Since 1952

Lutherans continued growing during this period. Their number of congregations doubled, while the number of total adherents increased by almost one-third to more than 418,000. Apparently, the Wisconsin Evangelical Lutheran Synod both created new churches and absorbed some existing congregations that had refused to join one or another of the mergers leading to the ELCA. Map 5-20 (p. 131) shows a wide scatter of counties across the Northeast and lower parts of the Midwest that, given general demographic trends in those regions, look suspiciously like ELCA defections (compare Map 4-16, p. 92). On the other hand, the development of new Wisconsin Lutheran congregations in Florida, Texas, and California is aligned with general patterns of migration and population growth.

The pattern for the Wisconsin Evangelical Lutheran Synod in 1990 is fairly clear. As seen on Map 5-19 (p. 131), the Wisconsin, Michigan, and Minnesota historic core region continued to be the most prominent feature. Indeed, more than three quarters of all Wisconsin Lutherans still resided in those three states, with 53 percent in Wisconsin alone. The dominance of the core area is softened a bit on the map by the existence of a number of largely metropolitan centers that fall in the highest category in areas outside the core region (e.g., Dallas-Fort Worth, metropolitan Denver, Phoenix, and San Diego among others). However, this multiregional sect is largely Midwestern. As seen in Table 3-3 (p. 59), in 1990, the Midwest was the only region where the Wisconsin Evangelical Lutheran Synod occupied more than 20 percent of counties (28 percent), and it was present in less than 10 percent of the counties in both the Northeast and Southeast.

The Wisconsin Evangelical Lutheran Synod has practiced a stubborn isolationism against efforts to unify American Lutheranism. As much for that reason as any other, it is classified here as a sect. Either it is the largest Lutheran sect or the smallest Lutheran denomination. We have used the designation sect here because the Wisconsin Evangelical Lutheran Synod has typified that category even in its relationship to other American Lutherans and because it constitutes only about 5 percent of American

Lutheranism. Despite the predominance of the original core area, the organization has expanded into the West in a fairly coherent pattern. Accordingly, the Wisconsin Evangelical Lutheran Synod may be viewed as the largest of the multiregional sects.

Reformed Church in America

The earliest European settlements along the East Coast of what was to become the United States included more than just English colonies. The most prominent non-English Colonial group was the Dutch, whose settlements were centered on what then was known as New Amsterdam in the Hudson Valley. Not surprisingly, the Dutch colonists brought their own brand of Calvinism with them and as early as 1623 had established what became colloquially as the Dutch Reformed Church. For more than two centuries this church continued to grow, and was the primary manifestation of Dutch-based Protestantism in North America. In the mid-nineteenth century, when a new wave of Dutch immigrants arrived and settled in western Michigan, the newer, more Midwestern contingent established a separate church (the Christian Reformed Church). This division between the two branches of Dutch Calvinism in the United States has persisted to the dawn of the twenty-first century. The Reformed Church in America, which is the descendant of the earliest Dutch settlers, remains dominated by its original core area in New York State. It has grown, though not spectacularly, and has expanded to a limited degree beyond the Northeast into the Midwest and other regions. Its retention of an ethnic identity and its specific version of Calvinist theology determine the Reformed Church in America's categorization as a sect. Table 5-11 presents the available county, church, and adherents data for the Reformed Church in America.

During the Colonial era, the original Dutch immigrant population continued to grow modestly, while also dispersing away from New York City into the Hudson River Valley and the interior of New York State, as well as moving westward into New Jersey. As a result, by 1776, 120 Dutch Reformed churches had

Table 5-11   Reformed Church in America

	1776	1850	1890	1952	1990
Number of counties	—	49	106	150	232
Number of churches	120	276*	670	773	917
Total adherents	12,870	46,239*	133,818	194,157	362,932

* With the Michigan settlement in place and the 1857 schism yet to occur, these numbers are a bit higher than appropriate for what will become the Reformed Church in America.

been established, virtually all of them in some proximity to the New York hearth. Our estimate of more than 12,000 adherents and some 120 churches for this organization in 1776 means that this community was a clearly recognizable element in the mid-Atlantic region. Moreover, due to the influx of substantial numbers of German immigrants, this mid-Atlantic region already was more diverse in cultural terms than was either New England or the Southern colonies.

Between the founding of the Republic and 1850, the Dutch Reformed population migrated slowly westward. Map 5-22 (p. 134) depicts rather graphically both the route taken and the rate of that migration. By 1850, the number of churches had almost tripled, and the number of adherents had more than tripled. This sect was well established in a virtually solid band of counties from New York City north to Albany, and from there, west to Buffalo along the Erie Canal. The pattern west of Buffalo was much more spotty and primarily centered in Michigan. The latter settlements would become the core region for the Christian Reformed Church and would be only a secondary region for the older parent organization, the Reformed Church in America.

The period from 1850 to 1890 saw both the separation of the Dutch Reformed movement into two separate organizations and the continued gradual expansion of the older Reformed Church in America. By 1890, the number of congregations had doubled, while the number of counties had reached more than 100. As seen on Map 5-22 (p. 134), most of the new counties lie in a scatter from western Michigan, across the upper Midwest, and into the Dakotas. Additionally, some modest expansion occurred along the margins of the New York core. In 1890, for the first time in the history of the Reformed Church, the number of adherents was greater than 100,000. The combination of total adherents, churches, and counties occupied established a pattern that has held true ever since. First, the average congregation size of 200 persons was relatively large, especially for this early date. Furthermore, there were more than six times as many congregations as counties, meaning that the average number of adherents per county occupied was more than 1,000. Thus, the Reformed Church in America became only moderately dispersed across regions, but strongly clustered and represented where it was found.

As shown on Map 5-22 (p. 134), the pattern of gradual and ever more widespread expansion of the Reformed Church in America has continued throughout the twentieth century. As might be expected, though a good part of that expansion was in the upper Midwest, the organization also began to shift still further westward. By 1952, it had entered areas in Arizona and California, and by 1990, it had expanded into an even larger number of counties. In the Southeast, in the most recent period, the only significant cluster of counties appeared in Florida. Like some of the areas further west, this acquisition may have represented a combination of both migration and retirement destination for populations originating in the Northeast or Midwest.

By 1990, the Reformed Church in America had reached a total adherents size of 362,932, but still had considerably less than 1,000 churches and was present in only 232 counties nationwide. The organizational pattern already established by 1890 still prevailed in 1990. Individual congregations were quite large and generally appeared in clusters. Map 5-21 (p. 134) indicates that one-third of the counties occupied by the Reformed Church in America contained a minimum of nearly 1,000 adherents. Those counties were a bit more widespread than might be expected. Yet, both the primary core region from New York City up the Hudson, as well as the secondary core in western Michigan, were easily discerned. As indicated by all of the previous discussion and confirmed by Table 3-3 (p. 59), as of 1990 the organization was present in more than 20 percent of counties only in the Northeast, and in more than 10 percent of counties in the Midwest. Elsewhere the Reformed Church in America barely was represented, although isolated individual sizable communities occurred in southern California and elsewhere. In summary then, the Reformed Church in America has been present in North America since the beginnings of European settlement, but it has grown relatively little beyond its ethnic and geographic origins.

Indeed, in 1990, fully one-third of all the Reformed Church in America's adherents resided in New York and New Jersey, with another quarter of them in Michigan. This bipolar distribution surely marks the organization as multiregional. In the present instance, a multiregional distribution appears to have evolved as a result of continued immigration of foreign nationals and general population migration westward during the nineteenth century. Although the Reformed Church in America is among the largest multiregional sects examined here, it does not appear to be moving toward either national or denominational status.

International Church of the Foursquare Gospel

The International Church of the Foursquare Gospel is both the newest and one of the most dynamically growing organizations covered in this atlas. With its roots in the evangelistic revival movement of the

Map 5-21

REFORMED CHURCH IN AMERICA

TOTAL ADHERENTS BY COUNTY 1990

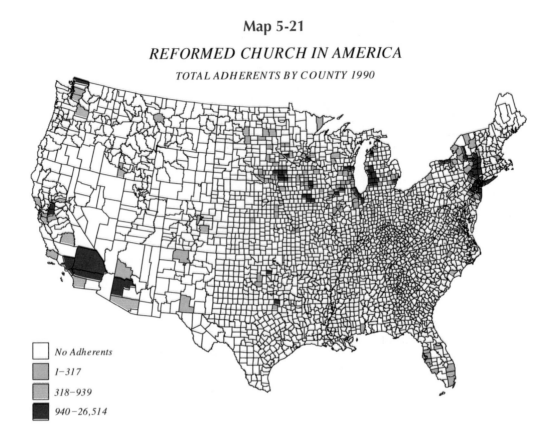

No Adherents

1–317

318–939

940–26,514

Map 5-22

REFORMED CHURCH IN AMERICA

GEOGRAPHIC CHANGE BY COUNTY 1850, 1890, 1952, 1990

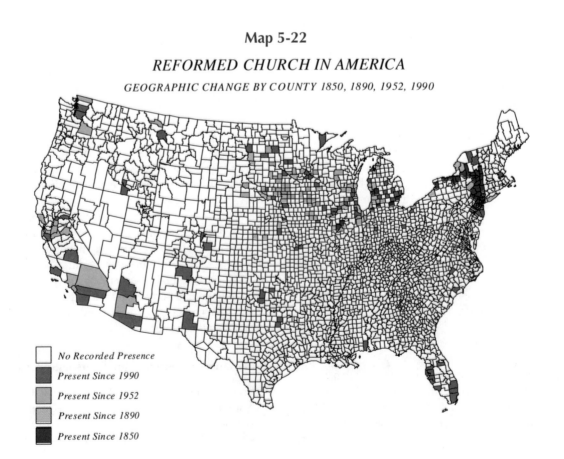

No Recorded Presence

Present Since 1990

Present Since 1952

Present Since 1890

Present Since 1850

early twentieth century, it traces its origins to one of the most widely recognized figures of that era, Aimee Semple McPherson. After a wildly successful series of tours during the World War I era, Ms. McPherson settled in Los Angeles. Between 1918 and 1923, she built a home church, the Angelus Temple, founded an evangelistic association, and created the International Church of the Foursquare Gospel. She wrote the "Declaration of Faith," which outlines the teachings of the church, and she remained the head of the church until her death.

Not surprisingly, the organization is described as fundamentalist, holding strongly to the truth of the Bible, believing in faith healing and speaking in tongues, and laying great emphasis on evangelism. As a result of its early charismatic leadership and continuing active evangelism, during the twentieth century, the International Church of the Foursquare Gospel has been one of the most rapidly growing and expanding of American sects. It surely will be one of the more interesting cases to follow during the twenty-first century. To what extent will continued growth (if it is sustained) and organizational maturity transform this unique American sect? Table 5-12 presents the available county, church, and adherents data for the International Church of the Foursquare Gospel.

Table 5-12 International Church of the Foursquare Gospel

	1952	1990
Number of counties	290	537
Number of churches	511	1,445
Total adherents	66,181	250,250

Considering that the organization had been founded only 30 years earlier, its distribution by 1952 is both surprising and a reflection of twentieth-century processes. In the brief time span between 1923 and 1952, the Foursquare Gospel Church established more than 500 congregations in almost 300 counties. Though this achievement is quite impressive, the pattern of geographic expansion, as seen on Map 5-24 (p. 136), is even more striking. Though the 1952 distribution displayed a clear West Coast orientation, additional pockets of churches were established from coast to coast in areas as disparate and separate from one another as rural Colorado, metropolitan Chicago, west Texas, and northeast Ohio. This far-flung distribution reflects not only the revival tour origins of the organization but also its leadership's early grasp of twentieth-century technology such as radio, which was a key element by which "the word" was spread prior to mid-century.

Between 1952 and 1990, this pattern of rapid adherent growth and spatial expansion continued. Indeed, an important indication of the vitality of any religious sect is its ability to thrive in the years after the demise of its charismatic founder. In that context, consider that the Foursquare Gospel Church almost quadrupled (376 percent increase) its number of adherents, while nearly tripling (282 percent increase) its number of congregations to more than 1,400 nationwide in this period. These measures of increasing strength were mirrored by the organization's entry into more than 200 additional counties, making it one of the most widely dispersed of small sects in the United States. As Map 5-24 (p. 136) demonstrates, the International Church of the Foursquare Gospel continued to expand both within its original western base and nationwide. In 1990, new counties were scattered across the Midwest and Southeast, as well as in New England. The spatial pattern of adherents in 1990, as depicted on Map 5-23 (p. 136), clearly revealed an emerging national distribution. Although the West Coast origin of the organization was apparent, counties in the highest category were located from coast to coast, and in all the four regions of the country. Table 3-3 (p. 59) indicates that in 1990, the International Church of the Foursquare Gospel was present in at least 10 percent of counties in all four regions. It was present in a quarter and a third of counties in the Northeast and West respectively. The apparent evenness of that distribution is offset by the fact that in 1990, almost 45 percent of the organization's adherents still were located in California, with an additional 20 percent in Washington and Oregon.

The International Church of the Foursquare Gospel has enjoyed dramatic growth and expansion in a very short period of time. In that process, it has begun to move beyond its original California base and beyond the personal charisma of its founder. If growth trends for this sect during the twentieth century are continued into the twenty-first century, the organization is likely to enhance its numeric and spatial reach. In 1990, the church's size, limited regional distribution, and especially its theological positions define it as a multiregional sect. Though numerical growth may well continue at a rapid pace, a theological softening seems less likely. As a consequence, the major question is whether this organization will attain national sect status in the twenty-first century.

Christian Reformed Church

As the religious movement inspired by John Calvin spread from Switzerland into Germany and the Low Countries, it generally adopted the name "Reformed,"

Map 5-23

INTERNATIONAL CHURCH OF THE FOURSQUARE GOSPEL

TOTAL ADHERENTS BY COUNTY 1990

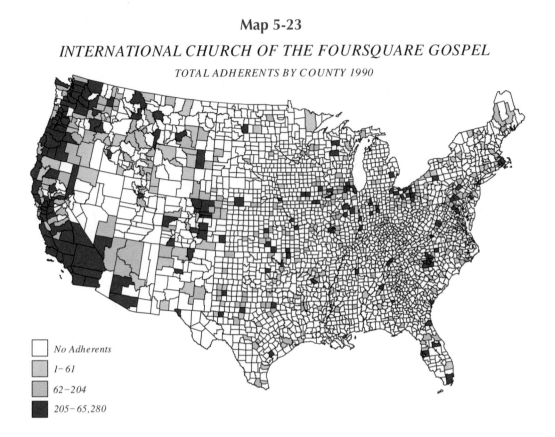

No Adherents

1– 61

62–204

205– 65,280

Map 5-24

INTERNATIONAL CHURCH OF THE FOURSQUARE GOSPEL

GEOGRAPHIC CHANGE BY COUNTY 1952, 1990

No Recorded Presence

Present Since 1990

Present Since 1952

while in Scotland it adopted the name "Presbyterian." Many immigrant churches arriving from the European continent retained "Reformed" in their name. However, most of those organizations by the end of the twentieth century have been subsumed in larger and more diverse merged denominations. The immigrants from Holland in this tradition largely have remained in separate and distinct churches carrying the name Reformed and, in fact, have even themselves divided into two religious organizations that are somewhat distinct from one another in location and, to a degree, in practice. They are the Reformed Church in America (see p. 132) and the Christian Reformed Church.

The parent organization known as the Dutch Reformed Church was a single body until 1857. At that time, some of the more recent immigrants who had settled in western Michigan separated themselves to create the True Holland Reformed Church, the predecessor of the contemporary Christian Reformed Church. Although in the latter half of the twentieth century, that organization undertook a number of home missionary efforts intended to diversify itself both geographically and ethnically, it has continued to be dominated by its founding ethnic community and its original core area in Michigan. The narrowness of both its cultural and geographic base defines the Christian Reformed Church as a multiregional sect. Table 5-13 presents the available county, church, and adherents data for the Christian Reformed Church.

Table 5-13 Christian Reformed Church

	1890	1952	1990
Number of counties	—*	121	235
Number of churches	106	346	716
Total adherents	17,557	155,355	225,852

* Only aggregate totals are available in the manuscript version of the 1890 United States Census.

Note: The Michigan Dutch Reformed churches were included in an all inclusive Dutch Reformed category prior to the 1857 split, and thus no 1850 data are available.

Again, the origins of the Christian Reformed Church date from the 1840s and 1850s with the immigration of Dutch settlers to western Michigan. Between the church's organization in 1857 and 1890, it grew relatively slowly, reaching totals of only 106 congregations and fewer than 18,000 adherents. It seems very safe to presume that the majority of these churches were located in close proximity to the organization's Holland, Michigan, base.

Growth and expansion were more in evidence between 1890 and 1952. By the latter date, the Chris-

tian Reformed Church had grown nine times larger in total adherents and had tripled its number of churches. Even so, by 1952 it was located in only 121 counties nationwide. As seen on Map 5-26 (p. 138), these counties appeared in a number of clusters in the Midwest, from Michigan westward into the Dakotas. Outside the Midwest, the pattern was more one of isolated counties scattered (in decreasing order) across the Western, Northeast, and Southeast. A comparison of the spatial pattern of the Reformed Church in America depicted on Maps 5-21 and 5-22 (p. 134) with those for the Christian Reformed Church reveals an interesting contrast and shows clearly the Colonial era core of the former and the nineteenth-century Midwestern core of the latter.

Between 1952 and 1990, the Christian Reformed Church expanded geographically at a healthy rate, though growing in adherents more slowly. While increasing its total adherents level by almost 46 percent, it doubled both its number of churches and the number of counties in which it was present. Although the organization is characterized by fairly large communities (see the key to Map 5-25, p. 138), it also is clear that by 1990, the Christian Reformed Church still was present in strength in only a small number of areas in the United States. As shown in Table 3-3 (p. 59), in 1990, it was present in between 10 and 12 percent of counties in three of the nation's regions, but barely was in evidence in the Southeast. This pattern of dispersal barely qualifies the Christian Reformed Church as multiregional given that in 1990 more than 40 percent of its national adherents were found in Michigan, with 19 percent in a single county in that state.

The Christian Reformed Church remains largely sect-like in both its distribution and behavior. The church is heavily concentrated in one small area of the country and is very thinly spread elsewhere. Like many of the sects in this study, it is the product of an organizational schism within a relatively small ethnic church, and it has not yet managed or chosen to move significantly beyond that base. Consequently, it appears destined either to remain essentially in the position of a multiregional sect or to contract spatially into the status of a classic sect.

Church of the Brethren

The Church of the Brethren began as a Pietist split in Lutheran ranks in the first decade of the eighteenth century. Before 1720, Brethren communities had begun a movement to the state of Pennsylvania, settling in Germantown under a land grant from William Penn. Growing out of religious-based conflict in Europe, the Brethren espoused pacifism,

Map 5-25

CHRISTIAN REFORMED CHURCH

TOTAL ADHERENTS BY COUNTY 1990

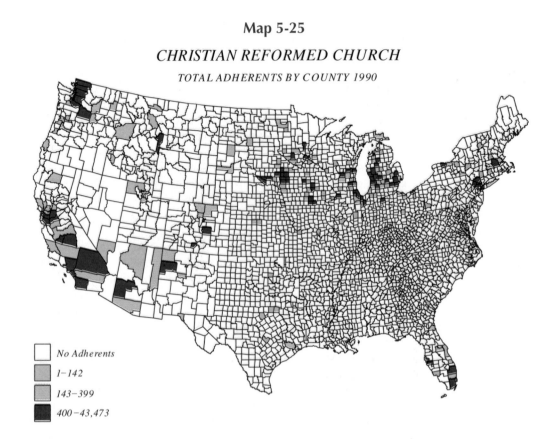

No Adherents
1–142
143–399
400–43,473

Map 5-26

CHRISTIAN REFORMED CHURCH

GEOGRAPHIC CHANGE BY COUNTY 1952, 1990

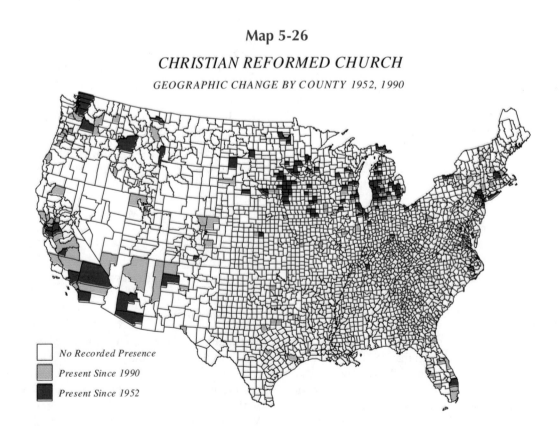

No Recorded Presence
Present Since 1990
Present Since 1952

temperance, and what often is referred to as the "simple life." Given these fundamental principles, the Church of the Brethren generally has been viewed as being outside the mainstream of American society. Their pacifist views led to their refusal to become involved in either the Revolutionary War or the Civil War despite their geographic proximity to both conflicts. Early in American history, these Pietists generally were called Dunkers or, in a more Germanic version, Tunkers, because of their practice of baptism by triple immersion. By the time of the Revolution, the Dunkers had grown to 24 congregations and approximately 2,500 adherents, mostly within the larger German community located in Pennsylvania. Table 5-14 presents the available county, church, and adherents data for the Church of the Brethren.

In the period from the Revolution to the middle of the nineteenth century, the Tunkers grew, but only modestly. By 1850, it numbered only 52 congregations and fewer than 23,000 adherents. Also by that date, more than half of these churches were located in Ohio and Pennsylvania, with a small scattering of congregations situated along the Shenandoah Valley into Virginia and across the Midwest. Between 1850 and 1890, the Brethren grew fairly impressively, despite some schisms that led to the development of splinter groups. The most significant of these led to the formation of the Church of the Brethren. Nonetheless, by 1890, the United States Census tallied more than 33,000 Brethren Church adherents in 152 counties. As Map 5-28 (p. 140) demonstrates, by 1890, Brethren churches stretch from the Pennsylvania core westward in an almost straight line that becomes thinner west of Ohio into Kansas and Iowa. Outside of that axis, there are only two small clusters of counties, one in Virginia and another in Arkansas.

The early part of the twentieth century brought continued growth and expansion of the Church of the Brethren. The 1952 tallies for the organization show a tripling of the number of counties to a total of 460, while the number of adherents grew even more impressively. As can be seen in Map 5-28, that geographic spread involved both expansion into areas adjacent to the ancestral core in a corridor from Penn-sylvania to Iowa and movement into new or previously unentered regions. Close to the core region, considerable expansion occurred in Virginia, as well as in Ohio and Michigan and into the Great Plains. By 1952, though, the Church of the Brethren had moved beyond the Northeast and Midwest, particularly into the West Coast states. With an adherent total of almost 190,000 people in 1,000 churches spread widely across the nation, the Church of the Brethren seemed poised for considerable growth.

However, the second half of the twentieth century ushered in stability and some decline. The totals for 1990 reveal a loss of several thousand adherents and a decline of more than 40 counties. Stability in the twentieth century seems to characterize several organizations in this study with roots in the Colonial period. It is clear that the Church of the Brethren "stabilized" somewhere near mid-century, and as such, it demonstrates that not all groups identified as sects sustain dynamic growth throughout their history. The Brethren movement has been plagued by divisions throughout its history, including schisms that have occurred as recently as the mid-twentieth century. These divisions have not been repaired, and the traditionalism of the organization apparently has not withstood the pressures of the mainstream culture very well.

In the aggregate then, the picture for the Church of the Brethren at the start of the twenty-first century reveals both numerical and geographic contraction. Map 5-27 (p. 140) depicts a highly concentrated pattern from Pennsylvania west into Ohio, and south into Virginia. Those three states held more than half of the organization's adherents. From this perspective, the designation of the Church of the Brethren as a multiregional sect is, in part, an accident of its spatial dispersion, which while highly confined and clustered, happens to straddle three of the nation's four regions. Its size surely is sect-like, and its cultural impact has been limited. Though the Church of the Brethren is one of many organizations that combine to give a unique cultural flavor to its core area, it has not progressed much beyond that niche culturally or geographically and, therefore, seems destined to straddle the criteria for a multiregional or classic sect.

Table 5-14 Church of the Brethren

	1776	1850	1890	1952	1990
Number of counties	—	45	152	460	420
Number of churches	24	52	338	1,019	1,121
Total adherents	2,574	22,400	33,234	189,277	186,588

Map 5-27

CHURCH OF THE BRETHREN

TOTAL ADHERENTS BY COUNTY 1990

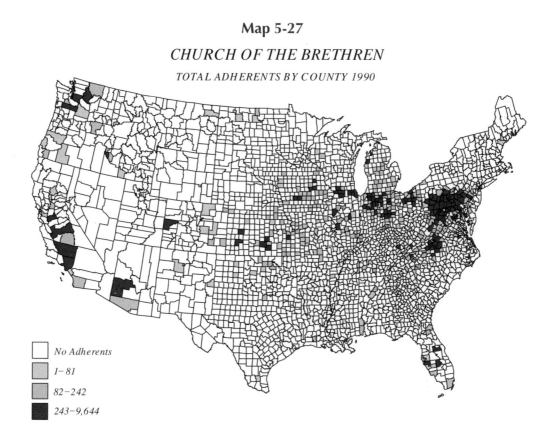

No Adherents
1– 81
82–242
243–9,644

Map 5-28

CHURCH OF THE BRETHREN

GEOGRAPHIC CHANGE BY COUNTY 1890, 1952, 1990

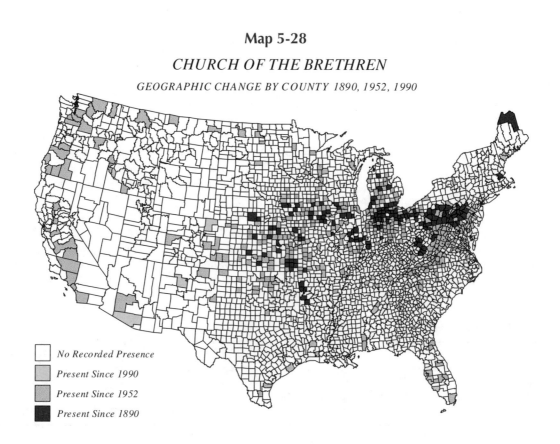

No Recorded Presence
Present Since 1990
Present Since 1952
Present Since 1890

Unitarian-Universalist Association

The term *sect* often calls to mind images of people shut off from the world or somehow railing against it. The members of the Unitarian-Universalist Association generally do not fit that mold. The Unitarian-Universalist Association is a product of a 1961 merger that connected two organizations with roughly similar origins in the United States, as well as compatible positions toward religion and society. Unitarianism began as a reform movement within New England Congregationalism at the end of the eighteenth century. It became more formalized as an independent organization after 1820. The Universalist movement originated in Europe also in the late eighteenth century but came to North America with the founding of a first congregation in Massachusetts in 1799. Thus, both organizations became established in New England at the beginning of the nineteenth century. Though many sects are viewed as right wing or conservative, these two organizations, from their outset, were more liberal both in theological terms and in their position toward the general society. This liberalism has been their distinguishing characteristic and places them on the left wing of American Protestantism. Table 5-15 presents the available county, church, and adherents data for the Unitarian-Universalist Association.

The New England roots of the Unitarian-Universalist Association are very clearly revealed by Map 5-30 (p. 142). By 1850, according to the United States Census, the two organizations had established a total of 1,162 congregations and accounted for more than 126,000 adherents. This represents strong growth in a relatively short period given their dates of origin. By 1850, these churches blanketed virtually all of New England and most of upstate New York. Beyond those regions, to both the west and the south, the incidence of Unitarians and/or Universalists was far more scattered. Nonetheless, it is quite clear that by 1850, the two organizations had become securely and broadly established, particularly in the Northeast.

By 1890, the two churches had added only 100 congregations, but could be found in almost 500 counties nationwide. Again, as seen in Map 5-30, most of that expansion occurred in the Northeast,

although since these two organizations already were well dispersed in the Northeast, most of the new growth appears to have been in the Midwest, and less so on the West Coast. The relative lack of movement into the Southeast is understandable in terms of the general liberalism of the two organizations, as well as general economic and social patterns in that region during the last half of the nineteenth century. Offsetting this pattern of fairly impressive geographic expansion, these two organizations added fewer than 40,000 adherents in a period when the national population grew by almost 40 million. By 1890, the Unitarians and Universalists accounted for 165,575 adherents scattered in congregations with an average size of 130 adherents and present in fewer than 500 of the nation's counties.

If the late nineteenth century was a period in which the Unitarian and Universalist churches were experiencing modest growth, the early twentieth century brought a reversal of fortune. Between 1890 and 1952, the two organizations lost more than 400 churches and disappeared from at least 125 counties. Though these numbers convey a sizable contraction, the number of total adherents dropped by *only* 5,000. Given the sizable losses in churches, this seems to be almost good news, until it is measured against a general population increase of 90 million, which represents a doubling of the U.S. population over those same years. Understandably, the two declining organizations might have been expected to attempt to stem this tide of real and relative decline, and so it was no surprise that during the 1950s they initiated a process that culminated in their merger in 1961.

Since mid-century and the merger, the Unitarian-Universalist Association has, in fact, reversed that earlier pattern of decline, but only to a limited degree. By 1990, its "county count" had risen sharply to a level above that reported a century earlier, while the number of churches grew by almost 150. Adherent growth was modest, involving an increase of only 14,000 people, with the net result that in some senses, the distribution became thinner and perhaps more sect-like. As seen on Map 5-29 (p. 142), one-third of all counties with Unitarian-Universalists present contained fewer than 64 adherents, and nationally, the median county

Table 5-15 Unitarian-Universalist Association

	1850	1890	1952	1990
Number of counties	154	490	365	546
Number of churches	1,162	1,256	819	965
Total adherents	126,720	165,575	160,336	174,004

Map 5-29

UNITARIAN-UNIVERSALIST ASSOCIATION

TOTAL ADHERENTS BY COUNTY 1990

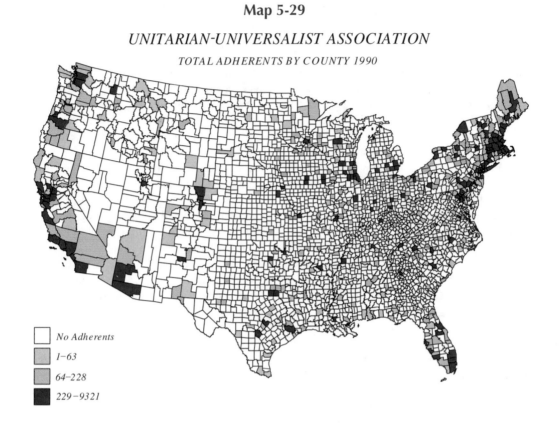

No Adherents
1–63
64–228
229–9321

Map 5-30

UNITARIAN-UNIVERSALIST ASSOCIATION

GEOGRAPHIC CHANGE BY COUNTY 1850, 1890, 1952, 1990

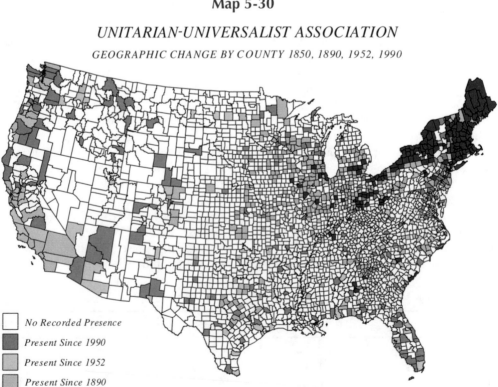

No Recorded Presence
Present Since 1990
Present Since 1952
Present Since 1890
Present Since 1850

(the midpoint of the second category in Map 5-29) registered only 150 persons. Though these were small communities to be sure, Map 5-29 also shows them to be scattered widely across the nation. Table 3-3 (p. 59) indicates that although the Unitarian-Universalist Association was still far more common in the Northeast than in the nation's other regions (with 56 percent of counties covered), by 1990, the organization was present in between 13 and 18 percent of the counties of the other three regions. As a result, though the combination of small numbers and unconventional theology define the Unitarian-Universalists as a sect, it is clear that it is more than a single-region phenomenon.

Thus, it may be argued that two small sects with limited presences outside their historic core region, to some degree, have maintained a multiregional status through organizational merger. If the twentieth century is to be understood as a time of organizational consolidation for American religious communities, then the Unitarian-Universalist Association demonstrates that the trend can be found among sects as well as denominations.

Baptist General Conference

The Baptist General Conference has had a complex organizational history. It originated in the 1850s as the result of the efforts of a Swedish immigrant, Gustaf Palmquist, who sought converts among other Swedish immigrants in Illinois and surrounding states. Those converts became organized and by 1879 formed the Swedish Baptist General Conference of America. Less than a decade later that organization became affiliated with the Northern Baptist Convention, an arrangement that would continue until 1944, when some of the remaining elements of the founding Swedish organization separated itself into what became the Baptist General Conference, dropping the Swedish identification. This change was more than cosmetic, as the new organization no longer was composed primarily of people of Scandinavian heritage. This checkered history makes it somewhat difficult to trace accurately the history of the Baptist General Conference between 1850 and 1952. In contrast, since 1945, the organization can be identified clearly as one of a number of smaller Baptist organizations that, for a variety of reasons, have remained apart from the larger Baptist denominations. In this instance, the organization has grown to sufficient size and is sufficiently dispersed geographically to be viewed as more than a classic sect. Consequently, we have designated it a multiregional sect. Table 5-16 presents the available county, church, and adherents data for the Baptist General Conference.

In order to be more certain that the discussion is focused on comparable entities, Map 5-32 (p. 144) portrays patterns for the Baptist General Conference only for 1952 and 1990. As the organization was re-established near mid-century, its roots in the upper Midwest are quite clear, with a primary cluster of counties that reached from northern Illinois through Minnesota to the Canadian border. Otherwise, the distribution is characterized by smaller pockets of counties scattered widely in Massachusetts and western Pennsylvania in the East, as well as in Colorado, California, and Washington in the West. In 1952, the Baptist General Conference, given its overall size, relatively localized geographic pattern, and its schismatic history, almost certainly would have been classified as a classic sect.

The patterns of growth and geographic expansion between 1952 and 1990 clearly justify classifying this organization as a multiregional sect. In that period, the Baptist General Conference more than doubled its number of churches and almost doubled the number of counties in which it was present. As seen on Map 5-32, most of that growth appears to have taken place in the vicinity of previously established locations, specifically, the Northeast, Midwest, and West, with limited entry into the Southeast. It appears that, although the Baptist General Conference had grown in regions populated by the American Baptist Churches with which it once was affiliated, it had not yet mounted a challenge to the Southern Baptist Convention in the latter's primary base in the Southeast. These impressions are reinforced by the data in Table 3-3 (p. 59), which indicate that in 1990, the Baptist General Conference was present in between 10 and 21 percent of counties in the Northeast, Midwest, and West, but in only 1 percent of the Southeast's counties.

Although this spatial growth is impressive, the strongest evidence of growth for the Baptist General Conference is its rate of increase in total adherents. That number more than tripled between 1952 and 1990, reaching a total of 167,874. Since this rate of increase exceeds that for the number of churches, it appears that average church size increased, in this case from 143 to 213. That increase should be

Table 5-16 Baptist General Conference

	1952	1990
Number of counties	181	352
Number of churches	343	786
Total adherents	49,127	167,874

Note: 1890 data are not available because this group was included in the "Regular Baptists, North."

Map 5-31

BAPTIST GENERAL CONFERENCE

TOTAL ADHERENTS BY COUNTY 1990

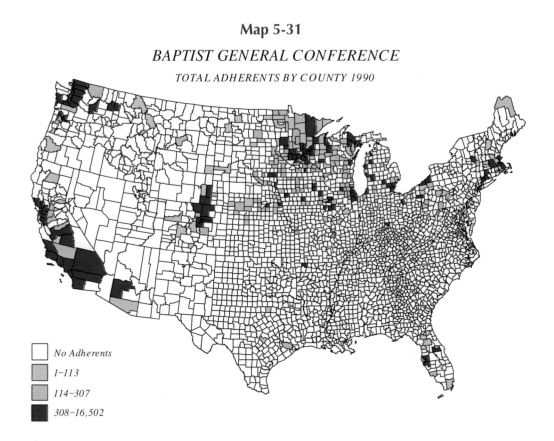

No Adherents
1–113
114–307
308–16,502

Map 5-32

BAPTIST GENERAL CONFERENCE

GEOGRAPHIC CHANGE BY COUNTY 1952, 1990

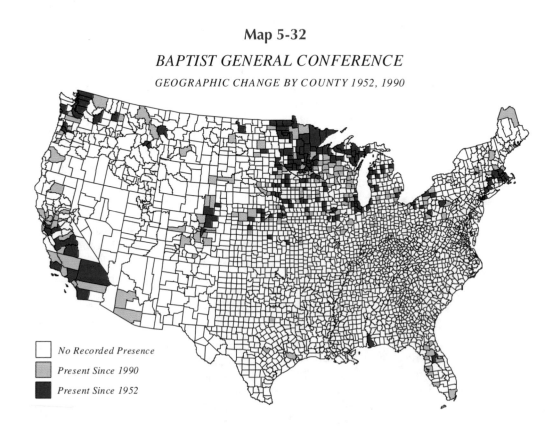

No Recorded Presence
Present Since 1990
Present Since 1952

interpreted as a manifestation of growing vitality and strength on a local level. Map 5-31 supports this view in at least two ways. First, the smallest category of counties reaches a maximum size of just over 100 persons. This category probably represents single churches, and though congregations of that size are not exactly robust, they are healthier than those of many other small sects. Second, the largest category of counties, many of which would appear to include multiple churches, are regionally quite dispersed, appearing in each of the regional clusters previously identified. This impression of dispersed strength is reinforced by the fact that the state with the largest body of adherents in 1990 was California, rather than one of the original core states in the Midwest. These patterns attest to the increasing strength and multiregional character of the Baptist General Conference. Although this organization cannot yet be viewed as national, or as a denomination, it has progressed a long way from its mid-century position as a relatively small schismatic sect parting company with a much larger parent organization. Throughout American history, the Baptist movement has been responsible for the emergence of a great number of sects and denominations. This particular instance reveals the ability of organizations that break from the mainstream in their denominational family to emerge with vitality from classic sect status and to move toward a more encompassing organizational form.

Pentecostal Holiness Church, International

The name of this organization identifies it as an outgrowth of the late nineteenth century revival movements variously described as Pentecostal or Holiness. These "purification" movements swept through many parts of the country around the turn of the century and resulted in the formation of a number of new religious bodies, among them the Pentecostal Holiness Church, the International Church of the Foursquare Gospel, the Assemblies of God, and the Church of the Nazarene. Though the Pentecostal Holiness Church, Int., has grown less than those other organizations, it has developed rapidly in the second half of the twentieth century, especially in terms of its number of adherents. Within the spectrum of Pentecostalism, the Pentecostal Holiness Church, Int., represents a moderate expression of this brand of American Protestantism. However, it does subscribe to both faith healing and speaking in tongues, practices that distinguish it as a sect, outside of the mainstream. Although it remains among the smaller organizations under discussion here, it is sufficiently widespread to be classed as a multiregional sect. Table 5-17 presents the available county,

church, and adherents data for the Pentecostal Holiness Church, Int.

The Pentecostal Holiness Church was organized in 1899 in the Carolinas. In 1911, and again in 1915, it absorbed through merger two other organizations, the Fire-Baptized Holiness Church (founded in 1898) and the Tabernacle Pentecostal Church. In that process, it created an organization with a primary core region in the Carolinas and a secondary core in Oklahoma and Texas. Those two areas stand in clear relief on Map 5-34 (p. 146), which shows the mid-century pattern to include those two regions, as well as smaller regional clusters in Florida and California. In its first half-century, the Pentecostal Holiness Church developed 932 churches in 371 counties. The fact that the organization claimed only 41,000 adherents in 1952 means that its average congregation had only 45 adherents, a tiny number almost more representative of a cell than a congregation.

As was common for the new churches arising from the Pentecostal or Holiness movements, the period from 1952 to 1990 was characterized by expansion and growth. During that interval, the Pentecostal Holiness Church established at least 558 new churches representing a 60 percent increase. Since the number of counties occupied increased by only 138, it appears that a large majority of these new churches were established relatively close to previously existing ones. That overall pattern is depicted on Map 5-34 (p. 146), which reveals the majority of counties newly entered by 1990 to be in the southern tier of states. Accordingly, in 1990, the Pentecostal Holiness Church, Int., was located primarily in a band of counties from California east to the Carolinas and Virginia. That visual impression is confirmed by Table 3-3 (p. 59), which indicates that the organization is present in 29 percent of counties in the Southeast and 21 percent of those in the West, while only infrequently in either the Midwest or Northeast. Clearly, this religious organization can claim only a two-region distribution.

If the geography of the Pentecostal Holiness Church, Int., has remained relatively stable, the growth in the number of adherents has been more dynamic. Between 1952 and 1990, its number of

Table 5-17 Pentecostal Holiness Church, International

	1952	1990
Number of counties	371	509
Number of churches	932	1,490
Total adherents	41,541	156,431

Map 5-33

PENTECOSTAL HOLINESS CHURCH, INTERNATIONAL

TOTAL ADHERENTS BY COUNTY 1990

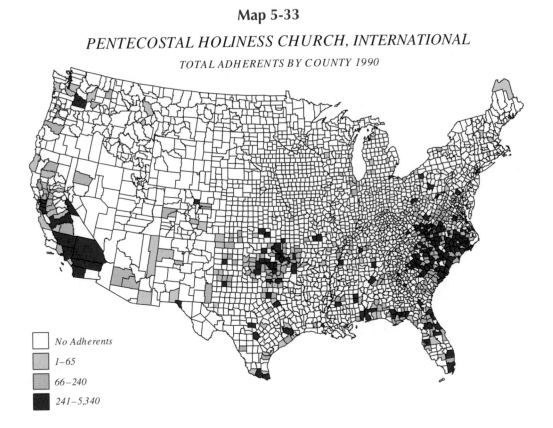

No Adherents
1–65
66–240
241–5,340

Map 5-34

PENTECOSTAL HOLINESS CHURCH, INTERNATIONAL

GEOGRAPHIC CHANGE BY COUNTY 1952, 1990

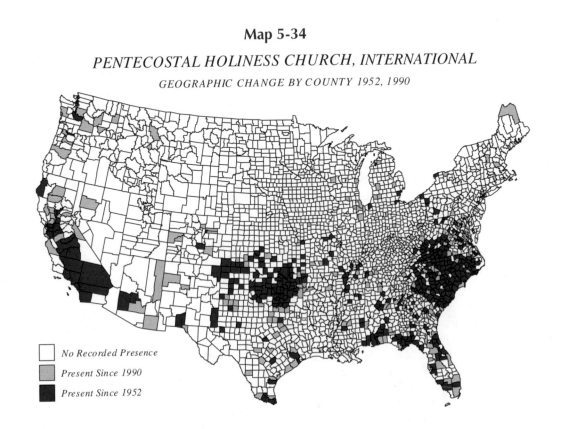

No Recorded Presence
Present Since 1990
Present Since 1952

adherents almost quadrupled, an increase that raised average congregation size from 45 to 105. These changes indicate that many individual congregations became more "established" and that, in many counties with multiple Pentecostal Holiness churches, this organization was becoming a more recognized element in the community. However, Map 5-33 reveals that this is not uniformly so. The lowest third of counties for the Pentecostal Holiness Church, Int., contained no more than 65 adherents, while the middle third reached only 240 persons. Populations of such small size surely did not play significant roles in defining local, let alone, regional culture.

Because the Pentecostal Holiness Church, Int., is widespread across the southern tier of states, it is classified as a multiregional sect. Prior to 1990, it was slow in reaching into the Midwest and Northeast and, therefore, does not yet seem to be moving toward national sect status.

Friends

The term *sect* carries with it many images beyond a simple passive recognition of being outside of the mainstream. When the Friends, or Quakers, were first established in England during the 1650s, members of the movement were persecuted, imprisoned, and even killed because of their beliefs. In fact, some of the first Quakers arriving in the American colonies were subjected to a similarly hostile reception. Despite this perilous start in North America, by the time of the Revolution, the movement had become relatively well established, especially in the mid-Atlantic region. Though their pacifist views set Quakers apart from the conflict of the Revolution, in many other ways they had become accepted, almost as a part of the dominant Anglo-Saxon Protestant mainline. With more than 300 congregations, or in their case "meetings," they ranked fifth among the religious bodies counted in 1776 (see Map 1-5, p. 21). Indeed, they were larger than either the Catholics or Methodists. In some ways, the combination of their long history here, their Anglo-Saxon roots, and their long record of commitment to "good works" has resulted in the sense that, if it is possible for a sect to

be part of the mainstream, the Friends would be so. However, in terms of their unique theological views, their organizational structure, and their demographic and geographic patterns since 1776, the Friends clearly are a multiregional sect. Table 5-18 presents the available county, church, and adherents data for the Friends.

As already noted, the Friends became securely established during the Colonial era, particularly in the mid-Atlantic states. Although the several modern-day associations use a variety of organizational names, we have adopted the generic term "Friends." The 1850 distribution of Map 5-36 (p. 148) reflects those origins. By that date, Friends had become widely established in New York, New Jersey, and Pennsylvania, as well as in many parts of New England. Reflecting fairly conventional migration routes, they also were present in a significant number of Midwestern counties, particularly in Ohio and Indiana. Given the Friends early and active anti-slavery position, it is not surprising that they were present in only a handful of Southern counties prior to the Civil War. In 1850, the United States Census tallied 728 churches (meetings), indicating that the movement had more than doubled in the early years of the Republic. Though the Friends had fallen significantly behind the growth rates of the Baptists, Methodists, and Presbyterians, their growth pattern was greatly different from either the Congregational or Episcopal churches. In most senses then, in the middle of the nineteenth century, the Friends still would have been viewed as an important secondary group in the dominant Anglo-Saxon Protestant religious culture.

The years from 1850 onward were to change that status and transform the Friends into a minor sect that nonetheless has continued to exert a disproportionate influence on the general culture in sociopolitical rather than religious ways. The period after 1850 was a difficult one for the Friends movement. Reflecting a theological focus on the individual, the movement both actively moved and passively drifted into a series of loosely connected, sometimes regional associations. As the nation expanded and settlement followed, accurate identification and labeling of movements like the various Friends meetings became

Table 5-18 Friends

	1776	1850	1890	1952	1990
Number of counties	—	151	319	260*	666
Number of churches	310	728	995	674*	1,296
Total adherents	33,247	82,002	155,664	95,029*	130,484

* The Friends are so loosely organized that it is difficult to determine or achieve comparability from date to date. The 1952 data most likely represent a significant undercount and will not be examined in detail here.

Map 5-35

FRIENDS

TOTAL ADHERENTS BY COUNTY 1990

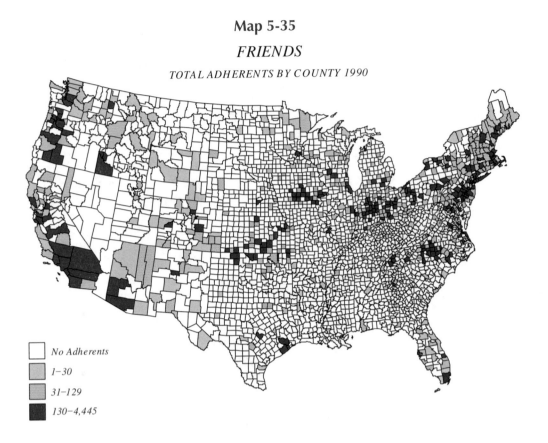

No Adherents
1–30
31–129
130–4,445

Map 5-36

FRIENDS

GEOGRAPHIC CHANGE BY COUNTY 1850, 1890, 1952, 1990

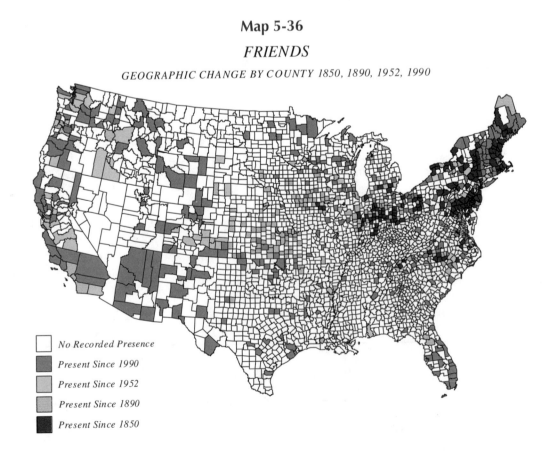

No Recorded Presence
Present Since 1990
Present Since 1952
Present Since 1890
Present Since 1850

progressively more problematic. Because the Friends did not develop a clergy, and frequently held their meetings in homes or halls not resembling "churches," they were not easily identified by census takers or readily contacted by volunteer enumerators relying on formal organizational structures to provide head counts. These problems mean that reported statistics for the Friends are reliable in only the most general sense.

Maps 5-35 and 5-36, and the numerical data, however, contain a portrait that, in its general pattern, does seem accurate. Between 1850 and 1890, the number of churches (meetings) increased by almost 270. However, this represents a much slower rate than in the preceding period. Map 5-36 indicates that expansion was strongest in the Great Plains but also included a limited number of new entries in both the West and the Southeast. The 1890 Census tallied 155,664 Friends in 319 counties nationwide. It is noteworthy that this 1890 estimated total exceeds by a good deal the estimate of a century later.

In the century between 1890 to 1990, the national pattern for the Friends appears to be best described as thinning rather dramatically. Their geographic distribution doubled from 319 counties to 666, and the number of individual meetings grew by an almost identical number, from 995 to 1,296. The startling change is that the adherents total declined by a bit more than 25,000 persons, or 16 percent. In short, many fewer people became spread across substantially more local meetings and a much greater area. Table 3-3 (p. 59) reveals that in 1990 this small body of individuals was present in at least one-fifth of the counties in the Midwest and West, and almost two-thirds of the counties in the Northeast. It is hardly surprising, then, that the average size of meetings is quite small, averaging only 100 persons. Map 5-35 indicates that by 1990, in fact, one-third of all counties with Friends present held 30 or fewer adherents. Although the tiny size of many Friends meetings may help explain why enumeration has been less than precise, it also substantiates their classification as a sect. Their broad dispersal across the country accounts for their classification as multiregional.

The future for the Friends is intriguing. Though greatly committed to helping others in many ways, the Friends have not actively sought converts. One writer (Mead 1975, 147) describes them as never being "great proselytizers." These positions have led to a long-term decline in membership that would not seem easily reversed, unless the Quakers were to become more assertive in seeking or incorporating new members. Like another American sect, with a similar name, the Shakers, the Friends may contain (in somewhat less dramatic fashion) the seeds for the ultimate demise of the movement. Clearly, longevity on American shores does not guarantee the survival of any religious community. Both the Friends and the Church of the Brethren provide examples of faith communities that were present at the nation's founding but subscribe to beliefs not compatible with the changing face of America's national religious or secular culture.

Salvation Army

The Salvation Army is without doubt, one of the most widely recognized and least understood sects operating in the United States. Most Americans readily summon images of Army bell ringers soliciting contributions at Christmas time, of second-hand stores or soup kitchens, or even of missions operating largely in an urban environment. Relatively few understand the beliefs or organization mounting this very considerable array of social service activities. The founder of the Salvation Army was an English Methodist minister named William Booth who was working in London's East End slums in the 1860s. As he sought to help many of "the lowly," he found that they were not welcomed in established regular churches. This prompted him to create a new organization that would provide both social and religious services. In 1878, the name Salvation Army was adopted along with a military style of organization. In the United Kingdom, the organization spread rapidly, especially in industrial areas, and by 1880, it had been transplanted to the United States. The Army's unique blend of social service activities and religious mission continues to mark it as a distinctive element in the constellation of American religious bodies. Table 5-19 presents the available county, church, and adherents data for the Salvation Army.

As can be seen in Table 5-19, the Salvation Army made a rapid "invasion" of the United States. Having arrived here in 1880, only a decade later, the United States Census found the Salvation Army operating in more than 200 counties. Map 5-38 (p. 150) shows

Table 5-19 Salvation Army

	1890	1990
Number of counties	238	778
Number of churches	27	1,167
Total adherents	13,018*	115,320*

* These numbers reflect only those people who "wear the uniform" and does not include any estimate of those who participate in Salvation Army services, religious or social.

Note: The Salvation Army was not included in the 1952 enumeration.

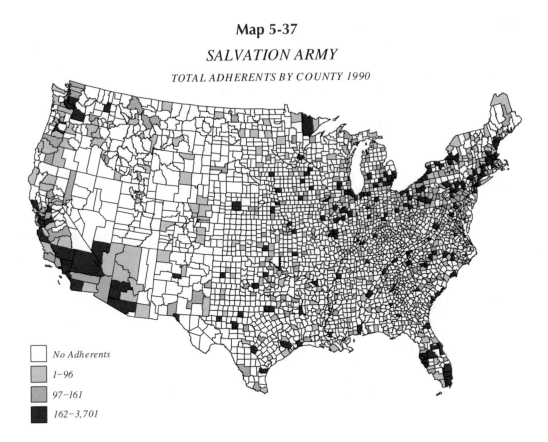

Map 5-37

SALVATION ARMY

TOTAL ADHERENTS BY COUNTY 1990

No Adherents
1–96
97–161
162–3,701

Map 5-38

SALVATION ARMY

GEOGRAPHIC CHANGE BY COUNTY 1890, 1990

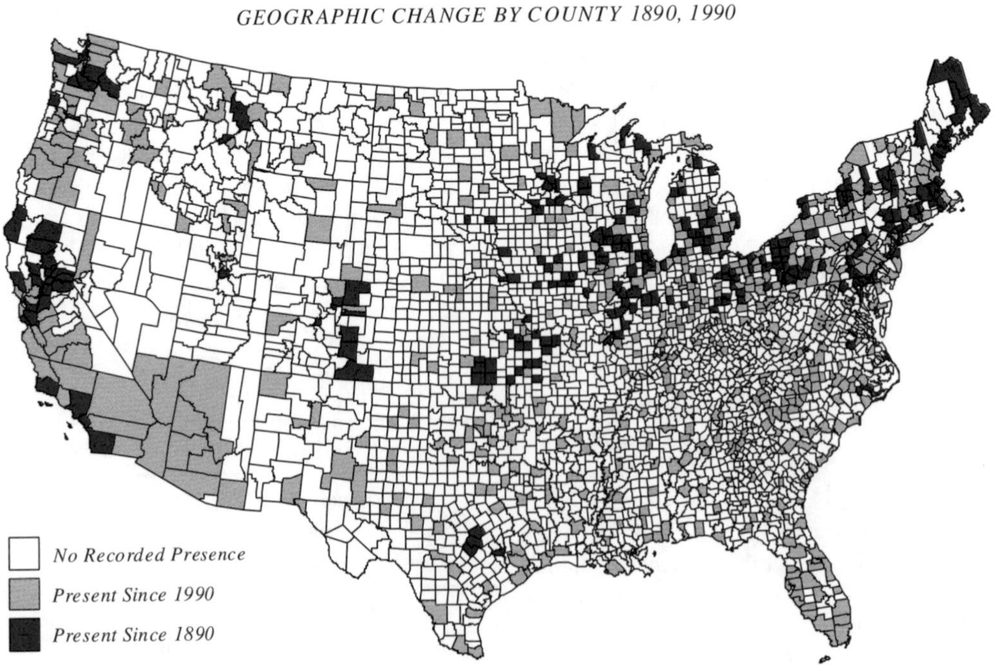

No Recorded Presence
Present Since 1990
Present Since 1890

that these areas of operation stretched from Maine to California, although they were most prevalent in the area from Minneapolis and Kansas City eastward to Baltimore and Boston. Even in 1890, a characteristic pattern already was established. The organization reported only 13,000 adherents, a relatively small number, given the number of counties in which it was present. Additionally, the primacy of its missionary and social service activities is revealed by the fact that, though operating in 238 counties, the organization reported only 27 "churches."

During the century from 1890 to 1990, the Salvation Army emerged as an enduring presence across the United States. By 1990, the Salvation Army reported operations and members ("soldiers," in this case) in 778 counties. As seen on Map 5-38, though in 1890 the Salvation Army had not entered the Southeast to any degree, by 1990 it had a more nationwide distribution. Table 3-3 (p. 59) reveals that in 1990 the movement was still anchored in the Northeast. However, it could be found in about one-fifth of all counties elsewhere in the nation. Map 5-37 shows that in many places, the organization was not large, as one-

third of all its counties contained fewer than 100 adherents, with the range for the middle third of counties reaching only 161 persons. However, "membership" here is limited only to the uniformed "soldiers" of the Salvation Army. Thus, the adherents numbers may be systematically lower than, and not exactly comparable to, those for the other religious organizations under discussion here. Nonetheless, the Salvation Army is a widespread organization, mostly focused on the nation's metropolitan areas. Clearly, this portrait matches conventional wisdom regarding this unconventional religious organization.

The Salvation Army remains a relatively unique body, both because of its style of operation and organization and its strong emphasis on service to the downtrodden. These special characteristics justify viewing the organization as a sect. Even if it is assumed that the available statistics entail an undercounting, it still seems reasonable to view this organization as multiregional rather than national. The latter category would require the Salvation Army to expand its operations more to the South and West and become more national in its distribution than it presently is.

National Sects

Jewish Population

Dating from their earliest communities in Newport, Rhode Island, and what was then New Amsterdam, the American Jewish population long has been among the largest and most conspicuous of the nation's non-Christian religious communities. This distinction alone might be sufficient for the Jewish population to be classified as a national sect. However, three other characteristics reinforce this categorization. First, though Jewish populations once were strongly identified with the Northeast, they subsequently have dispersed into all regions of the country. Conversely, although their distribution is now national rather than regional, Jewish Americans remain strongly clustered in metropolitan areas. As a result, despite their relatively large population size, the Jewish population is found in a comparatively small proportion (24.3 percent) of the nation's counties. Finally, the persistence of at least some level of anti-Semitism among the dominant community labels the Jewish population as "different" and reinforces Jewish self-identification as different. These reciprocal processes are entirely consistent with the sociological literature known as labeling theory (see our discussion, p. 57). For all these reasons, the Jewish Population is categorized here as a national sect.

The 1952 and 1990 data for American Jews more consistently resemble population counts rather than institutional memberships per se. They are, in fact, estimates of Jewish population assembled by community social service agencies and reported to the *American Jewish Yearbook*. We in turn have disaggregated these community statistics into counties. In this regard, these data are different from the organizational data available for the Christian communities examined here, but also are quite like the "adherents" data (as opposed to "members" data) that we have used for the latter. These matters have been discussed previously (p.48); see also Newman & Halvorson 1990). The data for 1776 for Jewish congregations are entirely compatible with other data utilized here, as they are taken from the same source (Paullin 1932). The 1850 data are drawn from the United States Census enumeration of "accommodations," which are the only available data (again, see our discussion on p. 48). This provides an estimate of the total adherents in what was, by any measure, a small population in 1850. The 1890 data are drawn from the same United States Census source as all other 1890 data and represent a combination of both Orthodox and Reform Jewish congregations. The greatest divergence in data aggregation is found in the

1952 and 1990 cases. The data utilized here are drawn from population estimates generated by Jewish community service agencies and reported in respective editions of the *American Jewish Yearbook*. As we've already noted, these data are closer to a culture count than a membership count, but in that sense, they are comparable to the adherents measure used for other religious communities. That degree of comparability resulted in their incorporation into the 1990 *Churches and Church Membership in the United States* enumeration (Bradley et al. 1992). Despite the differences in the enumeration process at different dates, the chronological and geographical patterns of change are clear and surely warrant description and analysis here. Table 5-20 presents the available county, congregation, and adherents data for the Jewish population in the United States.

By the time of the American Revolution, a Jewish presence in the emerging nation had been established, but to a very limited degree. Though two of the congregations were already more than a hundred years old, the 1776 data compilation reports a total of only five congregations, perhaps containing a population of roughly 500 persons. Clearly, this represents a small beginning, and the early years of the new nation brought only a modest expansion of these numbers. The 1850 United States Census reports a total of 37 congregations nationally, with only New York and Pennsylvania reporting as many as 3 congregations each. As shown on Map 5-40, the distribution of those congregations is already strongly urban. In addition to the expected locations in East Coast cities, other cities, such as Albany, Syracuse, Cleveland, Pittsburgh, Cincinnati, Louisville, and St. Louis, trace routes of travel and trade through urban networks into the interior of the nation. However, even with this apparent geographic dispersal, the total Jewish population remained quite small. The 1850 United States Census reports a total of 19,000 "accommodations." These "accommodations" were tallied by town clerks and most often mean "pew counts," or seats. By 1850, the total number of Jewish persons still was quite small and already was strongly

clustered in New York State, which had 14 of the total 37 congregations.

Between 1850 and 1890, the geographic pattern dispersed considerably, as can be seen in Map 5-40. By 1890, Jewish congregations were established in just over 200 counties, a more than tenfold increase. Much of this expansion took place in the Northeast and Midwest, where Jewish communities had settled in both newer industrial cities such as Detroit, Chicago, and Minneapolis-St. Paul, as well as in secondary cities such as Hartford; Binghamton, New York; and Erie, Pennsylvania. However, given conventional wisdom about the geography of the American Jewish population, it is surprising to note, by this early date, the relatively common establishment of Jewish congregations in the belt from the Carolinas to Texas. This pattern is strongly urban-oriented, as is further illustrated in North Carolina, Tennessee, and Texas. The number of congregations nationally also grew by a factor of almost 10 to just over 300, while the Jewish population was reported to be almost 200,000. Though this number is small compared to the national population of almost 63 million, it had increased much more rapidly than the general population and already was larger than that of most religious organizations that would be classified as sects in the United States today.

The period from 1890 to 1922 represents the high watermark of Jewish immigration into the United States. Consequently, the changes occurring on Map 5-40 between 1890 and 1952 are quite striking. Numerically, the Jewish population grew from less than 200,000 to more than 5,000,000, a growth rate of 2,500 percent. Just as striking, however, is the fact that by 1952, this tremendously expanded community was clustered in only 481 of the nation's more than 3,000 counties. Though it would have been impossible to match that rate of numeric growth, this represents a change of "only" 238 percent. The disparity in these two rates is central to an understanding of the social and geographic experience of American Jewry. During the first half of the twentieth century, this religious community came

Table 5-20 Jewish Population

	1776	1850	1890	1952	1990
Number of counties	—	15	202	481	748
Number of congregations	5	37	301	**	3,975
Total adherents	536	19,588*	193,708	5,146,634	5,982,529

*   The United States Census of 1850 reports "accommodations" rather than "members," while the *Baptist Almanac and Annual Register* provides no Jewish data.

** The number of congregations was not reported in 1952.

Map 5-39

JEWISH POPULATION

TOTAL ADHERENTS BY COUNTY 1990

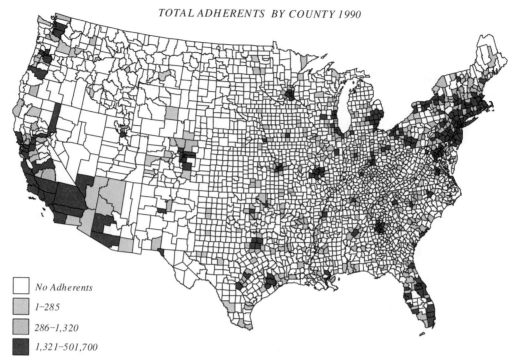

No Adherents

1–285

286–1,320

1,321–501,700

Map 5-40

JEWISH POPULATION

GEOGRAPHIC CHANGE BY COUNTY 1850, 1890, 1952, 1990

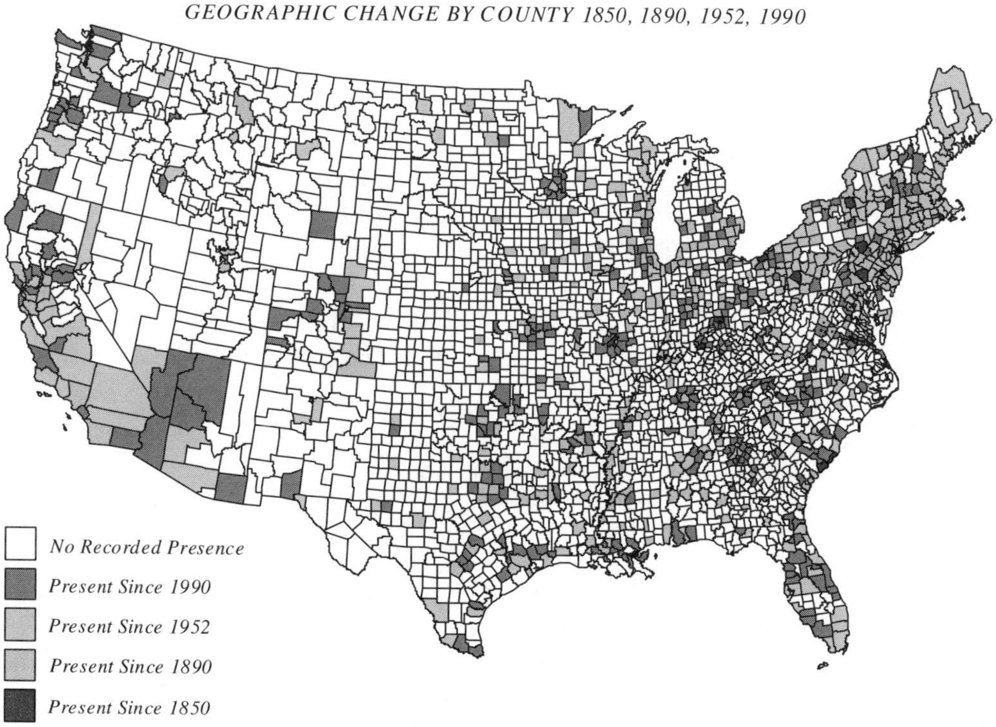

No Recorded Presence

Present Since 1990

Present Since 1952

Present Since 1890

Present Since 1850

to be identified with the metropolitan Northeast, especially New York City. This stereotype was both accurate and misleading. By 1952, 67 percent of all American Jews lived in the Northeastern states, with almost half of that number in metropolitan New York. However, the pattern revealed by Map 5-40 (p. 153) also shows a very significant dispersion not only into the Midwest, but also into the South, and even the Western states, most notably California. The tremendous degree of concentration around New York makes average numbers largely meaningless. However, it is clear that by mid-century, there were perhaps 200 Jewish communities across the country that included several hundred people. This dispersion toward a national distribution was largely masked by the dominance of the New York City core.

The period from 1952 to 1990, in stark contrast to the period that immediately preceded it, was dominated by geographic rather than numeric change. The American Jewish population has become noted for relatively low fertility rates. In the absence of sizable Jewish immigration in the latter half of the twentieth century, the Jewish population has grown slowly in a numerical sense and, in fact, some observers have even suggested that it may begin to decline in size. Between 1952 and 1990, the total of the Jewish population expanded by more than 800,000, representing a growth of only 16 percent during a period when the national population grew by 65 percent. Despite this relatively modest overall growth, the geographic distribution shifted dramatically in two ways. First, the regional distribution became far more even. Though the Northeast remained dominant, its proportion of the total Jewish population declined from 67 percent to 51 percent. As illustrated by data in Table 3-5 (p. 59) by 1990, just over 20 percent of counties in the Midwest and West had Jewish populations, and most surprisingly, 28 percent of all counties in the Southern region also contained Jewish communities. This regional pattern demonstrates that the Jewish population had been distributed more evenly across the nation. In most respects, this shift from the Northeast to the South and West reflects more general population shifts within the country during the period.

A second geographic shift occurring within the Jewish community also followed general population trends. Map 5-40 provides striking evidence of suburbanization. A cursory inspection of this map reveals interesting doughnut-shaped patterns in places such as St. Louis, Nashville, Minneapolis, and Atlanta. In each case, a central Jewish presence was established in the city prior to 1890, and the suburban ring of counties was added to the distribution between 1952 and 1990. This pattern accounts for a significant number of the counties newly added between 1952 to 1990 and surely is consistent with conventional wisdom about shifting patterns of general population distribution for the nation as a whole.

By 1990, then, the American Jewish population had grown to almost 6 million persons located in almost 25 percent of the nation's counties in every region of the United States. As Map 5-39 (p. 153) demonstrates, roughly 500 of those counties had Jewish communities of more than 300 persons, and 250 of the counties contained more than 1,300 Jewish people. Clearly, this religious community is not a classic sect, as it is large and regionally widespread. However, being Jewish still is considered distinctive or culturally non-normative, and the degree of clustering of the Jewish community in the largest metropolitan areas remains significantly greater than that of most "mainline" Christian groups. For these reasons, it is appropriate to categorize this distribution as typical of a national sect.

It is instructive to view the changing status of the American Jewish population through different historical periods. In Colonial times, Jews surely were a classic sect, small in numbers and spatially concentrated. By 1850, little had changed. However, by 1890, they might have been classified as a multiregional sect. As we've seen, between 1850 and 1890, both the spatial pattern and numeric extent of the Jewish population had begun a transformation. It is significant that these changes pre-date the second wave of the Great Migration from Eastern and Southern Europe. Unquestionably, the immigration that subsided in the mid-1920s provided the population growth among American Jews that would pave the way toward national status. On the eve of the twenty-first century, American Jews are primarily an American-born religious community. They have a national presence, but surely do not represent the religious norm. Thus, they are a sect holding national stature in the mosaic of American faith communities.

Church of Jesus Christ of Latter Day Saints (Mormons)

The Church of Jesus Christ of Latter Day Saints (hereafter referred to as the Mormons) is, at once, the most widely recognized and least understood of the religious movements arising out of the nineteenth-century American frontier. The broad outline of Mormon history involving Joseph Smith's revelation in upstate New York, the movement from New York through Ohio to Missouri and Illinois as a result of persecutions that culminated in the murder of Joseph Smith, followed by the Great Migration led by Brigham Young to the Salt Lake basin, where they settled and "made the desert bloom," is a widely recognized chapter in America's national chronicle. On the other hand, the Mormon claim to a new revelation as described in the Book of Mormon, their tightly hierarchical organization, as well as the practice of polygamy, which was deemed by the host society to be non-normative, all have made the Mormons the object of misunderstanding, fear, and persecution. Though these reactions took their strongest forms during the nineteenth century, the Mormon Church and Mormons still are perceived as apart from the mainstream of American religion. For that reason, they are classified as a sect, although some would argue that they have now progressed to the level of being a denomination. The rapid growth and expansion of the Mormon Church during the twentieth century brought Mormonism into much broader contact with the rest of American society. This, in turn, has helped diminish stereotypical fears, while increasing acceptance. On this basis, it could be argued that Mormonism has begun the transition from a national sect to a national denomination within the mainstream of American religious life. Table 5-21 presents the available county, church, and adherents data for the Church of Jesus Christ of Latter Day Saints.

In 1850, the Mormons were a movement in some degree of disarray. In the aftermath of their earlier persecution, and especially after the murder of Joseph Smith, they shattered into a number of splinter organizations, with Brigham Young leading the main body of the faithful well beyond the frontier into the wilderness of Utah. For these reasons, it is not entirely surprising that the Mormons were not even counted in the 1850 United States Census enumeration of minor sects. Thus, the *Baptist Almanac and Annual Register*'s estimate of 20,000 members is here adjusted upward to include children, resulting in a total estimate of 28,160. There were, of course, several smaller pockets of Mormons in other states, mostly in the Midwest. However, it is reasonable to presume that the majority of Mormon adherents settled in Utah.

The patterns of numerical growth and territorial expansion by 1890 are striking. First, in only 40

years' time, the number of Mormons increased by a factor of 10, to more than a quarter million. Given general perceptions about both typical Mormon family size and their aggressive missionary activity, this expansion is not entirely surprising. However, it remains impressive when compared to the rate of increase in the general population, which between 1850 and 1890, did not quite triple. Even more striking is the county coverage, as depicted on Map 5-42 (p. 156). Though the Utah core area is very obvious, the distribution is far more widespread than might be anticipated. By 1890, Mormons were reported in more than 300 counties nationwide. Not only had Mormon outposts been established along transportation routes leading to the Great Basin and along the West Coast, but even more impressively, large numbers of Midwestern counties and somewhat smaller numbers in both the Northeast and Southeast had established Mormon communities. Although Mormon life still was dominated by a focus on the Utah core region, Mormons also had begun to expand into other parts of the country in both rural and developing urban areas. In this sense, the 1890 data is striking both because of the substantial numerical increase reported and because of the wide dispersal of the Mormon Church.

These patterns of growth and expansion in the nineteenth century were only a prelude to more impressive expansion in the twentieth century. The absence of any data other than the total adherents number for 1952 of 845,689 limits discussion of the first half of the twentieth century. Obviously, there was a continued rapid increase in adherence. However, by 1990, the Mormons reported communities in 1,671 counties. As shown on Map 5-42 (p. 156), though those counties created a virtually complete cover of counties in the western third of the nation, they were plentiful nationwide. Table 3-5 (p. 59) also demonstrates that in 1990 the regional coverage of the Mormons was quite even, with Mormon churches in at least 40 percent of the counties in all four regions of the nation. There can be no doubt that in the twentieth century, the Mormons attained a national distribution.

Table 5-21 Church of Jesus Christ of Latter Day Saints (Mormons)

	1850	1890	1952	1990
Number of counties	—	316	**	1,671
Number of churches	—	266	—	9,208
Total adherents	28,160*	261,633	845,689	3,540,820

* This number is based on the *Baptist Almanac and Annual Register*. United States Census data are not available for total adherents or number of churches.

** In 1952, the Mormons reported only a national membership total and did not provide county-level data.

Map 5-41

CHURCH OF JESUS CHRIST OF LATTER DAY SAINTS

TOTAL ADHERENTS BY COUNTY 1990

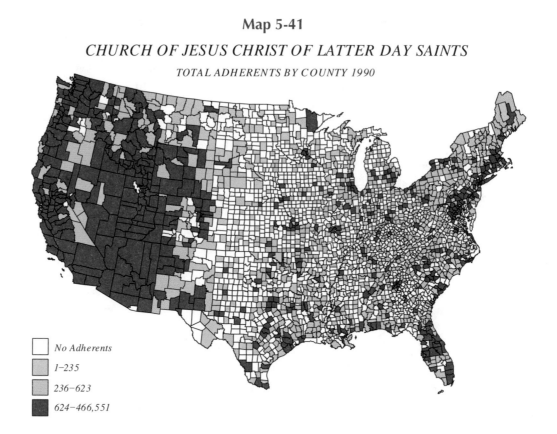

No Adherents
1–235
236–623
624–466,551

Map 5-42

CHURCH OF JESUS CHRIST OF LATTER DAY SAINTS

GEOGRAPHIC CHANGE BY COUNTY 1890, 1990

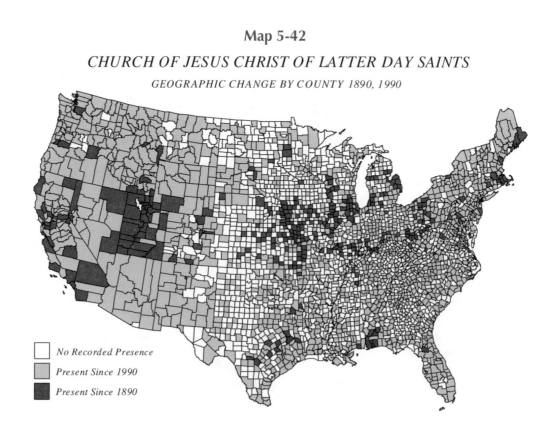

No Recorded Presence
Present Since 1990
Present Since 1890

Moreover, by 1990, the number of adherents had reached 3.5 million. As shown on Map 5-41, the smallest third of Mormon communities ranged upward to as many as 235 persons, while the average size of congregations was 384. This means that, as is widely recognized, Mormon congregations tend to be large and thus are visible elements in a community landscape. In places with two or more such congregations, as appears to be the case in more than 500 counties, the Mormons constituted an identifiable cultural element in community life. Given the continued emphasis on missionary outreach both foreign and domestic, sustained growth appears likely.

In any scientific activity involving classification, one must make "judgment calls." The Mormons represent a transitional case. They arrive on the American landscape in the early 1800s as a native religious movement whose unique beliefs and values shape them into a classic sect. However, from their sectarian enclave in Utah, they rapidly grow and disperse, transitioning from a multiregional sect to a national sect. At the beginning of the twenty-first century, only the issue of cultural normativeness prevents our reclassifying them as a national denomination. However, that final transition of Mormonism into the American religious mainstream hinges on processes of mutual perception and accommodation between Mormonism and the host society. Clearly, the Mormons are one of America's great religious success stories, and they progressively are becoming accepted as part of the mainstream culture and society.

African Methodist Episcopal Zion Church

The African Methodist Episcopal Zion Church is the only representative of the so-called black churches present in this study. This reflects a general problem within the voluntary collections of religious data between 1952 and 1990. The AME Zion Church, which numbered 1,142,016 adherents in 1990, is dwarfed by the 7.5 million adherents of the nation's largest black Protestant organization, the National Baptist Convention USA, Inc.; the 3.3 million adherents of the African Methodist Episcopal Church; and the 3.5 million adherents of the National Baptist Convention of America, Inc.(Jaquet, 1990). However, the AME Zion data available here does at least provide a first perspective on the role of America's black churches.

Two African Methodist Episcopal (AME) organizations originated in Northern cities among free blacks during the early years of the nineteenth century. The AME Church was started in 1787 in Philadelphia. The AME Zion Church originated in 1796 in New York. By 1821, the AME Zion Church organized

six congregations located in New York, New Haven, Newark, and Philadelphia into a larger organization using the name of the oldest congregation, Zion, to distinguish itself from the Philadelphia-based AME Church. Clearly, then, the AME Zion Church was present in a number of Northern cities prior to 1850. Yet, the 1850 United States Census study does not list these organizations as a distinct category and perhaps includes them in the general Methodist category. Table 5-22 presents the available county, church, and adherents data for the AME Zion Church.

Table 5-22 African Methodist Episcopal Zion Church

	1890	1990
Number of counties	289	448
Number of churches	1,587	1,962
Total adherents	599,836	1,142,016

Note: No data are available for 1850 or 1952.

In the absence of supporting data, it nonetheless must be presumed that the AME Zion Church, composed of free African-Americans, remained largely confined to Northern cities prior to the Civil War. In the aftermath of the war, the black population began to move between the South and North much more readily. The 1890 pattern for the AME Zion Church shown in Map 5-44 (p. 158) reflects this movement in two different ways. First, within the triangle from Boston to Cleveland to Washington, the AME Zion Church was widely established. However, there also were strong concentrations of adherents in the Carolinas and Alabama, two of the primary source areas for African-American migrants to Northeastern cities (recall the lyric from the closing scenes of *Porgy and Bess* set in Charleston, South Carolina, "There's a boat that's leavin' soon for New York"). Just as people moved in one direction, northward, so the religious organization moved backward through the migration stream to the communities from which they had come. As a result, by 1890, the AME Zion Church had become a sizable organization, with nearly 600,000 adherents in almost 1,600 congregations. Thus, in 1890, the average AME Zion congregation had more than 375 adherents. Since there were on average more than four congregations per county, in many places these religious organizations would have been quite a recognizable, if only occasionally integrated, element in local culture. Geographically, the three core areas of the metropolitan Northeast, along with the Carolinas and Alabama are the dominant locations, with only a few clusters elsewhere (e.g., central Florida and the lower Mississippi

Map 5-43

AFRICAN METHODIST EPISCOPAL ZION CHURCH

TOTAL ADHERENTS BY COUNTY 1990

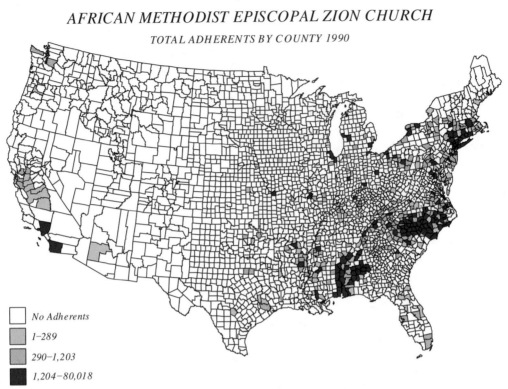

No Adherents

1–289

290–1,203

1,204–80,018

Map 5-44

AFRICAN METHODIST EPISCOPAL ZION CHURCH

GEOGRAPHIC CHANGE BY COUNTY 1890, 1990

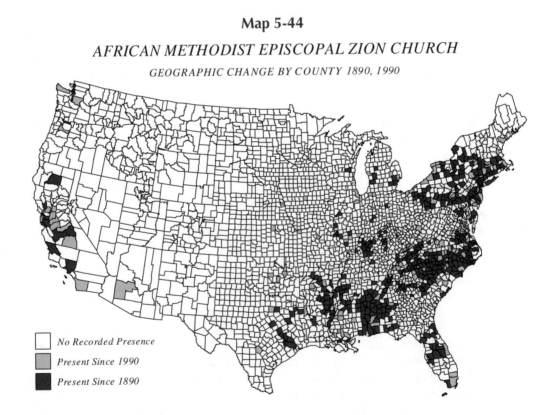

No Recorded Presence

Present Since 1990

Present Since 1890

Valley). A small handful of counties are present by 1890 in California as well. Already a striking feature of the distribution is that a relatively large number of adherents are contained in a relatively small number of counties.

This pattern of large adherent populations positioned in a very small number of counties is shared by the AME Zion Church and the American Jewish population. Both of these communities have been the objects of discrimination and residential segregation in American society. Though without question, it may be argued that especially in the twentieth century African-Americans have experienced these limiting social conditions much more than Jewish-Americans, it is little surprise that both communities' religious organizations exhibit broadscale patterns of geographic clustering and population concentration.

As noted earlier, one of the more unfortunate features of the voluntary religious data collections between 1952 and 1990 is the omission of the predominantly African-American ethnic churches. In the 1952 collection, this omission included the AME Zion Church with the result that only change patterns over a full century (1890 to 1990) are available for analysis. By 1990, the AME Zion Church had grown in total adherents by just over 90 percent to a total of 1.1 million. This expansion of more than 500,000 persons occurred with an addition of only 275 churches and within only 159 additional counties. In other words, most of the growth would appear to have been within previously existing churches or communities. This impression is reinforced by Map 5-4, which depicts many of the new counties as adjacent to previously occupied ones, although almost a quarter (13 of 59) of them were found in the far West.

The pattern revealed in Map 5-43 and the data in Table 3-5 (p. 59) may appear to call into question the classification of the AME Zion Church as a national sect. In 1990, the original core areas still were clearly evident, as shown on Map 5-43, and though AME Zion churches were present in significant numbers of counties in the Northeast and Southeast, they occupied only 4 percent of counties in the Midwest and West. What then accounts for their designation as a national sect? The answer lies in the degree to which the AME Zion distribution mirrors that of another national sect, American Jews. As already noted, both exhibit large total numbers of adherents found in a small number of counties nationally. In the AME Zion case, this pattern reflects relatively isolated but sizable AME Zion communities in metropolitan areas across the Midwest and in California. Midwestern cities such as Columbus, Cincinnati, Detroit, Chicago, St. Louis, and Kansas City all contain communities of more than 1,200 AME Zion adherents, as do San Diego and Los

Angeles. Thus, although the organization is still firmly rooted in the Northeast and Southeast, it is becoming a recognizable entity nationwide, despite its presence in only 15 percent of the nation's counties. It is this emerging national metropolitan network of AME Zion congregations that determines this church's designation as a national sect. Hopefully, future studies will produce data from the other large African-American religious organizations so that our assertions about the meaning of the AME Zion distribution pattern can be tested.

Seventh-Day Adventists

Most of the religious organizations defined here as national sects have their origins in the nineteenth century and in the United States. Rapid adherent and geographic expansion has transformed them into national organizations even as they continue to be sects. That sectarian status often is determined by a divergent view of some particular bit of theology or church life that sets them apart from the mainstream of American religion. The emergence of William Miller in upstate New York and his prediction of the Second Coming of Christ as occurring in 1844 typifies the sort of divergence that sustains the designation sect. In the aftermath of the failure of that predicted event to occur in 1844, some of Miller's followers developed an interesting theological revision in which Christ had entered *into* heaven at that time rather than coming out from it. Subsequently, they formed a new movement focused upon preparation for a Second Advent, as well as a sabbatarian orientation that perhaps was borrowed from the Seventh Day Baptists. Organizational headquarters were established in Michigan during the 1850s, and by 1860, they had adopted the name Seventh-Day Adventist. Table 5-23 presents the available county, church, and adherents data for the Seventh-Day Adventists.

As already noted, the origins of the Seventh-Day Adventists involve developments in upstate New York and Michigan prior to the Civil War, and these

Table 5-23 Seventh-Day Adventist

	1890	1952	1990
Number of counties	612	1,466	1,802
Number of churches	418	2,796	4,214
Total adherents	43,956	252,917	903,062

Note: A more general category of "Second Advent" is included in the 1850 United States Census category of minor sects, but otherwise there is no data available for 1850. However, in the 1890 Census, this rapidly growing body reported only 418 churches (edifices) but 995 congregations (organizations).

Map 5-45

SEVENTH-DAY ADVENTISTS

TOTAL ADHERENTS BY COUNTY 1990

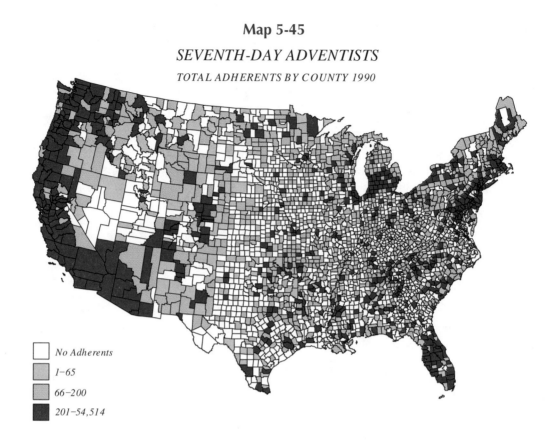

No Adherents
1–65
66–200
201–54,514

Map 5-46

SEVENTH-DAY ADVENTISTS

GEOGRAPHIC CHANGE BY COUNTY 1890, 1952, 1990

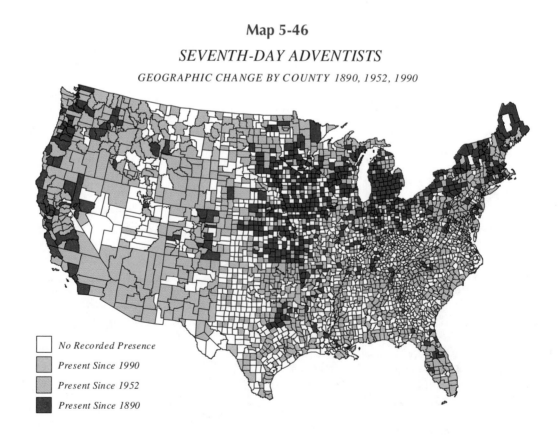

No Recorded Presence
Present Since 1990
Present Since 1952
Present Since 1890

locational features still are apparent in the 1890 patterns shown on Map 5-46. The organization had spread fairly continuously across the tier of states from Maine to Iowa, and from Iowa, north and south into the Plains states. Though the Northeast clearly is the core area, there also was significant movement into the West Coast from border to border. This dispersion for a religious organization not yet 40 years old is quite impressive. However, these adherents also were rather thinly spread. With fewer than 44,000 adherents in more than 600 counties, the average number of Adventists per county was barely 70 persons, and the average congregation would have been even smaller than that. Nonetheless, especially for a religious movement with highly distinctive theological views, the general patterns of their growth by 1890 are impressive.

Between 1890 and 1952, even more dramatic growth occurred. The number of adherents increased by a factor of five, to a quarter of a million, and the geographic expansion involved an increase of more than 800 counties, bringing these Adventists into almost half of the nation's counties. Map 5-46 reveals a general Northern and Western geographic bias. In the zone from Maine to Maryland on the East Coast, and from Washington to New Mexico along the West Coast and southwestern borders of the country, only two sets of gaps appeared in what becomes a relatively complete blanket of occupied counties. The most obvious of these was in the Mormon territory of Utah and Nevada, while the second entailed a large number of presumably thinly populated rural counties mostly located in the Great Plains. Although many of the new counties probably held relatively small congregations of Adventists numbering significantly fewer than 100 people, the average church size had more than doubled to 173. These changes indicate that in addition to being present in many more locations, the Seventh-Day Adventists also were becoming a more noticeable presence in many communities.

The growth and expansion typical of the earlier years has continued during the second half of the twentieth century. Between 1952 and 1990, the Seventh-Day Adventists expanded into more than 300 additional counties, bringing their total to just over 1,800 or more than 58 percent of the national total. Again, consulting Map 5-46, it is apparent that most of these new counties are in the Southeast, giving this organization a clearly national distribution, as shown in Table 3-5 (p. 59). In 1990, Adventists occupied more than 50 percent of the counties in each of the nation's four regions. The total adherents figure expanded even more dramatically to approximately 900,000, or 3.5 times the 1952 total. Additionally, the number of churches grew by more than

1,400, yielding a 50 percent expansion since 1952. Thus, two types of growth took place. The Seventh-Day Adventists expanded geographically quite vigorously, while also increasing impressively the size of their local churches. By 1990, the average Seventh-Day Adventist county population was more than 500 persons, while their average congregation size was more than 210 people. As shown on Map 5-45, the number of adherents in two-thirds of their counties remained less than that, with many hundreds of them claiming fewer than 66 persons. Thus, much of the distribution remained characterized by a thin, or sect-like pattern. Yet, in a significant number of communities, the Seventh-Day Adventists had become a sizable population element. This is perhaps most true in California, which contained about 25 percent of the nation's Seventh-Day Adventists, as well as the largest single concentration of them, more than 50,000 in Los Angeles county.

These sharp differences mark the Seventh-Day Adventists as an organization in transition. In 1990, although it is clear that the Seventh-Day Adventists' distribution is national, it is less clear whether the organization will remain a sect or become a denomination. If the general society comes to accept their theology as mainstream, it is indeed possible that in the twenty-first century the Seventh-Day Adventists could join the small circle of national denominations in the United States.

Church of God (Cleveland, Tennessee)

The Church of God (Cleveland, Tennessee), like several of the other national sects examined here, developed late in the nineteenth century. This Church of God originally was organized as the Christian Union in 1886, and then reorganized in 1902 as the Holiness Church, a name that reveals its basic theological orientation. A variety of doctrinal issues as well as a series of problems of internal politics resulted in a number of schisms during the twentieth century, with the Church of God (Cleveland, Tennessee) emerging as the largest of the surviving organizations. The origins of this organization as part of the Holiness movement in America's so-called Bible Belt is reflected in its "born again" fundamentalist theology, including a belief in faith healing and the practice of speaking in tongues. Table 5-24 (p. 162) presents the available county, church, and adherents data for the Church of God (Cleveland, Tennessee).

Despite several schisms, by 1952 the Church of God (Cleveland, Tennessee) had developed rather strongly, with considerably more than 100,000 adherents in more than 2,600 churches located in one-third of the nation's counties. As shown on

Table 5-24 Church of God (Cleveland, Tennessee)

	1952	1990
Number of counties	1,073	1,497
Number of churches	2,617	4,996
Total adherents	136,461	691,563

Map 5-48, very clearly, the Church of God (Cleveland, Tennessee) is centered in the Southeast, with a virtual blanket of counties across the area of the "Old South" bounded by the Ohio and Mississippi River valleys. By 1952, this organization's northward and westward expansion, though much more spotty, had occurred particularly in the mid-Atlantic and industrial Midwest regions, as well as in southern California. Thus, by mid-century, the Church of God (Cleveland, Tennessee) evidenced strong growth, not only attaining considerable size, but both filling the region of its origin and beginning to spread beyond it into the other regions of the country.

The period from 1952 to 1990 saw these patterns continued, especially in terms of increasing numbers of adherents. The Church of God (Cleveland, Tennessee) added more than 2,300 new churches and more than 400 new counties between 1952 and 1990. These changes represent 90 percent and 40 percent increases, respectively. As seen in Map 5-48, the geographic expansion largely (and of necessity) took place outside of the Southeast. The visual impression is that much of this dispersion occurred in the Western states. However, closer inspection also reveals a good number of newly occupied counties in the Midwest and Northeast. The end product by 1990, as seen in Table 3-5 (p. 59), was a national distribution covering almost 50 percent of the nation's counties and exceeding 30 percent of counties in all four regions, despite the continued strong concentration of this organization in the Southeast. Certainly, though the Church of God (Cleveland, Tennessee) was not yet "everywhere," this emergent national sect was gaining on that target rapidly.

This impressive spatial expansion pales in comparison to the organization's numerical growth, which showed a fivefold increase during the 1952–1990 period, reaching just a little less than 700,000 adherents by 1990. This indicates that individual congregations grew rapidly. Whereas average congregation size in 1952 was only 52, by 1990 it had increased to 138, with an average county population of more than 400 adherents. As Map 5-47 demonstrates, those averages may be a bit misleading, since one-third of all the counties containing Church of God (Cleveland, Tennessee) churches had fewer than 102 adherents. Clearly, most such

counties were located outside the Southeast. On the other hand, a surprising number of counties in the highest category (containing at least 340 adherents) most likely contained multiple congregations and had developed in a good number of locations in the other regions as well.

Although the Church of God (Cleveland, Tennessee) is a strong component in the organizational mix that defines the religious character of the Southeast, clearly it had grown beyond that region by 1990. Its distribution has become increasingly national, although it remains either absent from or small in a majority of the nation's counties. Like a number of other national sects of relatively recent origin, over the next generation, the Church of God (Cleveland, Tennessee) may continue to experience growth and expansion, achieving national denominational status in the twenty-first century. Of course, a key factor here is the extent to which institutional growth is accompanied by a moderation of the more extreme practices of "born again" Christianity; or conversely, the extent to which Holiness and fundamentalist Christianity become more socially normative in the American twenty-first century.

Church of the Nazarene

It is an accident of the classification scheme employed here that places the Church of the Nazarene adjacent to what is both its closest historical parallel case and most interesting comparison, the Church of God (Cleveland, Tennessee). The Church of the Nazarene, like the Church of God (Cleveland, Tennessee), is an outgrowth of the nineteenth-century Holiness movement. However, where the Church of God represents a regional organization that has expanded to national status, apparently through proselytizing, the Nazarenes, through a series of organizational mergers, became national almost at the time of their organizational founding. In 1907, an organization called the Association of Pentecostal Churches in America, which was based primarily in New England and New York, merged with a West Coast sect called the Church of the Nazarene. They formed a new organization under the name Pentecostal Church of the Nazarene. Only one year later, a third regional body called the Holiness Church of Christ, centered in Texas, joined the merger, almost immediately creating the skeleton framework for a national sect. The latter was further augmented by a merger with the Pentecostal Mission in 1915. The Nazarenes' attainment of virtual instantaneous nationwide status through merger suggests comparison with the more limited success of several other merged religious organizations. Consider, for example, the United Church of Christ, which in 1990 occupied only

Map 5-47

CHURCH OF GOD (CLEVELAND, TENNESSEE)

TOTAL ADHERENTS BY COUNTY 1990

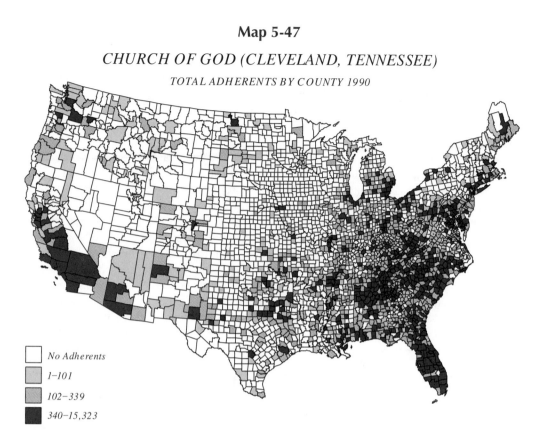

No Adherents
1–101
102–339
340–15,323

Map 5-48

CHURCH OF GOD (CLEVELAND, TENNESSEE)

GEOGRAPHIC CHANGE BY COUNTY 1952, 1990

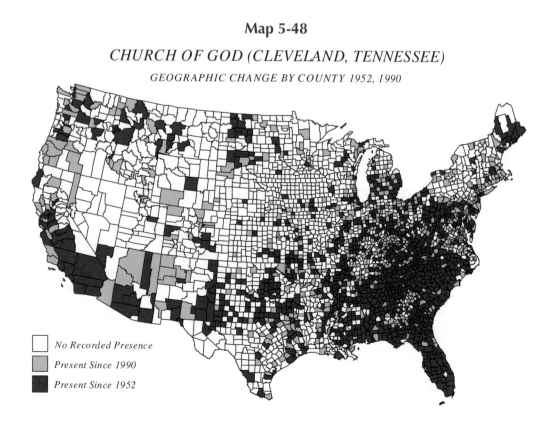

No Recorded Presence
Present Since 1990
Present Since 1952

two-thirds as many counties as the Nazarenes and which exhibits a far more regionalized pattern. In 1919, the Church of the Nazarene dropped "Pentecostal" from its name as a way to dissociate itself from the Pentecostal practice of speaking in tongues. This decision reveals the Church of the Nazarene to be a bit closer to the mainstream than some of the more theologically extreme organizations growing out of the Holiness movement. However, the Nazarenes do adhere to most of the central beliefs of that movement. Despite two different organizational paths, and different theological positions, it is intriguing that after almost a century of change, the Church of God (Cleveland, Tennessee) and the Church of the Nazarene, both products of the Holiness movement, have arrived at rather similar positions. Table 5-25 presents the available county, church, and adherents data for the Church of the Nazarene.

Table 5-25 Church of the Nazarene

	1952	1990
Number of counties	1,680	1,852
Number of churches	3,818	5,167
Total adherents	249,033	683,245

As might be expected from its multiregional origins, by 1952, the Church of the Nazarene already was quite widespread, appearing in more than half of the nation's counties. Map 5-50 reveals a generally national distribution, with gaps most noticeable in two types of location: areas with strong religious competitors, specifically in the Southeast and in the Mormon heartland, and areas characterized by population decline such as the Great Plains. By mid-century, the Nazarenes had grown numerically and expanded spatially. However, they did so from a more balanced point of departure than do most sects. With almost a quarter million adherents and nearly 4,000 churches, in 1952, the Church of the Nazarene already had moved well beyond the regional character of any of its founding organizations.

Between 1952 and 1990, the Church of the Nazarene continued to grow, although somewhat less rapidly than some of its fellow Holiness Movement organizations. Already widespread by 1952, the organization entered only 172 new counties by 1990. Yet, it created more than 1,300 new churches leading to the conclusion that most of the growth was taking place within communities that already had a Nazarene presence. The location of new counties appears to be largely in coastal areas of the Southeast and in the western Mountain States. These changes between 1952 and 1990 do little more than supple-

ment an already national distribution pattern. As documented by Table 3-5 (p. 59), the Church of the Nazarene is one of the most strongly and evenly distributed of the religious organizations in this study excepting, of course, the national denominations. Only in the Southeast does it occupy fewer than 60 percent of the region's counties. This is indeed a "national" distribution.

The rate of numeric increase between 1952 and 1990 was quite impressive, involving the addition of more than 400,000 new adherents for a 274 percent increase—a figure far greater than the roughly 65 percent increase in the general population. Obviously, the Church of the Nazarene developed a program that was able to attract large numbers of new adherents at a rate that doubled congregational size from 65 persons in 1952 to 132 in 1990, a configuration that more resembles a mainline denomination than a sect. However, as demonstrated by Map 5-49, in 1990 fully one-third of the Nazarenes' counties held fewer than 85 adherents, meaning that in more than 400 counties, the Church of the Nazarene was a very small and sect-like presence. Moreover, its churches were absent from more than 1,200 counties. In contrast, in more than 400 counties, the Nazarenes apparently had two or more congregations and adherents that number well into the hundreds. Like their fellow Holiness group, the Church of God (Cleveland, Tennessee), the Church of the Nazarene might well attain national denomination status in the twenty-first century. Their more moderate version of Holiness religion certainly moves them in the theological direction of the mainstream.

Church of God (Anderson, Indiana)

Many religious bodies in the United States and Canada employ the name "Church of God." A number of these share a common origin in the various late nineteenth century movements described as Holiness or Pentecostal, including, for example, the Church of God (Cleveland, Tennessee). The Church of God (Anderson, Indiana) differs from most other "Church of God" organizations in several ways. The Anderson body views itself as a movement or association within which local congregations are autonomous. In this view, the churches are not an organization as such. To the degree that this movement has a consistent theology, it is opposed to many of the practices of the Holiness or Pentecostal churches, including speaking in tongues and faith healing. Consequently, although originating as a reform movement at much the same time (1880s) as many of the Holiness or Pentecostal organizations and sharing a name common to them, the Church of God (Anderson,

Map 5-49

CHURCH OF THE NAZARENE

TOTAL ADHERENTS BY COUNTY 1990

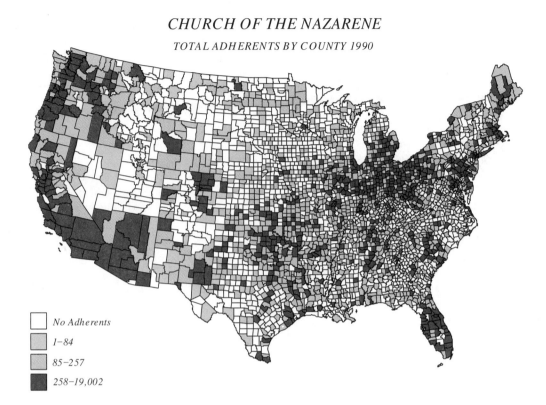

No Adherents
1–84
85–257
258–19,002

Map 5-50

CHURCH OF THE NAZARENE

GEOGRAPHIC CHANGE BY COUNTY 1952, 1990

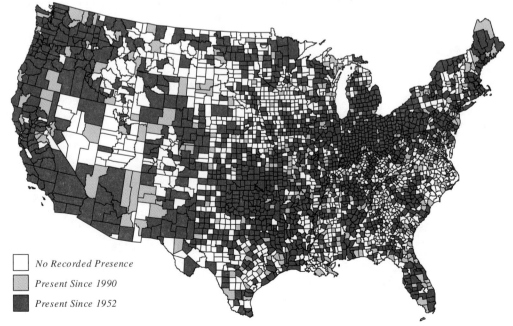

No Recorded Presence
Present Since 1990
Present Since 1952

Indiana) must be understood as quite different from them. Table 5-26 presents the available county, church, and adherents data for the Church of God (Anderson, Indiana).

Having only originated during the previous decade and reluctant to impose organizational order above the level of the individual congregation, the Church of God (Anderson, Indiana) understandably was not included in the 1890 United States Census enumeration. Despite the lack of detailed statistics, it is known that the movement originated within congregations in the Midwest, where it has maintained what passes for its headquarters. This is not stated disparagingly, but rather in recognition of the group's staunchly local orientation, which has mitigated against the development of a large-scale central organization. Despite, or perhaps in some part because of that, the movement took root rather quickly in a widespread variety of areas. As can be seen on Map 5-52, prior to 1952, Church of God (Anderson, Indiana) congregations were located in substantial numbers of counties in most parts of the nation. Occupying about 1,000 counties nationally by 1952, they had expanded beyond their central Midwest core area, into areas as diverse as Florida and Oklahoma, Louisiana and California, Colorado, and even in the Northwest. With total adherents of only just over 100,000, distributed across nearly 1,000 counties and 2,000 congregations, the general pattern suggests very small churches and a very limited, albeit widespread, presence in local communities.

As was common for several of the religious organizations that started in the late nineteenth century and survived into the twentieth, the Church of God (Anderson, Indiana) continued to grow fairly rapidly into the last half of the twentieth century. However, its growth rate lagged behind those of most other religious movements (especially Adventist and Holiness organizations) that emerged in this period. As a result, in 1990, they were the smallest of the national sects examined here. Between 1952 and 1990, the Church of God (Anderson, Indiana) gained more than 300 churches and more than doubled its number of adherents. Spatially, it added only 30 more counties. Obviously, growth for this Church of God has been associated primarily with increasing the size of existing congregations or developing new congregations close to previously existing churches. As might be expected, the change in the organization's distribution between 1952 and 1990, as portrayed on Map 5-52, showed little or no distinct regional shifts, in

Table 5-26 Church of God (Anderson, Indiana)

	1952	1990
Number of counties	990	1,020
Number of churches	2,015	2,336
Total adherents	105,564	227,887

Note: This largely informal movement was not sufficiently defined by 1890 to be included in the 1890 United States Census.

that new counties were both small in number and quite scattered. The picture conveyed by Map 5-51 confirms the view of this movement as a sect-like religious minority in most communities. By 1990, one-third of the counties occupied contained 60 or fewer adherents, while the middle category of counties ranged from 61 to only 171 adherents. These ranges of adherent sizes reinforce the impression that in most places across the country the Church of God (Anderson, Indiana) was absent or, where present, was in the form of rather small individual churches. This aspect of the church's general pattern combined with a distinctive anti-organizational theology marks this movement as largely sect-like. At the same time, the Church of God (Anderson, Indiana) came to be located in one-third of the nation's counties in an exceptionally balanced regional pattern (see Table 3-5, p. 59). In 1990, the Church of God (Anderson, Indiana) occupied a low of 26 percent of Western counties, and a high of 34 percent of Southeastern counties. Therefore, on a regional basis, the organization had a presence in most sections of the nation, although it surely represented a minor religious element where it is encountered.

Several of the other national sects examined here seem to be on the threshold of moving from the status of sect to denomination. That surely is true of the Church of the Nazarene, and the Church of God (Cleveland, Tennessee), and perhaps the Seventh-Day Adventists, all of which have theological positions a bit outside the mainstream. The Church of God (Anderson, Indiana) is further removed from that point because of its strongly local orientation. This pattern suggests that the future will bring more of the same for the Church of God (Anderson, Indiana): steady moderate growth within existing congregations. Therefore, though it is reasonable to cast them as a national sect here, there is little indication that they are headed toward national denomination status anytime soon.

Map 5-51

CHURCH OF GOD (ANDERSON, INDIANA)

TOTAL ADHERENTS BY COUNTY 1990

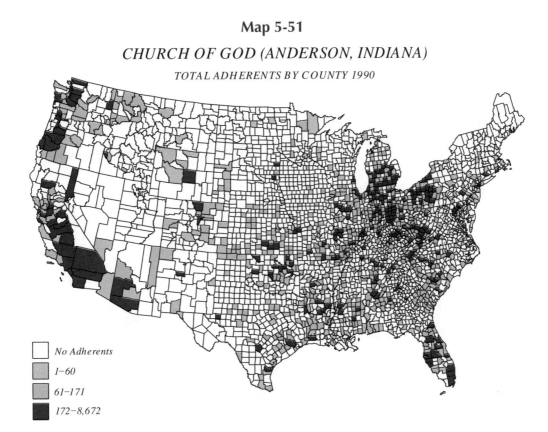

No Adherents
1–60
61–171
172–8,672

Map 5-52

CHURCH OF GOD (ANDERSON, INDIANA)

GEOGRAPHIC CHANGE BY COUNTY 1952, 1990

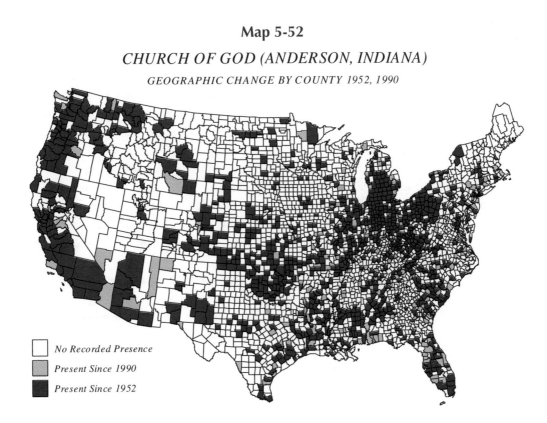

No Recorded Presence
Present Since 1990
Present Since 1952

Epilogue

Twenty-five years ago we set out to chronicle changes in American religion. The period we tackled covered barely twenty years, from 1952 to 1971. We tried to call attention to what we thought was a valuable and underutilized data source, the Churches and Church Membership studies. That effort initiated a collaboration that, with this work, now has focused upon more than two centuries of the American religious experience and has entailed the greater part of our professional lives. What can we now say based on that perspective?

Co-authors often wrestle with phrasing. In our case, one recent phrasing bout has debated over the "end of the twentieth century" as opposed to the "beginning of the twenty-first century." These phrases may provide a framework from which to view our subject and our work. Current scholarship on American religion has given much attention to the "competition" of various faiths for the "hearts and minds" of the American public. This focus presupposes a fundamental truth about American society, that diverse religious communities have found a wide variety of forms of expression. Organized religion has flourished in this setting, where people enjoy the freedom to pick and choose how they will practice their faiths. The various religious organizations have trod very different pathways and pursued them to rather different positions within society. This has resulted in the complex histories and geographies that we have attempted to portray here. Obviously, we think it is a fascinating set of stories about the American collective past.

However, the old adage that the "past is prelude" also is true. At each of the earlier benchmark dates we have employed, 1775, 1850, 1890, and 1952, we have been able to discern a basic set of patterns in American religion, only to see them significantly altered in the ensuing period. This demonstrates an important fact, but also signals a warning. The patterns of religious organizations in the United States have been as dynamic and changeable as the weather in New England. This has been true both because of the arrival of new peoples with different religious traditions, and because of the native or indigenous development of new expressions of religion. There is every reason to assume that the future will bring dynamic changes to the most recent patterns we have portrayed here.

Significantly, the processes of data collection continue to lag behind social reality with regard to religion in American life. In this volume we have discussed the lack of data for most of the large African-American Christian churches, and also have noted the absence of data on Eastern Orthodox churches. Recently, scholars have described the development of community-based churches identified as megachurches, about which there exist only isolated case studies. Additionally, in recent decades there has been a proliferation of mosques, evidencing a very rapidly growing Islamic faith community in the United States. Increased immigration from Asia has brought still other traditions in greater number than ever before. The size and distribution of all these religious communities are yet to be charted. Clearly, there is much to be done.

For all these reasons we recognize that our work in many respects stands as only a prelude to the work of others yet to come. We know that the religious tapestry we have described remains a work in progress, because American society is a work in progress. We hope we have advanced the task of portraying the role and scope of organized religion in American society, and that some few scholars may be motivated to tell the continuing story from here.

Bibliography

American Jewish Committee
    1990   *American Jewish Yearbook.* New York, American Jewish Committee.
American Baptist Publication Society
    1850   *Baptist Almanac and Annual Register.* Philadelphia, American Baptist Publication Society.
Ammerman, Nancy
    1990   *Baptist Battles: Social Change and Religious Conflict in the Southern Baptist Convention.* New
          Brunswick, N.J., Rutgers University Press.
Bainbridge, William Sims
    1997   *The Sociology of Religious Movements.* New York, Routledge.
Becker, Howard
    1963   *The Outsiders: Studies in the Sociology of Deviance.* New York, Free Press.
Bellah, Robert
    1967   "Civil Religion in America." *Deadalus* 96:1–21.
Bonomi, Patricia U.
    1986   *Under the Scope of Heaven: Religion, Society and Politics in Colonial America.* New York,
          Oxford University Press.
Bonomi, Patricia U., & Peter R. Eisenstadt
    1982   "Church Attendance in the Eighteenth-Century British American Colonies." *William and Mary*
          Quarterly 3 (39):245–86.
Bradley, Martin B., Norman M. Green, Jr., Dale Jones, Mac Lynn, and Lou McNeil
    1992   *Churches and Church Membership in the United States, 1990.* Atlanta, Glenmary Research Center.
Bureau of the Census
    1854   Seventh Census of the United States, 1850. Washington, D.C., Government Printing Office.
    1864   Eighth Census of the United States, 1860. Washington, D.C., Government Printing Office.
    1874   Ninth Census of the United States, 1870. Washington, D.C., Government Printing Office.
    1894   Eleventh Census of the United States, 1890. Washington, D.C., Government Printing Office.
    1910   Religious Bodies, 1906. Washington, D.C., Government Printing Office.
    1919   Religious Bodies, 1916. Washington, D.C., Government Printing Office.
    1930   Religious Bodies, 1926. Washington, D.C., Government Printing Office.
    1941   Religious Bodies, 1936. Washington, D.C., Government Printing Office.
    1975   *Historical Statistics of the United States: Colonial Times to 1970.* Washington, D.C., Government
          Printing Office.
    1958   *Religion Reported by the Civilian Population of the United States, March 1957.* Series P-20, Number
          79, Washington, D.C., Department of Commerce.
Carroll, Jackson W., Douglas W. Johnson, & Martin Marty
    1979   *Religion in America, 1950 to the Present.* San Francisco, Harper & Row Publishers.
Christiano, Kevin
    1987   *Religious Diversity and Social Change: American Cities, 1890–1906.* New York, Cambridge
          University Press.
DeVita, Carol J.
    1996   "The United States at Mid-Decade." *Population Bulletin* 50 (March): 4.
Finke, Roger, & Rodney Stark
    1986   "Turning Pews into People." *Journal for the Scientific Study of Religion* 25:180–92.
    1992   *The Churching of America 1776–1990: Winners and Losers in Our Religious Economy.*
          New Brunswick, New Jersey, Rutgers University Press.
Gaustad, Edwin
    1962   *Historical Atlas of Religion in America.* New York, Harper & Row Publishers.

Glock, Charles Y., & Rodney Stark
    1965   *Religion and Society in Tension.* Chicago, Rand McNally.
Goen, C.C.
    1985   *Broken Churches, Broken Nation.* Macon, Georgia, Mercer University Press.
Haggett, Peter
    1983   *Geography: A Modern Synthesis.* Revised third edition. New York, Harper Collins.
Hale, Russell J.
    1977   *Who Are the Unchurched?* Washington, D.C., Glenmary Research Center.
Halvorson, Peter L., & William M. Newman
    1978   *Atlas of Religious Change in America, 1952–1971.* Washington, D.C., Glenmary Research Center.
    1987   *Atlas of Religious Change in America, 1971–1980.* Atlanta, Georgia, Glenmary Research Center.
    1994   *Atlas of Religious Change in America, 1952–1990.* Atlanta, Georgia, Glenmary Research Center.
Harrison, Paul
    1959   *Power and Authority in the Free Church Tradition.* Princeton, Princeton University Press.
Hawthorne, Nathaniel
    1850   *The Scarlet Letter.*
Herberg, Will
    1955   *Protestant-Catholic-Jew.* Garden City, New York, Doubleday and Company.
Hilliard, Sam B.
    1987   "A Robust New Nation, 1783–1820." In Mitchell, R. D., & P. A. Groves (eds.), *North America.* Totowa, New Jersey, Rowman & Littlefield, 149–71.
Hoge, Dean, Benton Johnson, & Donald Luidens
    1995   "Types of Denominational Switching Among Protestant Young Adults." *Journal for the Scientific Study of Religion* 34:253–58.
Jacquet, Constant (ed.)
    1990   *Yearbook of American and Canadian Churches.* Nashville, Abingdon Press.
Johnson, Benton
    1957   "A Critical Appraisal of the Church-Sect Typology." *American Sociological Review* 22:88-92.
    1963   "On Church and Sect." *American Sociological Review* 28:539–49.
    1971   "Church and Sect Revisited." *Journal for the Scientific Study of Religion* 10:124–37.
Johnson, Douglas, Paul Picard, & Bernard Quinn
    1974   *Churches and Church Membership in the United States, 1971.* Washington, D.C., Glenmary Research Center.
Jones, Maldwyn Allen
    1960   *American Immigration.* Chicago, University of Chicago Press.
Lee, Robert
    1960   *The Social Sources of Church Unity.* New York, Abingdon Press.
Lemert, Edwin M.
    1967   *Human Deviance, Social Problems and Social Control.* Englewood Cliffs, New Jersey, Prentice-Hall.
Lewis, Pierce
    1987   "America Between the Wars: The Engineering of a New Geography." In Mitchell, R. D., & P. A. Groves (eds.), *North America.* Totowa, New Jersey, Rowman & Littlefield, 441–37.
Littell, Franklin
    1962   *From State Church to Pluralism: A Protestant Interpretation of Religion in American History.* Garden City, New York, Doubleday & Company.
Mathews, Donald
    1969   "The Second Great Awakening as an Organizing Process 1780–1830: An Hypothesis." *American Quarterly* 21 (1): 23–43.
Mead, Frank S.
    1975   *Handbook of Denominations in the United States.* New sixth edition. Nashville, Abingdon.
Mead, Sidney E.
    1963   *The Lively Experiment: The Shaping of Religion in America.* New York, Harper & Row.

Miller, Perry

    1965   *The Life of the Mind in America: From the Revolution to the Civil War*. New York, Harcourt, Brace and World.

Mueller, Samuel, & Angela Lane

    1972   "Tabulations from the 1957 'Current Population Survey on Religion.'" *Journal for the Scientific Study of Religion* 11:76–98.

Nelson, Clifford E. (ed.)

    1975   *The Lutherans in North America*. Philadelphia, Fortress Press.

Newman, William M.

    1976   "Religion in Suburban America." In Barry Schwartz (ed.), *The Changing Face of the Suburbs*. Chicago, University of Chicago Press, 265–75.

Newman, William M., & Peter L. Halvorson

    1980   *Patterns in Pluralism: A Portrait of American Religion, 1952–1971*. Washington, D.C., Glenmary Research Center.

    1982   "Updating an Archive: 'Churches and Church Membership in the United States, 1959–1980.'" *Review of Religious Research* 24 (1): 54–58.

    1984   "Religion and Regional Culture: Patterns of Concentration and Change Among American Religious Denominations, 1952–1980." *Journal for the Scientific Study of Religion*. 23 (3): 304–15.

    1990   "An American Diaspora? Patterns of Jewish Population Distribution and Change, 1971–1980." *Review of Religious Research* 31 (3): 259–67.

    1993   "The Church Membership Studies: 'Four Decades of Institutional Research.'" *Review of Religious Research* 35 (1): 74–80.

Newman, William M., Peter L. Halvorson, & Jennifer Brown

    1977   "Problems and Potential Uses of the 1952 and 1971 National Council of Churches' *Churches and Church Membership in the United States* Studies." *Review of Religious Research* 18 (2): 167–73.

Niebuhr, H. Richard

    1929   *The Social Sources of Denominationalism*. New York, Holt, Rinehart & Winston.

Niemi, Albert W., Jr.

    1980   *U.S. Economic History*. Second edition. Chicago, Rand McNally.

O'Dea, Thomas

    1957   *The Mormons*. Chicago, University of Chicago Press.

    1966   *The Sociology of Religion*. Englewood Cliffs, New Jersey, Prentice-Hall.

Paullin, Charles O.

    1932   *Atlas of the Historical Geography of the United States*. Washington, D.C., New York, Carnegie Institution and American Geographical Society.

Petersen, William

    1962   "Religious Statistics in the United States." *Journal for the Scientific Study of Religion* 2:165–78.

Quinn, Bernard, Herman Anderson, Martin Bradley, Paul Goetting, and Peggy Shriver

    1982   *Churches and Church Membership in the United States, 1980*. Atlanta, Glenmary Research Center.

Roof, W. Clark, & William McKinney

    1987   *American Mainline Religion: Its Changing Shape and Future*. New Brunswick, New Jersey, Rutgers University Press.

Shortridge, James R.

    1976   "Patterns of Religion in the United States." *Geographical Review* 66 (4): 420–34.

    1977   "A New Regionalization of American Religion." *Journal for the Scientific Study of Religion* 16 (2): 143–53.

Sopher, David

    1967   *Geography of Religion*. Englewood Cliffs, New Jersey, Prentice-Hall.

Stark, Rodney, & Roger Finke

    1988   "American Religion in 1776: A Statistical Portrait." *Sociological Analysis* 49 (1): 39–51.

Stark, Rodney, & Charles Y. Glock

    1968   *American Piety: The Nature of Religious Commitment*. Berkeley, University of California Press.

Stark, Werner

  1967   *The Sociology of Religion: A Study of Christendom, Volume II, The Sect.* New York, Fordham University Press.

Stump, Roger W.

  1984   "Regional Migration and Religious Commitment in the United States." *Journal for the Scientific Study of Religion* 23 (3): 292–303.

  1986   "Regional Variations in the Determinants of Religious Participation." *Review of Religious Research* 27 (3): 208–24.

Swatos, William

  1979   *Into Denominationalism.* Storrs, Connecticut, Society for the Scientific Study of Religion, Monograph Series #2.

  1998   "Denomination/Denominationalizing." In William Swatos, *Encyclopedia of Religion and Society.* Walnut Creek, California, AltaMira Press, 134–36.

Sweet, William Warren

  1952   *Religion in the Development of American Culture, 1765–1840.* New York, Charles Scribner's Sons.

Tocqueville, Alexis de

  1835–39   *Democracy in America.*

Troelstch, Ernst

  1912   *The Social Teachings of the Christian Churches.* Trans. Olive Wyon (1931). New York, Macmillan Company.

Weber, Max

  1904   "Objectivity in Social Science and Social Policy." In *The Methodology of the Social Sciences.* Trans. Edward Shils & Henry Finch (1949). New York, The Free Press.

  1904–5 *The Protestant Ethic and the Spirit of Capitalism.* Trans. T. Parsons (1958). New York, Charles Scribner's Sons.

  1922   *Virtschaft und Gesellschatf.* J.C.B. Mohr (ed.). Trans. Guenther Roth & Claus Wittich (1968). New York, Bedminster Press.

Wiebe, Robert H.

  1975   *The Segmented Society; An Introduction to the Meaning of America.* New York, Oxford University Press.

Whitman, Lauris, & Glen Trimble

  1956   *Churches and Church Membership in the United States, 1952.* New York, National Council of Churches of Christ.

Wilson, Bryan

  1959   "An Analysis of Sect Development." *American Sociological Review* 24:3–15.

  1961   *Sects and Society.* Berkeley, University of California Press.

  1970   *Religious Sects.* New York, McGraw-Hill.

Winter, Gibson

  1961   *The Suburban Captivity of the Churches.* Garden City, New York, Doubleday and Company.

Yinger, J. Milton

  1946   *Religion in the Struggle for Power: A Study in the Sociology of Religion.* Durham, North Carolina, Duke University Press.

  1970   *The Scientific Study of Religion.* New York, The Macmillan Company.

Zelinsky, Wilbur

  1961   "An Approach to the Religious Geography of the United States: Patterns on Church Membership in 1952." *Annals of the American Association of Geographers* 51 (2): 139–93.

Index